Reiner Schulze/Dirk Staudenmayer (eds.)

Digital Revolution: Challenges for Contract Law in Practice

HART PUBLISHING

Nomos

The Deutsche Nationalbibliothek lists this publication in the Deutsche Nationalbibliografie; detailed bibliographic data are available on the Internet at http://dnb.d-nb.de

ISBN 978-3-8487-2956-2 (Print)
978-3-8452-7348-8 (ePDF)

British Library Cataloguing-in-Publication Data
A catalogue record for this book is available from the British Library.

ISBN HB (Hart) 978-1-5099-0733-5

Library of Congress Cataloging-in-Publication Data
Schulze, Reiner / Staudenmayer, Dirk
Digital Revolution: Challenges for Contract Law in Practice
Reiner Schulze / Dirk Staudenmayer (eds.)
271 p.

ISBN 978-1-5099-0733-5 (hardcover Hart)

1. Edition 2016

Foreword

On 1–2 October 2015 a workshop on 'Digital Challenges for Contract Law in Practice' was held at the Centre for European Private Law (CEP) of the Westfälische Wilhelms-Universität Münster. The creation of the Digital Single Market, one of the European Commission's top 10 priorities, and the changeover to the digital economy were the inspirations for this workshop. The workshop was dedicated to the effects and requirements of the digital economy on European private law, in particular in the fields of 3D-Printing, Share Economy and the Internet of Things. The results are contained in this volume.

We kindly thank the speakers for their willingness to publish their contributions in this volume, the moderators – Hugh Beale (Warwick), Marco Loos (Amsterdam) and Jerzy Pisuliński (Cracow) – and the workshop participants for their valuable contributions to the discussions.

Particular thanks are owed to the research assistants Benedikt Beierle, Cristina Pardo and Jonathon Watson for their enthusiastic and invaluable support in the organisation of the workshop and publication of this volume.

Münster, December 2015 *Reiner Schulze & Dirk Staudenmayer*

Contents

Introduction

The Challenges of Digitisation for Consumers 11
Gerd Billen

Digital Revolution – Challenges for Contract Law 19
Reiner Schulze / Dirk Staudenmayer

3D-Printing and Contract Law

Conformity of 3D prints – Can current Sales Law cope? 35
Christian Twigg-Flesner

3D Printing: The Limits of Contract and Challenges for Tort 67
Geraint Howells / Chris Willett

Share Economy & Internet Platforms

Regulation of Share Economy: A Consistently Changing Environment 89
Larry A. DiMatteo

Share Economy and the Consumer Concept 111
Rafael Illescas Ortiz

Share Economy and Consumer Protection 119
Caroline Meller-Hannich

Internet of Things

Profiling and Targeting Consumers in the Internet of Things – A New Challenge for Consumer Law 135
Natali Helberger

Contractual Duties and Allocation of Liability in Automated Digital Contracts 163
Rolf H. Weber

Consumer Contracts and the Internet of Things 189
Christiane Wendehorst

Liability and Risk Management in Robotics 225
Erica Palmerini / Dr. Andrea Bertolini

Panel Discussion on the Internet of Things

Statement 263
Rolf H. Weber

Statement 265
Robert MacDougall

Introduction

The Challenges of Digitisation for Consumers

Gerd Billen[*]

Thank you for giving me the opportunity to kick off this workshop by outlining the consumer-protection challenges that will have to be mastered in connection with the process of digitalization. As all of you know, we live in times of dramatic change. Perhaps the only historical periods comparable in this regard are the dawn of the printing press or the age of industrialisation. The rapid pace at which digitisation is penetrating all of our daily lives is breathtaking, to say the least. And while many people are enjoying the almost limitless possibilities and benefits that a digitised and networked world can bring, others regard it with dread.

This conference comes at exactly the right time. After all, the European Commission announced that the digital single market will be one of its top priorities and released a strategy paper in May that defined no less than 16 initiatives. Since recommendations for individual measures to promote this digital single market are to be submitted this year and the next, I suspect that the Commission is hard at work on these proposals at this very time. Perhaps this conference will generate valuable ideas and suggestions that might facilitate the Commission's work, as well as future debates on the subject.

So what are the main aspects of digitisation from the consumer's point of view? If I had to identify a single starting point and recurrent theme for any consumer-protection policy that is oriented by consumer interests, it would be trust. In fact, the trust that consumers place in the digital markets can be regarded as the very key to these markets' success. The question we have to ask ourselves, therefore, is this: How can we ensure that consumers – regardless of their age group, educational level or buying patterns – are able to find their way in the digital world in a manner that makes them feel comfortable? For unless we can ensure that consumers have a sufficient degree of trust and confidence – and I hope we all agree

---

* Gerd Billen is State Secretary to the Federal Minister of Justice and Consumer Protection. The contribution was held as opening speech during the conference on which this volume is based.

on this – we will not be seeing any strong and sustainable growth in this field. And a major factor for boosting this trust of consumers is to give them a sense of self-determination, transparency, and security when dealing with the internet. The process of digitisation with all its benefits – not least economic benefits – can only succeed if the rights of consumers are safeguarded. Only then will new business models as well as digital services and products find widespread acceptance on the internet.

If we look at today's digital world we see highly dynamic markets with a constant succession of new business models. Practically on a daily basis, some new product or service is being offered to a broad range of consumers who differ widely from one another in terms of their interests or the degree of protection they require. Take children and youths, for example. Clearly, this is a key target group for digital offerings, but one that is also particularly vulnerable to any number of risks.

As protectors of the consumer, our task is threefold: We must see to it that all consumer groups are able to use and exploit the opportunities and benefits of the digital world. We must provide them with the means of themselves defining the offerings available in that world. And at the same time, we must ensure that their participation in it does not place at risk the interests of the individual consumer, general consumer rights, or the special protected status of personal data. I should note that for all of these objectives, the key factor will be not only how the markets behave, but also how consumers themselves behave.

Many market players like to play up the importance of the so-called 'responsible consumer', one who evaluates every offer in detail and carefully weighs all the corresponding risks and benefits. This is a lofty ideal, but unfortunately it hardly conforms to the reality of the digital world. Digital markets are much too complex and dynamic for that. And let's be honest: How many of you really feel you are fully up to the task of meeting 100% of the challenges posed by the internet?

A much more realistic conclusion about the digital world is that many consumers act as 'trusting consumers'. As such, they tend to click on the 'I agree' button to confirm general business terms, terms of use or data protection terms without actually having read them – or at least having gained a basic understanding. Instead, they simply trust that it will all work out in the end, somehow. But what if this leads to a situation where the consumer's trust is abused and remains permanently damaged? It should be clear to everyone, therefore, that the steady growth of digital markets is not a self-perpetuating phenomenon. Rather, it is an ongoing process for which consumer trust will mean the difference between success and failure.

Accordingly, effective and comprehensive consumer-protection policies will require more than simply ensuring that consumers receive comprehensible information. On certain points, the law will have to be very clear in the provisions it stipulates. Two such points that specifically come to mind here are special consumer-protection rights with respect to digital applications, as well as the right to retain data sovereignty, in other words, the ability to maintain control over one's own data.

But these safeguards alone will not suffice. Unless consumer protection is effectively implemented in practice, all the vested rights in the world will be of no avail. As I see it, the rights of consumer associations constitute an important building block in this context. In Germany, the legislature intends to extend a consumer association's right to bring legal action to cover cases of data-protection infringement. The corresponding legislative process is currently under way and I hope it will be adopted in an expedited manner. Another very important milestone, in my opinion, is that Germany's negotiation position on this point has prevailed, so that it now looks as if this important consumer-protection tool, which has proved its worth in Germany time and again, will also find applicability in the future European General Data Protection Regulation.

A particular challenge for consumer protection in the digital world consists in the fact that we cannot simply transpose the rules and customary practices of the 'analogue' world to the digital world on a one-to-one basis. This is due to the very specific nature of the products and services on offer in the digital world. One salient characteristic, for example, is that consumers communicate with counterparts whom they essentially perceive in virtual form only. This means that everything takes place in 'distance contract' mode, as this phenomenon is known in legal terminology. Just how specialised the issues associated with digital products and services are, can be illustrated by a few case examples:

Just consider the many open questions that apps give rise to, for instance – those mobile applications for our smartphones that we can easily obtain from so-called 'app stores', either free of charge or for a fee. Which rights of usage and which functions and restrictions am I actually buying? Which of my personal data will be processed when and for what purpose? Will I have any control over how this is done? If it turns out that an app is not to my liking or does not perform as promised, can I return it? What sort of customer support will I receive and over how long a period?

Or take streaming services. A recent survey revealed that every fourth user of streaming services has a problem to report, such as frequent reception disruptions, issues relating to price or membership, or copyright-related difficulties – for example, when it comes to distinguishing between legal and illegal offers of products and services.

We also encounter just as many questions when it comes to the Internet of Things, as practically all of the physical objects we use in our daily lives become mutually interconnected. What will my consumer rights be like once my refrigerator is able to independently shop for groceries? What will be my liability if my autonomously driving car causes an accident? Who will compensate my damages if my home technology is hacked? Or take 3D printers: What contractual rights and duties apply when a consumer receives a digital printing template but the corresponding 3D product fabricated by the printer proves to be deficient? Who is the 'producer' in this case, legally speaking? And what are the implications in terms of quality assurance and liability – for instance, when a spare part made by a 3D printer is installed in an automobile?

Which brings me to another point that I would like to highlight: Personal data. At best a sideshow in the analogue world, they often represent the core business in the digital world. In fact, one can safely say that personal data has become the very currency of the internet. You are all familiar with the phrase 'Facebook is and remains free of charge'. We know what this really means: You actually pay for your use of the social network by turning over your data – and quite handsomely! Of course Facebook is not alone in this regard. Practically every market player is hard at work to find ways of securing a piece of the big-data pie for itself. By now, it is an open secret that consumer data are regarded as 'marketing gold' that is available in plentiful supply and merely needs to be mined. So here, as well, we will need clear rules if full transparency and consumers' right of self-determination are to be ensured. But that alone will not be enough. Unless the media competence of consumers keeps pace with new digital developments and trends, success will prove elusive.

Data processors are probably pleased as punch that so many consumers are not yet fully aware of how valuable their data actually is – although this is beginning to dawn on more and more people. The measures we will need to take to rectify this situation will include a sustained effort to educate the buying public, particularly vulnerable consumer groups such as children and senior citizens. For these groups, in particular, do not realise that the price they are paying for an ostensibly free product or service could be nothing less than their own personal data. This lack of awareness is not entirely surprising, given that the benefits and drawbacks of a digital offering may arise at different times, and that often, the drawbacks remain hidden. Take a free-of-charge app, for example: Once I download the app, I can use it right away. The disadvantage of having my data collected and exploited may not become apparent until much later, since it occurs unnoticed behind the scenes.

In the vast majority of cases, the user does not even know how or for what purpose his or her data are actually being used. Add to this the fact that certain providers enjoy significant market power and that many consumers feel hopelessly overwhelmed by the complexity of digital technology. It is something practically all of us have experienced: An automatic update suddenly starts running in the background, or we notice that our basic settings have inexplicably changed, or that a different search engine has become the default setting. Or there's a pop-up window on our screen that simply cannot be closed unless we choose one of the options available.

So I think it is plain to see that providers and consumers have not been facing one another across a level playing field for quite some time now. The imbalance that prevails is major and structural in nature, and it threatens to create substantial disadvantages for consumers. Thus, the concept of the 'see-through consumer' whose lifestyle choices can be tracked at all times is no longer a frightening scenario, it has become stark reality. We already know what the consequences are, of course: When consumers visit an online shop, the search results, advertising content, and even the purchase prices they see displayed are algorithmically determined based on their personal data. Even the consumer's creditworthiness can be determined in this fashion. This makes it all the more important for policymakers in the area of consumer protection to focus their efforts on restoring consumers' sovereignty over their own data.

The conference will examine three specific topics relating to digitalisation. The first of these pertains to the challenges posed by the digital world in terms of contract law. As part of its strategy for a digital single market, the European Commission has announced to propose by the end of 2015 legislation to harmonise the contractual provisions of contracts on the supply of digital content as well as on the online sales of tangible goods. The objective here is to promote cross-border commerce by standardising certain areas of contract law. An interesting aspect in this regard will be the online purchase of digital content, in other words downloads, streaming films and music, apps, online games – content that will make up the mass market of the future, in other words. As it happens, not all of these types of content are currently subject to uniform regulations throughout Europe. Bringing about further harmonisation is not likely to be easy, however – new regulations should be adopted only where they are actually needed. Also, unless a high level of consumer protection is ensured, the digital single market will simply not become attractive for consumers. At the same time, any such regulations must be made 'future-proof' so as to not be rendered obsolete by the headlong pace of digital development. All of which means that we can look forward to spirited and interesting discussions at the European level!

Another new business model that has given rise to increased digitisation is the so-called 'sharing economy'. This model promises consumers a wider range of choices, stronger community cohesion, and greater environmental protection. But in order for this to work in practice, the corresponding framework conditions will first have to be created by politicians and the business sector. They will have to see to it that security, public interest, and privacy are protected. Another challenge posed by the sharing economy is the difficulty of drawing a clear distinction between the commercial and private realms. Thus, each consumer must be able to determine whether he or she is dealing with a commercial provider or a private one. And even when interacting with private providers, consumers must enjoy a minimum standard of protection. On the other hand, lawmakers will also have to make it easier for private individuals to offer their sharing services. As in the case of all the digital world's new business models, the guiding principle is here as well that consumers must retain full control over their rights. So can you see, I think, how much remains to be accomplished in this area. At present, the German Federal Ministry of Justice and Consumer Protection is preparing a consumer-specific survey and analysis of the new business models associated with the sharing economy. I am confident that the contributions to the conference will give me all kinds of interesting and helpful food for thought on this topic as well.

The Internet of Things, i.e. the communication among objects, presents yet another of the key challenges for consumer protection in the digital age, and I have already touched on this topic briefly. Although the Internet of Things may not appear to loom large in our daily lives quite yet, it is developing rapidly and is, in the end, only a matter of time.

The business sector, for one, has been quick to recognise the Internet of Things as a promising area of commercial endeavour, but is also wrestling with the problems that it entails. Problems that, unless resolved, will make it impossible to create the consumer trust that is indispensable for end-to-end networking. Early this year, a number of leading US firms from the field of the Internet of Things came together to form a so-called 'Online Trust Alliance', and to draft a self-regulatory code of ethics for manufacturers, developers, and dealers of electronic devices. The goal was to introduce uniform security and data-protection standards so as to better safeguard privacy within the Internet of Things. This code could well be a first step in the right direction.

Social networks have a very special role to play in this regard. They provide users with a forum that fundamentally allows them to freely disseminate their views and opinions, enabling them to reach a large audience in a direct and immediate manner. However, if the messages posted are punishable under law, this will require prompt action to be taken. Social networks may not be abused for the mass dissemination of illegal hate speech. As recent incidents in connection with the influx of refugees into the European Union have made quite clear, the platforms concerned have a responsibility towards society at large. Social networks who pronounce in their Community Standards that spreading racist messages or content inciting to hatred is prohibited must allow themselves to be measured by their own standards. At present, we are pursuing intense talks to achieve improvements in this arena.

Digital Revolution – Challenges for Contract Law

*Reiner Schulze / Dirk Staudenmayer**

I. Challenges for Contracting

The digital revolution is one of the ground-breaking trends of our century which will change fundamentally our economy and our society.[1] This development will also extend to many aspects of law. Legislators, scholars, legal practitioners and legislators are faced with the key question whether the current legal framework is suitable for its purpose or if perhaps an adapted or even a new framework is necessary. Such question concerns many areas of law, especially contract law due to its central role for a functioning market economy.[2] Contracts are the tool which makes transactions work in our economy; private law provides the general framework within which these transactions take place. It is an area of law which is already experiencing a rapid and profound change due to the influence of the digital revolution, yet at this time it is not possible to predict all the consequences thereof. The impact covers a variety of matters, such as the communication in contract preparation, the conclusion and performance of a contract, as well as to new matters and forms of trade, together with the associated new contract types (such as the supply of digital content).

Contract law could in this regard thus be facing a new phase of modernisation which extends beyond the modernisation since the second

---

* Reiner Schulze is Professor of German and European Civil Law at the Westfälische Wilhelms-Universität Münster and Director of the Centre for European Private Law. Dirk Staudenmayer is Head of Unit Contract Law, DG Justice, European Commission and Honorary Professor at the Westfälische Wilhelms-Universität Münster. The present editorial expresses only the personal opinion of the author and does not bind in any way the European Commission. Both authors thank the research assistants, Benedikt Beierle and Jonathon Watson, for their support in managing the conference and for their preparation of this chapter.

1 Reiner Schulze and Dirk Staudenmayer, 'Editorial' (2015) 6 EuCML 215.

2 On this function of contract law and the stage of development of European contract law see Reiner Schulze and Fryderyk Zoll, European Contract Law (Nomos 2015) 1.

half of the 20th century, more specifically the research by *Ernst Rabel*[3] which formed the starting point for extensive reforms and measures at international and national level.[4] This research had combined civil law and common law perspectives and linked the experiences from the study of Roman law with a clear view of the needs of the 20th century. At first, the research provided a basis for the Hague Conventions[5] and ultimately for the 1980 Vienna Convention on Contracts for the International Sale of Goods (CISG). The CISG has not only since entered into force in over 80 countries[6] but its new approaches (such as the concept of 'conformity' and the catalogue of 'remedies' etc.) have also influenced the development of national contract laws – from Chinese contract law[7] to the 'New Civil Code' in the Netherlands[8], from the reforms in central and Eastern European countries[9] to the 2002 modernisation of the German law of obligations[10] and to other present reform projects in France[11] and Spain[12].[13] The

---

3 Ernst Rabel, *Das Recht des Warenkaufs* vol. I (1936, reprinted de Gruyter 1964). See also Ernst Rabel, 'A Draft of an International Law of Sales' (1938) 5 University of Chicago Law Review 453

4 Reiner Schulze, 'The New Shape of European Contract Law' (2015) 4 EuCML 139.

5 Hague Conventions of 1 July 1964: Convention relating to the Uniform Law for the International Sale of Goods (ULIS); Convention relating to the Uniform Law of the Formation of Contracts for the International Sale of Goods (ULF).

6 For a comprehensive overview see Franco Ferrari (ed), *The CISG and its Impact on National Legal Systems* (Sellier 2008). A list of all CISG Member States is available online under <http://www.uncitral.org/ uncitral/en/uncitral_texts/ sale_goods/1980CISG_status.html> accessed 27 November 2015.

7 In general on the relationship between CISG and Chinese Law see Michael Will (ed), *CISG and China – Theory and Practice (An International Exchange)* (Faculté de droit/ Unité de droit allemande 1999).

8 For an overview see Sonja Kruisinga, 'The Impact of Uniform Law on National Law: Limits and Possibilities – CISG and its Incidence in Dutch Law' (2009) 13 Electronic Journal of Comparative Law 1.

9 E.g. Romania, Lucian Bojin, 'The Law of Obligations in Romania' in Reiner Schulze and Fyderyk Zoll (eds), *The Law of Obligations in Europe – A New Wave of Codifications* (Sellier 2013) 377, 382–383.

10 Carsten Herresthal, '10 Years after the Reform of the Law of Obligations in Germany – The Position of the Law of Obligations in German Law' in ibid 193; Reiner Schulze and Hans Schulte-Nölke, 'Schuldrechtsreform und Gemeinschaftsrecht' in Reiner Schulze and Hans Schulte-Nölke (eds), *Die Schuldrechtsreform vor dem Hintergrund des Gemeinschaftsrechts* (Mohr Siebeck 2001) 3; Peter Schlechtriem, '10 Jahre CISG – Der Einfluss des UN-Kaufrechts auf die Entwick-

inspirational effect of the CISG can also be clearly seen in the development of European contract law, both in regard to academic drafts (such as the Principles of European Contract Law from the 'Lando Commission'[14] and the Draft Common Frame of Reference[15]) and EU legislation (in particular the Consumer Sales Directive[16]).[17]

However, fundamental changes to contract practice arose soon after the CISG was signed due to the spread of the Internet; the digital revolution over the following decades has led to further new challenges for contract law. It is evident that it will not be possible to respond to these challenges with national law alone; legal answers will also be necessary at European and international level alongside the national changes. European solutions, which take account of the conditions and potential of the internal market, will be needed as marketing and contracting through such new technologies are of key importance for the development of the internal market and

---

lung des deutschen und des internationalen Schuldrechts' (2001) 1 Internationales Handelsrecht 12.

11 'Projet de loi relatif à la modernisation et à la simplification du droit et des procédures dans les domaines de la justice et des affaires intérieures' available online under <http://www.senat.fr/leg/pjl14-076.pdf> last accessed on 27 November 2015. On the history of the draft see Hélène Boucard, 'The curious process reforming France's law of obligations' (2015) 1 Montesquieu Law Review 1.

12 'Propuesta para la modernización del Derecho de obligaciones y contratos' available online under <http://www.mjusticia.gob.es/cs/Satellite/1292338914438?blobheader> last accessed 27 November 2015. See also Nieves Fenoy Picón, 'The Spanish Obligation and Contract Law and the Proposal for its Modernisation' in Reiner Schulze and Fryderyk Zoll, *The Law of Obligations in Europe – A New Wave of Codifications* (Sellier 2013) 397.

13 Ingeborg Schwenzer and Pascal Hachem, 'The CISG – A Story of Worldwide Success' in Jan Kleinemann (ed), *CISG Part II Conference* (Iustus Förlag 2009) 125.

14 The Commission on European Contract Law, Ole Lando and Hugh Beale (eds), *The Principles Of European Contract law. Parts I and II* (Kluwer Law International 1999); Part III edited by Ole Lando et al (Kluwer Law International 2003).

15 Christian von Bar, Eric Clive and Hans Schulte-Nölke (eds), *Principles, Definitions and Model Rules of European Private Law. Draft Common Frame of Reference (DCFR Outline Edition)* (Sellier 2009)

16 European Parliament and Council Directive 1999/44/EC of 25 May 1999 on certain aspects of the sale of consumer goods and associated guarantees [1999] OJ L171/12 (Consumer Sales Directive).

17 Reiner Schulze, 'The New Shape of European Contract Law' (2015) 4 EuCML 140.

thus for prosperity in Europe. As a relatively young 'law in progress', European contract law was able over the past two decades to react relatively quickly and with flexibility to the new challenges. A series of directives[18] provided a response to the changes in practice and may – alongside other instruments[19] – provide the starting point for suitable approaches also for the future tasks that arise through the development of digitalisation.

Accordingly, it is hardly surprising that the promotion of a connected Digital Single Market is one of the ten priorities of the European Commission. The European Commission has recognised that a functioning Digital Single Market could be a largely untapped potential for economic growth. Preparing a framework that creates the necessary technical, legal and other conditions would help to allow new business models to flourish while creating the users' trust necessary for them to embrace the advantages of the Digital Single Market. In its Digital Single Market Strategy[20], it announces a number of initiatives to create a favorable framework for the digital economy and thereby ultimately to promote economic growth in Europe. Various aspects of contract law which concern its vital role for the Digital Single Market, are also included in the public consultations launched by the European Commission. This includes, for example, the consultation on the regulatory environment for platforms, online intermediaries, data and cloud computing and the collaborative economy.[21] In the context of this public consultation the workshop, which provided the basis for this volume, discussed several pressing challenges for contract law

18 Inter alia Directive 97/7/EC of the European Parliament and of the Council of 20 May 1997 on the protection of consumers in respect of distance contracts [1997] OJ L144/19; Directive 1999/93/EC of the European Parliament and of the Council of 13 December 1999 on a Community framework for electronic signatures [2000] OJ L103/12; Directive 2000/31/EC of the European Parliament and of the Council of 8 June 2000 on certain legal aspects of information society services, in particular electronic commerce, in the Internal Market ('Directive on electronic commerce') [2000] OJ L178/1; Directive 2002/65/EC of the European Parliament and of the Council of 23 September 2002 concerning the distance marketing of consumer financial services [2002] OJ L271/16.

19 Inter alia the work undertaken in preparation for the – since withdrawn – proposal for a Common European Sales Law (COM (2011) 635 final).

20 Commission, 'A Digital Single Market Strategy for Europe' COM (2015) 192 final.

21 Consultation text available online under <https://ec.europa.eu/eusurvey/runner/Platforms/> last accessed on 27 November 2015.

which are posed by some of the new developments of digitalisation and the digital economy: 3D-Printing, Share Economy, and Internet of Things (IoT).

II. 3D-Printing

Technological developments in 3D-Printing have a profound effect on the future of production and manufacturing. 3D-Printing will lead to a situation where users for goods which are not used in a mass market will no longer buy such goods, but rather the corresponding digital files which will allow them to 3D-print the goods at home or to instruct a 3D-print shop to print for them. At first glance, particular practical advantages associated with this new technology are easily identifiable, for instance the facilitation of innovation, the contribution to sustainability and ease and speed of distribution, as well as clear disadvantages such as affording access to legally-restricted or prohibited items (such as firearms).[22]

Accordingly, 3D-Printing gives a new dimension to a broad variety of legal implications and issues in different fields of law. In this regard, the main contributing factors to this problem of the digital age are not only the relatively affordable access to the (physical) 3D-printer, thereby taking manufacture out of the factory and into homes, hospitals and even the International Space Station, but also the access to the (digital) code of the item to be printed. A glance through a legal lens clearly shows a multitude of issues anchored in intellectual property (copyright, patents etc.), tort law (e.g. product liability) and even criminal law.[23] Whereas within the scope of this brief introduction it is not possible to give a detailed insight into all of these individual issues in each area of law the focus is directed

---

22 See further Devan Desai and Garard Magliocca, 'Patents, Meet Napster: 3D Printing and the Digitalization of Things' (2014) 102 The Georgetown Law Review 1691, 1700–1703; Banning Garrett, '3D Printing: New Economic Paradigms and Strategic Shifts' (2014) 5 Global Policy 70, 71–72; Phil Reeves and Dinusha Mendis, 'The Current Status and Impact of 3D-Printing in the Industrial Sector' (March 2015) 1–2.

23 See the contribution by Geraint Howells and Chris Willett, in this volume, 67. See also Deven Desai and Garard Magliocca, ibid, 1705–1713; Nora Engstrom, '3D Printing and Product Liability: Identifying the Obstacles' (2013) 162 University of Pennsylvania Law Review Online 35; Phil Reeves and Dinusha Mendis, ibid, 49–53.

towards the legal implications of 3D-Printing for the present legal framework in contract law.[24]

The purchase of a 3D-printer and the required printing material sits quite neatly in the framework of a sales contract and the protection already in place under existing European legislation for the sale of goods. However, the acquisition of the 'digital' instructions needed to produce the tangible end-product is problematic from a number of different perspectives, not just from an intellectual property standpoint.[25] It is noted that the issues surrounding 3D-Printing are merely a specific manifestation of the general legal problems and challenges underlying digital content as a whole rather than a particular area that may require separate, targeted regulation.[26] However, in comparison to other digital media files such as games, films or music, the notable characteristic of 3D-Printing is the use of such digital files in the manufacturing process. In other words, the 3D-printer – and its 'ink' – represents the medium to transform the series of intangible binary code into a tangible object. It is the gateway between the virtual and physical worlds. From a doctrinal standpoint it contains elements which have implications both in contract and also in tort liability regimes, more specifically the liability (and classification) of the producer of the 3D-printed good. In this context, 3D-Printing may make a further contribution not only to the continuous debate on the definition of a consumer, but also the role of both parties in general.[27]

The distinction between contractual and tortious liability in relation to any harm caused either by the digital content or the printed good is of great importance. Nevertheless, it is apparent that the various regulatory facets within these two schemes do not provide concrete solutions as to the rules applicable to more general aspects of 3D-Printing or the narrower, individual constellations which arise through activity in both the

---

24 See also the contribution by Christian Twigg-Flesner, in this volume, 35. For tort law see Geraint Howells and Chris Willett, in this volume, 67.

25 Deven Desai and Garard Magliocca, 'Patents, Meet Napster: 3D Printing and the Digitalization of Things' (2014) 102 The Georgetown Law Review 1691, 1705–1713. Phil Reeves and Denusha Mendis, 'The Current Status and Impact of 3D-Printing in the Industrial Sector (March 2015) 49–53. See also Denusha Mendis, Davide Secchi and Phil Reeves, 'A Legal and Empirical Study into the Intellectual Property Implications of 3D-Printing' (March 2015) 7.

26 See Christian Twigg-Flesner, in this volume, 35.

27 See Geraint Howells and Chris Willett, in this volume, 67; Christian Twigg-Flesner, in this volume, 35.

virtual and physical world. A legislative response may thus not just be limited to contract, but may also be necessary in aspects of tort law, in particular in the area of producer's liability. The challenges posed for contract law by 3D-Printing may in some instances be – more fundamentally – remaining as the system for regulating liability.

Irrespective of the liability regime there is a need to close regulatory gaps regarding digital content. However, a core question at this early stage in the legislative process relates to the methodology in drafting such rules. Gaps could be plugged with specific rules; alternatively it may be necessary to extend the scope of existing general rules in favour of a principle-based approach. As is highlighted for various issues in this volume, the impact of the digital revolution may appear to strike specific areas of law, yet the ripples it creates will spread across different fields; this is especially apparent for 3D-printing.

It is a general issue whether current rules for goods can be extended to cover digital content. However, for 3D-Printing in particular, the question whether the purchase of the digital code equates in essence to the purchase of the product to be 3D-printed;[28] the buyer's expectations are ultimately not limited to the digital content itself but extend to the physical manifestation of this content. Under this approach, the provider of the digital content may not just be liable for the conformity of the digital file but also its content, i.e. the 3D-printed good. Consequently, the wider question can arise in respect of the protection of the buyer's legitimate expectations and the extent to which the law should extend to the broader expectations arising under the contract for CAD files.

Although some of the various constellations related to 3D-Printing may be covered by the current legislative regime in contract, the new dimension 3D-Printing gives to current contract law may therefore be in a *sui generis* contract for the situation in which the consumer purchases digital content and 3D-prints, i.e. manufactures, the good himself. It may suffice to adjust accordingly the traditional forms of contract. This reflects the general discussion surrounding the classification of the contract for digital content, yet it also has broader implications for rules concerning 'mixed' or 'hybrid' contracts in general. In comparison to such contracts comprising goods and service elements, the law for both areas is established – at least at national level – whereas the combination of goods and

28 See Geraint Howells and Chris Willett, in this volume, 67.

digital content is only partially established. A priority at present is therefore to clarify the applicable law on digital content as a whole. However the increase in accessibility to 3D-Printing will ultimately require legislative or judicial clarification of the relationship between the rules on the virtual and physical elements and thus the scope of protection. 3D-Printing may well reflect general issues concerning digital content, yet its peculiar gateway function shows that the relationship between rules for digital content and rules for goods could to be taken into account in future legislative steps.

The European Commission has clarified in its very recent proposal for a Directive on contracts for the supply of digital content[29] clarified that this Directive would also apply to the supply of visual modelling files required in the context of 3D-Printing. However, it has explicitly not yet regulated goods produced with the use of 3D-Printing technology or the damage caused to them. Given the fast moving pace of technology and the limited knowledge and legal discussion available on this subject, this is understandable as the proposal for a Directive as the first deliverable under the Digital Single Market Strategy focuses on issues which are indispensable to be regulated now. Therefore this proposal is a sensible first step. However, in the medium term, this issue will need to be tackled in legal doctrine and possibly also in legislation.

III. Share Economy

Share economy has become a commonly used term for different forms of economic acts in the manufacture, sale or consumption whereby the traditional roles of producer and consumer are not played. Such acts are often said to be linked as much as possible to the goal of a community-based, resource-saving and sustainable performance.[30] Share economy appears, for example, in the form or Crowdfunding, Couchsurfing or Car-sharing.[31]

---

29 Commission, 'Proposal for a Directive of the European Parliament and the Council on certain aspects concerning contracts for the supply of digital content of 9 December 2015' COM (2015) 634 final, Recital 16.

30 Caroline Meller-Hannich, 'Zu einigen rechtlichen Aspekten der "Share Economy"' [2014] WM 2337.

31 See Larry DiMatteo, in this volume, 89; see Caroline Meller-Hannich, in this volume, 119.

In the sharing economy consumers conclude contracts with service providers who are often not professional traders but other private persons. However, such contracts are frequently concluded through a platform. Customers will often not realise that their contracting partner is not the platform itself but another private person. Existing consumer contract law legislation applies however only in business-to-consumer transactions. It is thus necessary to examine whether the scope and the contents of the legal framework are adequate or if there are problems that imply a need to act.[32]

Questions are not only raised for consumers concluding contracts in the sharing economy, but also for businesses. For instance, a small start-up app developer contracting with a platform with considerable bargaining power is sometimes faced with a contracting partner which prescribes standard terms and conditions determining most of the competition parameters, such as price, quality control, remedies of the user. This could possibly be problematic if one takes as a point of departure the principle of freedom of contract in a business-to-business transaction. More generally, there is the task to determine more precisely the responsibility of an operator of an internet platform within the relationship seller (or service provider)–buyer (or customer)–platform operator. The sales contract (or services contract) may be a contract between non-commercial parties, however the platform is a commercial third party who organises and controls the communication between the parties, has the main information and broadly stipulates the conditions for the preparation and conclusion of the contracts. Consequently, the question is posed of the extent to which it must perform information duties, the breach of which can lead to its liability, and furthermore whether it – with regard to the principle determination of a legal position – it is not simply viewed as a typical 'third party' in the relationship between the parties who have concluded a sales or services contract via the platform.[33]

---

32 See Rafael Illescas Ortiz, in this volume, 111.

33 Specific questions concerning online platforms were discussed at a later conference 'Platform Services in the Digital Single Market' held in Osnabrück on the 19–20 November 2015 and organised by Christoph Busch, Hans Schulte-Nölke, Aneta Wiewiórowska-Domagalska and Fryderyk Zoll. A project group was formed following this conference and will prepare a discussion paper for EU legislation on online platforms.

IV. Internet of Things

The notion of the Internet of Things presents a new challenge for business, society and law; it is a concept which was described in American literature as 'ubiquitous computing'[34]. The IoT is linked to the vision of a network of day-to-day objects that can communicate with one another. Over time, the term 'ubiquitous computing' has been joined by many others that feature various differences, yet have the same core: the internet leaves the purely digital world and enters the physical. However, it does not suffice to say that this stage is possible merely when an object has internet capabilities. The object must rather be programmed with a level of artificial intelligence that also allows for it to act autonomously. The advancements in technology have resulted in smaller and more powerful micro-processors which gave rise to the recent category of 'smart phones'. Now, just a short time later, there are new categories of so-called 'wearables', not to mention the mass suitability of RFID-technology or the advancements in the field of self-driving vehicles, which show the extent of the technological progress. Together with further developments – such as 'cloud computing' and 'big data' – the technological promises enormous potential, considerable increases in efficiency and possibilities for growth. Such potential is so far-reaching that there are numerous references to the next stage of the industrial revolution, an Industry 4.0 or simply a *digital* revolution.[35]

Legal problems and particularly questions of contractual and extra-contractual liability can easily arise in many different IoT scenarios from self-driving cars to the use of robotics in smart factories or the use of apps linked to household appliances in smart houses.[36] For example, who is responsible for damage caused by a self-driving car if a child crosses the street and the self-driving car can only run over the child or damage another car parked on the street: The producer, the seller, the owner, the 'driver', the infrastructure providing the data to the car, the child? This simple example highlights why the Digital Single Market Strategy

---

34 Mark Weiser, 'The Computer for the 21st Century' [1991] (9) Scientific American 94.

35 According to the German association, Bitkom, the term 'Industrie 4.0' became one of the main topics of the year, see press release 15/01/22.

36 On the scope of these questions see Christiane Wendehorst, in this volume, 189.

considers clarification of liability as an important pre-condition for the roll-out of IoT.[37]

Beside the fact that it was adopted in 1985 when nobody thought about rules for the internet, not to talk about IoT, the approach of the Product Liability Directive is probably not an adequate or at least an insufficient solution for liability questions in the IoT.[38] One may be able to find solutions based on the existing private law regimes for cases where a human intervention is at the origin and a causality link can be established, but even this may require adaptations or further development of the existing legal approaches. Questions about liability become however really pertinent if they are linked to completely autonomous systems such as self-driving cars or autonomous robotics. A regulatory clarification seems to be unavoidable.

This raises however quite a number of more complicated questions. If such regulatory clarifications are necessary, the question arises as to the approach in a legal-systematic context and in relation to the legal technique. On a substantive level, one will have to consider the criteria for determining liability, not just in relation to the criteria but also to the party.[39] Due to the number of participants there is also the question whether each individual is liable or whether there should be a kind of joint liability, perhaps depending on contributions to the risk which materialised in the damage. Numerous further questions are also posed for the reason and legal nature of liability: Can there be at all a somehow fault-based liability approach if actions are determined by software and algorithms? Should liability be based on a principle that somebody running an autonomous system has created a risk and should therefore be liable for possible damage when this risk has materialised? Should liability be strict?[40] Should there be caps or the possibility to take into account

---

37 Commission, 'A Digital Single Market Strategy for Europe' COM (2015) 192 final.

38 Cf Erica Palmerini and Andrea Bertolini, in this volume, 225.

39 The concept of an 'Electronic Person' is probably not well suited as a solution, on this suggestion see Susanne Beck 'Über Sinn und Unsinn von Statusfragen – zu Vor- und Nachteilen der Einführung einer elektronischen Person' in Eric Hilgendorf and Jan-Philipp Günther (eds) *Robotik und Gesetzgebung* (Nomos 2013).

40 In this direction e.g. Peter Bräutigam and Thomas Klindt, 'Industrie 4.0, das Internet der Dinge und das Recht' [2015] NJW 1137; Malte-Christian Gruber, 'Gefährdungshaftung für informationstechnologische Risiken: Verantwortungszurechnung im „Tanz der Agenzien"' [2013] KJ 356; Jochen Hanisch,

external factors? Should liability be coupled with a – possibly mandatory – insurance solution?

While clarification of liability in IoT is important, the legal questions do not stop there. For example, one will also have to consider the consequences arising for consumer law (especially consumer protection in competition law) from the new possibilities of greater personalised advertising in IoT (including new forms of profiling and targeting).[41] The same also applies to the means of payment enabled by IoT, including the new chances and dangers of the exercise of rights to 'self-help' via IoT (for instance, the 'smart fridge' that is programmed not to contract when the consumer is late in paying an installment in the purchase price).[42]

Another set of questions deals with 'machine-to-machine' contracts. If a smart fridge orders food from the local supermarket or a machine orders spare parts from a machine in the supplier's smart factory, how is the contract concluded and what are the legal implications? Such questions are not entirely new due in light of automated conclusion of contract and have already gained in significance due to the increased importance of e-commerce.[43] The discussions on this topic will however become more relevant due to the advances in technology arising from digitalization. Having automated conclusion of contracts is different from contracts concluded by autonomous systems that interact with their environment in an independent manner. Further, advances in technology, such as the blockchain technology, may make it possible that a truly automated conclusion of contracts takes place when a decentralised infrastructure processes a contract because it has noted that two sets of standards terms and conditions fit together[44]. Ultimately, it will not just be concerned with building bridges between the traditional models of conclusion of contract via offer and acceptance and modern forms of automated conclusion of contract.

Haftung für Automation (Cuvillier 2010); Herbert Zech, 'Gefährdungshaftung und neue Technologien' [2013] JZ 21.

41 See Natali Helberger, in this volume, 135.

42 See Rolf Weber, in this volume, also with regard to digital cryptocurrencies, 163.

43 E.g. Joachim Lieser 'Die zivilrechtliche Haftung im automatisierten Geschäftsverkehr' [1971] JZ 759; Kai Cornelius, 'Vertragsabschluss durch autonome elektronische Agenten' [2002] MMR 353.

44 Florian Graillot, 'The Blockchain Might Be The Next Disruptive Technology' (*TechCrunch*, October 2015) <www.techcrunch.com/2015/10/03/the-blockchain-might-be-the-next-disruptive-technology> accessed 01 December 2015.

V. Conclusion

While at the present situation, there are more questions than answers, some conclusions seem already plausible. Firstly, as the impact of those questions and answers do beyond the national level, the discussion should take place at European and international level. Secondly, the discussion about the answers to those questions needs to be interdisciplinary: it should involve law, IT and other technology and all market players. Only such an interdisciplinary discussion would ensure that law finds the answers the economy needs for what technology can deliver.

In this framework, the present volume can only be a start in a longer discussion that will allow us to understand the private law questions related to the challenges of digitalisation and the data-driven economy. The answers to be given will necessarily be diverse. Once the questions properly understood, undoubtedly a more or less large part of the answers will be provided by the existing European and national laws which just have to be applied or adapted in their application with the new circumstances in mind. Awareness of the new challenges is all what is needed here. In other cases, soft law approaches like model contract terms could help market participants, in particular SMEs. Finally, new laws may be necessary in other cases. Again, such new laws could be of a different nature. They could only adapt existing laws to a more or less minor extent or simply clarify certain issues. They could also provide genuinely new rules. An important requirement of such new rules would be that their contents have to be coherent within contract law as whole and with neighboring areas that are partially overlapping or which share common borderlines as data protection law, copyright law and telecommunications law.

The proposal of the European Commission on contracts for the supply of digital content is the first example of such a new law. It is a further development of the already existing rules on the sales of tangible goods.[45] This proposal limits itself voluntarily to some key issues to prevent existing or forthcoming legal fragmentation. It therefore leaves many issues unregulated where it perhaps at present better not yet to interfere in the fast-moving pace of technological and commercial progress of the

45 European Parliament and Council Directive 1999/44/EC of 25 May 1999 on certain aspects of the sale of consumer goods and associated guarantees [1999] OJ L171/12 (Consumer Sales Directive).

digital economy.[46] Besides the above-mentioned opening to 3D-Printing, it also states explicitly that specific issues related to IoT, such as machine-to-machine contracting, should be addressed separately.

One of the major achievements of this proposal is to include in its scope the supply of digital content against a counter-performance other than money. This will set a clear landmark in EU and national laws that data is already a currency of today, but even more a currency of tomorrow. It also shows the way to the recognition that data are not only a currency but also the lifeblood of or the basis for the data-driven economy. The aim should be to ensure that data can flow so freely that new business models can flourish. At the same time, the interests of all contracting parties need to be safeguarded so that the access to and transfer of data is as smooth as possible. Furthermore, data protection is – especially in relation to privacy – one of the main concerns which European legislation is tackling in light of the new challenges,[47] as is shown by the proposed General Data Protection Regulation[48].

Taking this into consideration, contract law in the digital age is thus also faced with the task of ensuring the fundamental freedoms (especially the free movement of goods and freedom to provide services) also in respect of the free flow of data in the internal market. Seen from this broader angle, the proposal of the European Commission on contracts for the supply of digital content could possibly be only a first step in writing the future private law of the digital economy.

---

46 A further workshop on this topic will take place in Autumn 2016.

47 With regard to the importance of this issue see Rolf Weber, in this volume, 163.

48 Commission 'Proposal for a Regulation of the European Parliament and of the Council on the protection of individuals with regard to the processing of personal data and on the free movement of such data (General Data Protection Regulation)' COM (2012) 11 final.

3D-Printing and Contract Law

Conformity of 3D prints – Can current Sales Law cope?

Christian Twigg-Flesner[*]

I. Introduction

This contribution focuses on the contract law issues of an exciting technological development: the wide-spread use of 3D-printing as a new manufacturing process. As will become apparent, this is much more than just another new technology that can be used to improve current manufacturing processes – rather, this is the kind of development which Clayton Christensen would regard as a 'disruptive technology'.[1] The objective of this paper is to consider how the arrival of 3D-printing might require us to re-think current law particularly with regard to contract law, specifically the sale of goods. Much has been written about the intellectual property implications of this development,[2] but the implications for the law on sales contracts are under-explored. In order to identify these, this paper will first give a brief overview of the process of 3D-printing, before considering the most common types of transaction where 3D-printing is likely to have, or already has, a sustained application. Based on this, the particular legal issues this creates are considered, before examining the extent to which current law is able to address these and suggesting aspects where there might be a need either to clarify the law, or to introduce new provisions to fill a gap in existing legislation. The focus of this analysis is primarily on

---

* Christian Twigg-Flesner is Professor of Commercial Law at the University of Hull.
The author is grateful to participants at the *Digital Revolution – Challenges for Contract Law in Practice* workshop and attendees at a staff seminar at City University Hong Kong for their comments, as well as to Hugh Beale for commenting on an earlier draft of this paper.

1 Clayton M Christensen, *The Innovator's Dilemma – When New Technology Causes Great Firms to fail* (Harvard Business Review Press 1997).

2 See e.g. Anne Lewis, 'The Legality of 3D Printing: How Technology is Moving Faster than the Law' (2014) 17 Tulane Journal of Technology and Intellectual Property 303, and Preeta Reddy, 'The Legal Dimension of 3D Printing: Analyzing Secondary Liability in Additive Layer Manufacturing' (2014) 16 Columbia Science and Technology Law Review 222.

the position of a (consumer) buyer who acquires an item produced by 3D-printing technology. However, it needs to be acknowledged that the way 3D-printing could be utilised also raises wider questions about how contract law might need to respond more generally beyond the scope of this paper.

II. What is 3D-printing?[3]

In this section, I will provide a brief overview of what 3D-printing is and its potential applications.[4] On the basis of this section, I will then explore the most common types of transaction where 3D-printing is already being utilised. The implications of any new technology are two-fold: first, it can have a significant practical impact by 'disrupting' established ways of manufacturing; and secondly, it might reveal that existing laws are insufficiently equipped to deal with the implications of this new technology. Although the focus of this paper is primarily on legal issues, a few words about the technological aspects are needed by way of context.

1. 3D-printing: the main ingredients

Any 3D-printing process requires three main ingredients:[5]

(1) The design: this will be a file created using Computer-Aided-Design (CAD) software. It contains all the necessary information about the item to be printed to enable a 3D-printer to turn the design into a tangible item. Often, these CAD-files are shared as open-source files, allowing others to download the files for free and also to develop the design further.

---

3 For this section, I benefitted from the very clear explanation of the 3D-Printing technology and potential market applications in Chris Anderson, *Makers – The New Industrial Revolution* (Random House 2012), and Christopher Barnatt, *3D Printing – The Next Industrial Revolution* (ExplainingTheFuture 2013).

4 See also Lucas S Osborn, 'Regulating Three-Dimensional Printing: The Converging World of Bits and Atoms' (2014) 51 San Diego Law Review 553, 558–562.

5 For a more detailed account, see Nicole D Berkowitz, 'Strict Liability for Individuals? The impact of 3-D printing on Products Liability Law' (2014) 92 Washington University Law Review 1019, 1023–1027.

(2) A 3D-printer: this is the device that interprets the CAD-file containing the design to make the physical item. There are a variety of 3D-printers available already, and the various technologies are explained below. Most 3D-printers are only suitable for an industrial or commercial setting, although desktop printers suitable for home use are already being offered, and it is likely that more consumer-focused 3D-printers will become available rapidly.
(3) The material used for printing: As explained below, there are various materials which can be utilised for 3D-printing, particularly plastic and certain metals. Although most 3D-printers will print using a single material, there are some printers capable of 3D-printing an item using more than one type of material.

2. *The Technology*

Although commonly referred to as 3D-printing, the process which leads to the creation of a three-dimensional object using technology which resembles the familiar process of printing a document on a printer is properly known as 'additive manufacturing', or 'additive layer manufacturing'. In essence, an item built up in very thin layers, with each new layer added to the previous layers already printed. Thus, in order to make an item, its design has to be broken down into very thin layers, and the 3D-printer then has to be instructed to make layer upon layer to create the finished item. Although '3D-printing' is a popular label given to this process, not all additive manufacturing processes really are like 'printing'. At the present time, there are three principal additive manufacturing technologies:[6]

Thermoplastic Extrusion: This resembles the familiar idea of printing most closely. This type of 3D-printer uses a print-head not dissimilar to a standard inkjet printer, but with the ability to move up and down as well as left and right. Material (usually plastic) is heated to melting point and then extruded through the print nozzle onto a platform to make a layer. The platform is then slightly lowered and the process is

6 For a more detailed explanation of the variations within these three broad categories, see Christopher Barnatt, *3D Printing – The Next Industrial Revolution* (ExplainingTheFuture 2013) ch 2.

repeated to make the next layer until the item is completed. This process is particularly suitable for simple objects which do not have any overhanging or orphan parts,[7] although where there are such parts, it is possible to print thin support structures which have to be removed after the printing process has been completed

Photopolymerisation: In this process, the material is liquid inside a container, and a laser is used to solidify a thin layer of material for the item to be made. A platform within the container is then lowered slightly and the process is repeated. The advantage of this approach is that it is possible to make more complex objects, especially those with overhanging or orphan parts. It is also possible to use a wider range of materials.

Granular materials binding: This type of process uses a powder and a means of binding powder particles together to form a layer. One way of doing this is similar to photopolymerisation in that a laser is used for binding together particles to make a layer. An alternative way is to spray a layer of a bonding agent onto the powder to make a layer, then to add a thin layer of the material and repeat the process.

It would go far beyond the scope of this paper to explore these different technological approaches in full detail. It is a continuously emerging technology, and it remains to be seen which processes will emerge to be utilised widely. The technology has already reached a stage to allow 3D-printing of detailed objects at a microscopic level.[8] Also, the range of materials in which 3D-printing is possible is broadening: as well as plastics and metal, there are recent examples of objects 3D-printed in glass.

3. *Why use 3D-printing?*

The arrival of a new technology does not create immediate issues if its application remains confined to the experimental stage, but once a new technology is utilised widely, it will attract the attention of regulators, policy-makers and lawyers. Several areas for using 3D-printing have

7 Overhanging parts and orphan parts are elements of the item to be made which would be unsupported during the printing process: see Christopher Barnatt, *3D Printing – The Next Industrial Revolution* (ExplainingTheFuture 2013) 35.

8 Using a process called 'Two-Photon Polymerisation': see Christopher Barnatt, *3D Printing – The Next Industrial Revolution* (ExplainingTheFuture 2013) 50–54.

already emerged.[9] One of the earliest uses for 3D-printing has been the rapid prototyping of new products: once a design has been created, a 3D model can be printed and studied for any aspects that would benefit from further development.[10] More recently, it has gained popularity as a new means of manufacturing goods, a development described by some as revolutionary[11] and as 'democratising' the creation of new goods,[12] although there are also cautionary voices.[13]

3D-printing is already used for items supplied as consumer goods[14] and there are a number of uses of 3D-printing in the consumer context: first, it enables customisation of items to suit the preferences or particular requirements of a customer. Secondly, 3D-printing can be utilised to make items which are not suitable for mass-production by more traditional manufacturing methods such as injection moulding. It is well-known that mass production benefits from economies of scale, i.e., the more units of one particular item are made, the cheaper the process becomes. If there is limited demand, then the cost of setting-up a mass production run will not

9 The applications of 3D-printing are growing in number at an exponential rate. For recent examples, visit <http://3dprint.com/> accessed 27 November 2015.

10 It has also been used to help with the completion of Gaudi's Sagrada Familia in Barcelona: see e,g. Becky Chung, '3D Printing Accelerates Construction on Gaudí's Sagrada Família' (The creators project, 20 March 2015), <http://thecreatorsproject.vice.com/en_uk/blog/3d-printing-accelerates-construction-on-gaudis-sagrada-famlia> accessed 27 October 2015.

11 For example, Chris Anderson, *Makers – The New Industrial Revolution* (Random House 2012) charts the rise of the 'maker movement' which utilises the potential of information technology, the internet, and new production processes such as 3D-printing.

12 Nora Freeman Engstrom, '3-D Printing and Product Liability: Identifying the Obstacles' (2013) 162 University of Pennsylvania Law Review Online 35.

13 Elizabeth J Kennedy and Andrea Giampetro-Meyer, 'Gearing Up for the Next Industrial Revolution: 3D Printing, Home-Based Factories, and Modes of Social Control' (2014) 45 Loyola University Chicago Law Journal 955 discuss concerns about workplace protection, environmental risks, and safety.

14 As well as having many useful applications, 3D-printing can also be used for less welcome purposes, such as producing guns. This has already created significant attention in the U.S. – see e.g., Katie Curtis, 'A Wiki Weapon Solution: Firearm Regulation for the Management of 3D Printing in the American Household' (2015) 41 Rutgers Computer and Technology Law Journal 74 and Jeffrey T Leslie, 'The Internet and its Discontents: 3-D Printing, the Commerce Clause, and a Possible Solution to an Inevitable Problem' (2014) 17 SMU Science and Technology Law Review 195.

be recouped by subsequent sales. However, items for which there is limited demand could be made using 3D-printing technology. In contrast, 3D-printing would not be suitable for mass production, because the cost for making each item remains the same, i.e., there are no economies of scale for 3D-printed products. Unsurprisingly, therefore, 3D-printing has already become very popular for making gadgets, art work and jewellery.

A third application is to permit the localised production of products which could be 3D-printed. For example, a business based in Hong Kong might offer for sale goods which can be produced using 3D-printing technology. A customer from Germany places an order on the website of that business, and the business then arranges for a 3D-printing service in Europe to make and despatch the item.

Another potential application is achieved through combining 3D-printing with 3D-scanning technology. Such scanners can scan an item and turn it into a CAD-file. It is then possible to modify the item (if necessary), and make a copy using a 3D-printer. A useful application of this would be to make spare parts for goods on demand, or to make spare-parts where these are no longer available.

Finally, it seems that in the medical context, 3D-printing is likely to become increasingly useful.[15] For example, it has already been utilised to scan organs on which a surgeon will perform an operation to allow the medical team to rehearse the operation on a 3D-printed model of the organ. Also, it is possible to make some prostheses using 3D-technology to suit the specific requirements of a patient. The use of such technology in the medical context could have significant benefits, although it will also raise questions for regulators who impose very strict controls over medical devices such as implants. This issue is beyond the scope of this chapter.

Having outlined the nature of 3D-printing and possible applications, the next section will examine several types of transaction through which 3D-printed items can be supplied to a final customer. This will help to identify the specific legal issues created by the utilisation of this new technology.

15 It was recently reported that human tissue was created using 3D-printing technology. See BBC News, 'Consumer 3D Printer used to create human tissue' (BBC News, 28 October 2015) <http://www.bbc.co.uk/news/technology-34505242> accessed 29 October 2015.

IV. Common 3D-printing arrangements

In order to identify whether the advent of widespread utilisation of 3D-printing will have specific implications for contract law, it will first be necessary to consider several types of transaction through which 3D-printed goods are supplied to a (consumer) buyer. There is potentially quite a range of such transactions, so for the purposes of this discussion, the most common forms have been divided into 3 types of transaction. These will now be explained in turn. The specific legal issues arising in respect of each of these types will be explored afterwards. The classification below looks at these arrangements from the perspective of the final buyer (who will usually be a consumer).

Type 1:

The first type involves transactions which are really no different from the paradigm sales contract: a buyer concludes a contract with a trader for the sale/supply of goods. In the standard sales contract situation, the trader will either have those goods in stock or acquire them from his supplier and then deliver the goods to the buyer. In this context, 3D-printing technology may be used in several ways:

(i) by the manufacturer to make all or parts of the item;
(ii) by the retailer to make the item once an order has been received;
(iii) by either manufacturer or retailer to print an item which is customised in some way to meet the specific requirements of the buyer;
(iv) by the trader (who may be based anywhere in the world and operating on-line), who will forward the CAD-file containing the design to a 3D-printing facility near when the buyer is located, to have the item printed there and delivered to the consumer (reducing transportation distances and cost).

With this type of transaction, the buyer's contract essentially resembles the familiar sales contract, and all of these transactions should therefore be treated no differently from a sales contract involving goods manufactured by traditional methods (although in situation (iii), the extent of customisation might turn this into a different contract if a particular jurisdiction maintains such a distinction[16]).

Type 2

In this group, there are transactions where the buyer does not enter into a contract to buy a finished item, but instead the buyer first acquires the design CAD-file and then, as a second step, arranges for the design to be printed.

As far as acquiring the CAD-file containing the design is concerned,[17] there are generally two options:

(i) Purchase a CAD-file
(ii) Obtain the CAD-file through an open-source website

Then, in order to turn the CAD-file into a physical item, the main options are:

(i) Print the item at home on a 3-D desktop printer, if possible
(ii) Forward the CAD-file to a professional 3D-printing service

Although these two stages will result in the consumer eventually acquiring a physical item, there are several differences compared to the paradigm sale contract. First, the buyer does not have a single contract for the supply of the final item, so this no longer fits with the usual understanding of a contract of sale. Instead, with this type of transaction, there may two, one, or even no contracts: there will be two contracts where the buyer pays for the CAD-file and then arranges for a professional 3D-printing service to make the finished item. There might only be one contract where the pays for the CAD-file and then 3D-prints the item at home, or where the CAD-file is obtained through an open-source website and then turned into a physical item by a professional 3D-printing service.[18] Finally, there might

16 In the United Kingdom, the effect of Part 1 of the Consumer Rights Act 2015 is that the historic distinction between different types of supply transactions has become all but redundant in the consumer context.

17 Acquiring the CAD-file essentially means that the consumer obtains a copy of that file and, if a fee is paid, the right/licence to use that file to 3D-print the actual item.

18 Whether a free download can be a transaction regarded as a contract will vary between jurisdictions.

not be a contract at all where the CAD-file is obtained from an open-source website and the item is then 3D-printed at home.

Where there are contracts, none will be a standard sale of goods contract. Thus, the first contract would be for the acquisition of the CAD-file. In essence, this is a contract for the supply of digital content, and will essentially be a licence to use the CAD-file for specific purposes (primarily to 3D-print the item). Contracts involving the supply of digital content have given rise to extensive debate about how such contracts should be classified, especially with regard to conformity issues and remedies:[19] in some jurisdictions, the supply of digital content might be treated as a sale of goods to engage provision of conformity of goods with the contract and relevant remedies,[20] but in others, it might be regarded as a contract for the supply of digital content and be subject to separate rules.[21] The second contract is for the production of the finished item based on the CAD-file supplied, and it would once again depend on how this type of contract is classified in a particular jurisdiction whether this is a contract for a service, or a contract for the sale of the finished item, or a combination of both. These issues will be discussed in more detail below.

Type 3

The third type involves arrangements which are a more complex version of the arrangements referred to as Type 2. Here, the buyer visits a particular website which operates as a 'collaborative economy platform', or a peer-to-peer service. For the purposes of this discussion, it is assumed that there are two broad types of such platforms:

(i) A *selling* platform where individuals can offer goods they have made themselves for sale, which includes goods made using 3-D print technology (e.g., etsy.com)

---

19 For a discussion in the US context, see Lucas S Osborn, 'Regulating Three-Dimensional Printing: The Converging World of Bits and Atoms' (2014) 51 San Diego Law Review 553, 567–9, 571–2.

20 E.g., under the Consumer Guarantees Act 1993 in New Zealand, the definition of goods includes 'to avoid doubt…computer software' (s 2(1)(vi)).

21 E.g., under Part 1, chapter 3 of the Consumer Rights Act 2015 in the United Kingdom.

(ii) A *production* platform which is dedicated to sharing designs for 3D-printing and offers the facility to print items on-demand and ship these to a buyer. Such a platform combines offering a 3D-printing service (see above) with the possibility of marketing and selling designs to third parties (the main platform at present is shapeways.com).[22]

The buyer visits such a site/platform, and chooses a particular item. The order is placed on the site and processed by the platform. As noted above, depending on the type of platform, on placing the order, one of these things might happen:

(i) On a selling platform, the item will be listed as a physical item, which may have been produced as a 3D-print. It will be despatched directly by the seller
(ii) Also on a selling platform, the item might be listed with options for customisation. The seller will arrange to 3D-print the item to the customer's specifications on receiving the order, and the seller will despatch the physical item when printed.
(iii) On a production platform, the platform itself will 3D-print the item, either based on a standard design or customised to the customer's requirements, and despatch the physical item directly to the customer.

As noted above, the main difference between Type 2 and Type 3 arrangements is that Type 3 arrangements involve the buyer ordering a finished item, whereas Type 2 concerns the separate stages involved in making a 3D-printed item. From the perspective of the buyer, the Type 3 transactions are not that dissimilar to the Type 1 transactions, although there is one crucial difference between these two types. Type 1 transactions will involve a trader, i.e., a business seller of goods. In Type 3, the items acquired by the buyer are designed by an individual (or a group of individuals) and made available via a P2P platform. The person creating the design and/or the CAD-file which is used to make the item using 3D-printing technology could be doing so purely as a 'hobbyist', but could also be a small business using the P2P platform services to sell goods to

22 The complete service offered by such platforms to designers, reducing their costs in selling their designs, makes it likely that the impact of 3D-printing will most likely be felt in this context: see Charles W Finocchiaro, 'Personal Factory or Catalyst for Piracy? The Hype, Hysteria and Hard Realities of Consumer 3-D Printing' (2013) 31 Cardozo Arts & Entertainment Law Journal 473.

the public.[23] So, in contrast to Type 1 transactions, the buyer in Type 3 transactions does not necessarily know whether the person selling the goods is a hobbyist or a professional seller. This situation is further complicated by the active involvement of the production platform, which might mean that the buyer is contracting with the platform itself.

V. 3D-printing – contract law issues

The purpose of the preceding section has been to identify the main types of transaction through which 3D-printed items could be supplied to a final buyer (assumed to be a consumer in the three groups discussed above, although it is equally possible that the buyer could be a professional, particularly with regard to Type 2 transactions). In this section, the specific contract law issues to which these various arrangements give rise will be discussed more fully. The following section will then consider the extent to which current EU law is able to deal with these issues.

Type 1

(a) Buyer – Trader contract

As already noted, the contract between the buyer and the trader fits the paradigm sales contract – the buyer contracts to buy a final item from the trader. The trader, or the manufacturer from whom the trader acquires the item, may utilise 3D-printing for this purpose, but this is ultimately not of concern to the buyer. Familiar legislative provisions on the sale of goods will apply to the contract between the buycr and the trader. If the buyer is

23 For example, on its website, Etsy states that "Etsy sellers range from hobbyists to professional merchants, and have a broad range of personal and professional goals. Some Etsy sellers just want some extra pocket money, while others depend on their shops to support themselves and their families. Our 2014 Seller Survey reveals a unique population of Internet-enabled creative entrepreneurs who are building businesses on their own terms—prioritising flexibility, independence and creativity. 76% of US sellers consider their Etsy shop to be a business and for almost a third, their creative business has become so well established that they are able to focus on it as their sole occupation." <https://www.etsy.com/uk/about/> accessed 24 September 2015.

a consumer, then these will be the national rules implementing the Consumer Sales Directive (99/44/EC). The item supplied to the buyer has to be in conformity with the contract (Art 2). If it is not, then the buyer can rely on the remedies provided in Art 3. It matters not, as far as this contract is concerned, whether the cause of the non-conformity is due to the information in the CAD-file or to problems with the 3D printer.

(b) The trader's position when reselling goods made by manufacturer

The trader's liability to the buyer was set out above. If the trader in turn obtained the goods from a manufacturer who utilised 3D-printing technology, then the trader may have a corresponding claim against the manufacturer for any non-conformity in the goods.

(c) The trader's (or manufacturer's) position when 3D-printing

As explained earlier, the trader may have his own 3D-printing facility, whether at a central facility or in locations around the world (where this is done to reduce transportation costs). The non-conformity which has arisen in the contract between the buyer and the trader could be caused by one of three things:

(i) there could be a problem with the CAD-file itself, which means that every time an item is printed using that file, the non-conformity occurs;
(ii) the 3D printer itself might cause the problem; or
(iii) the material used to print the item might not have been of the right standard.

Whether the trader will have any recourse in such circumstances depends on the cause of the problem, and whether there is a third-party supplier who might be liable towards the trader for this. For example, if the CAD-file was created by a third-party supplier and the file is the source of the non-conformity, then there might be contractual liability of the CAD-file supplier towards the trader.

It does not seem that any of these matters pose novel problems from a legal point of view, with the exception of the more general question whether there are, or ought to be, general conformity requirements for digital content akin to those that apply to goods. This point is considered below.

Type 2

Whereas Type 1 transactions do not seem to create a major challenge for existing law, the same cannot be said for Type 2 transactions. As explained above, there are essentially two separate stages which by which a buyer obtains a physical item made by 3D-printing. The first stage is the acquisition of the CAD-file which contains a particular design. Here, there buyer may have the option of buying a file on-line, or simply downloading an open-source CAD-file. If there is a problem with the design contained in the CAD-file, the buyer may wish to assert that there is a non-conformity which gives rise to specific remedies. The first challenge in considering conformity issues is that it will depend on how the applicable law[24] classifies a contract involving the supply of CAD-files. In essence, these files are a form of 'digital content', and so it will depend on how national law treats such contracts when it comes to questions of conformity. Few jurisdictions presently have rules dealing with digital content,[25] although many have found a way of drawing a parallel with the sale of goods – albeit not necessarily convincingly so.[26] So it may be possible to have recourse in law if there is a problem with the CAD-file, or the design contained in that file, but that is far from clear.

There are three additional issues with regard to the CAD-file: first, if the buyer pays for access to the file, then there will be a contract, which provides some legal basis for asserting remedies for a lack of conformity. But if a CAD-file is downloaded for free from an open-source site, the position might be less clear, and it is possible that there is no contract at all. This means that there would be no basis for claims relating to prob-

24 A consideration of the various potential issues that could arise from a private international law perspective if the parties to these contracts are from different jurisdictions is beyond the scope of this paper.

25 For a concise survey of both theoretical and practical aspects, see Natalie Helberger, Marco B M Loos, Lucie Guibault, Chantal Mak and Lodewijk Pessers, 'Digital Content Contracts for Consumers' (2013) 36 Journal of Consumer Policy 37, 42–44.

26 Contrast the positions in New Zealand under the Consumer Guarantees Act 1993 and the United Kingdom under the Consumer Rights Act 2015.

lems with the design, unless it is possible to somehow bring an action in the law of tort.[27] Secondly, these files are created by both professional and private designers, and so it may not always be clear whether downloading a particular file will, in fact, allow the buyer to rely on rights which would be available against a trader. Conversely, private designers may not realise that their activities might be regarded as constituting a business activity once the threshold from private to business is crossed. This, then raises the further question how the point of crossing that threshold should be determined. A third issue arises particularly with regard to open-source CAD-files, which by their nature are not created by one person, but shared with others with the express intention that the design can be developed further and the CAD-file modified by others, and so it will not always be easy to identify which (if any particular) person might have created the aspect of the CAD-file which subsequently gives rise to a non-conformity.

The second stage involves the process of turning the CAD-file into a printed item. The buyer may do so on his own desktop printer. As with the trader making his own 3-D prints in the case of Type 1 transactions, here there may be issues of non-conformity which are created not by the design, but rather by the way the printer operates (both mechanically and how it interprets the information in the CAD-file), or the material used for printing. Assuming it is possible to identify what caused the non-conformity in the finished item, the buyer will be able to hold liable either the printer manufacturer or the supplier of the material used for printing the physical item.

However, the buyer may also wish to utilise the services of a commercial 3D-printing service, e.g., because of the complexity of the design, or the desired material in which the finished item is to be made. There will therefore be a separate transaction for 3D-printing the design in the CAD-file to make the finished item. This raises the question of how this contract is best classified – it might still be a contract for the sale of goods, or it could be much more like a contract for a specific service. This might affect the rights of the buyer if the finished item is not of the quality or fitness for purpose expected. If the contract is treated as a contract of sale (which might be the case in many jurisdictions – see below), then it will be necessary to identify the source of the non-conformity. If the CAD-file is the problem, then liability for the non-conformity of the finished item

27 See the discussion by Chris Willett and Geraint Howells, in this volume, 67.

should not be imposed on the 3D-printing service.[28] However, if the CAD-file (and therefore the design) is not the cause of the non-conformity, then the non-conformity will be the result of the 3D-printing process itself. Generally, the cause could be either with the printer and/or the materials used for 3D-printing the item. As far as the consumer is concerned, liability for a non-conformity should be imposed on the 3D-printing service provider in these circumstances. In turn, the 3D-service may have a claim against the supplier of the 3D-printer or of the materials used.

Group 3

Finally, there are the transactions in Group 3. As already suggested above, from the perspective of the buyer, there is a contract of sale for the finished item, and so the ordinary rules applicable to such contracts would also apply here.

However, one difficulty is being able to identify whether the seller is acting in a professional capacity or is simply a private individual, a 'hobbyist', selling a few home-made 3D items online. Generally, sellers seeking to utilise a platform will do so by creating a profile, or shop on a platform which then allows potential customers to browse what is offered and to place an order. Some platforms then process the order and the final item is made and despatched by the seller. If that seller is a professional seller, then the relevant consumer sales law rules will apply, but it is sometimes not clear whether an individual has crossed the line from hobbyists to professional.

This is particularly difficult to establish in the case of on-line platforms where the platform itself provides all the relevant aspects of turning the CAD-file uploaded by the seller into the 3D-printed item, and despatching it to the buyer.[29] This allows designers both to have their designs printed and to market them to third-party customers. Some platforms may take

---

28 It may be possible that liability could arise in tort law if the 3D-printing service company has failed to recognise an obvious problem.

29 Shapeways.com operates an all-inclusive service for designers, which means that the platform will deal with all customer service issues, and even refund buyers if there is a problem. If it turns out that the problem is caused by the design, then the platform will work with the designer to improve this. See <http://www.shapeways.com/tutorials/shops/how-we-pay> accessed 24 September 2015.

quite an active role in managing all aspects of the production and marketing process, which means that the 'seller' will only create and modify the design, and then make it available via the platform to be produced as desired. The significant involvement of such platforms in that process raises the question whether there should be direct liability of the platform towards a buyer for any non-conformity issues, rather than the buyer having to pursue the seller directly (bearing in mind the possible uncertainty about their status as a hobbyist or professional seller).

VI. 3D-printing: the key legal issues

Based on the analysis of the legal issues to which the various arrangements discussed above give rise, a number of common legal issues can be identified.

1. Sales Law and 3D-printed products

First, a consumer buying an tangible item which was 3-D printed will be in the same position as a person buying an item manufactured by other means, so this will be a straightforward contract of sale. The rules applicable to the sale of tangible goods will apply.

2. Digital Content and Conformity

Secondly, a person who has acquired a CAD-file and 3D-printed the item himself who has a non-conforming tangible item will need to identify the cause of that non-conformity. Generally speaking, the possibilities are: (i) the CAD-file; (ii) the 3-D printer itself or (iii) the materials used for printing. As far as (ii) and (iii) are concerned, liability for any non-conformities are already covered by current sales law rules. However, (i) is the key legal issue: a non-conformity which has its source in the CAD-file itself. This could be because the design contained in the file has a flaw, or it could be that the instructions the file provides to the printer are inadequate. So one question is whether there are already clear conformity requirements and related remedies with regard to digital content and whether these are sufficient, or whether a new set of rules is required. In addition, it was explained earlier that CAD-files can be obtained for free from open-source websites or be received in return for payment. As associated question is whether a conformity requirement should only be imposed in respect of digital content/CAD-files made available in return for payment, or more generally.

3. 3D-Printing Services

The third issue arises with regard to the use of a commercial 3D-printing service to make a tangible item based on a CAD-file provided by a consumer. The 3D-printing service will carry out all of the stages of making the item based on the CAD-file. If there is a non-conformity in the finished item, then this will raise questions both of whether and how far the printing service should be liable for the non-conformity. One option is to apply the general level of service liability, which is often based around requiring performance of the service with reasonable care and skill. Alternatively, as the service involves the production of a tangible item, a better option might be to extend the rules on conformity and associated remedies to items made by a 3D-printing service, at least to the extent that the non-conformity is the result of the printing process rather than because of a problem with the CAD-file. If the CAD-file itself is the source of the non-conformity, it would be appropriate to exclude this from the scope of liability imposed on the 3D-printing service. This could be combined with a duty to warn the consumer of problems with the design apparent to the 3D-printing service before production commences.

4. The threshold from hobbyist to business/trader

Fourth, there is the difficulty of identifying whether the other contracting party is a business or a hobbyist, and, indeed, at which point the activities of a hobbyist become a business activity. This is crucial because the nature of the supplier will both determine the specific obligations they might be under and the rights a buyer (especially a consumer buyer) might have. A clear test for identifying when the activities of a hobbyist cross the line and become a business activity needs to be developed. One might be us the volume of transactions concluded by an individual with others to determine whether the threshold has been crossed. However, this might not be a good criterion, as Osborn explains:

> 'Suppose a college student designs a CAD file for a simple widget in her dorm room for fun. She uploads it to a website and puts a price of five dollars for the CAD file, thinking little of it. For the first three months, she sells only one – to her mother. Is she a merchant at this point? It would seem not. To her amazement, in the next three months – while she does nothing but study for classes – the widget goes viral and she sells 20,000. Is she now a merchant? In one sense, yes, because she has sold 20,000 of the same widget. In another sense, no, because she expended no more effort and became no more sophisticated than when her mother was her only customer.'[30]

This example neatly illustrates how using a 'volume of transactions' criterion would be inappropriate in the context of 3D-printing, at least when it comes to selling CAD-files. Osborn goes on to suggest that 'factors such as the sophistication of the seller, the number of transactions, and the expectations of the buyer'[31] could all be relevant to determining when someone offering CAD-files or 3D-printed products becomes a business/ trader. These are useful factors, although including a 'number of transactions' criterion might not be the best approach: rather, one should consider (a) the regularity with which the individual offers CAD-files or 3D-printed items for sale and (b) the range or variety of designs on offer. Taking this criterion, combined with the other two factors (sophistication and expectations of the buyer), would offer a helpful means of working out when the threshold from hobbyist to business/trader is crossed. The inclusion of the buyer's expectations can be useful in view of the very different ways in which CAD-files and 3D-printed items are sold, especially if relevant criteria for establishing what those expectations might be are included. Two essential criteria can be mentioned here: first, this should be an objective standard, rather than a subjective one. Secondly, it should take into account the method by which the CAD-file or finished items are supplied. There might be other factors. Thus, whilst it should not be determinative how the seller presents himself on the website, information on the seller's profile (which many websites feature) could be a relevant consideration.

---

30 Lucas S Osborn, 'Regulating Three-Dimensional Printing: The Converging World of Bits and Atoms' (2014) 51 San Diego Law Review 553, 573.

31 Lucas S Osborn, 'Regulating Three-Dimensional Printing: The Converging World of Bits and Atoms' (2014) 51 San Diego Law Review 553, 575.

Berkowitz goes one step further and argues that the law should recognise 'micro-sellers' as an intermediate category between a hobbyist ('occasional seller') and a trader.[32] According to her, "this 'micro-seller' category would cover those sellers who surpass 'occasional seller', but are not quite enterprise sellers."[33] Her objective is to provide small-scale designers with a defence against strict liability claims, and the criteria she puts forward for determining who might be a micro-seller suit that context,[34] but are more difficult to apply at a general level. In any event, introducing an intermediate category would not solve the problem of identifying when the activities of an individual are such that they should no longer be treated in law as a hobbyist.

A clear test for when the line from hobbyist to business is crossed is needed, and a test along the lines of Osborn's suggestion might work best. Beyond this narrow question, there is also a wider question as to whether some degree of liability should be imposed on hobbyists for the quality of the items they sell, but this is beyond the scope of this discussion.[35]

5. *On-line platforms for selling/producing 3D-prints*

Finally, the role of on-line platforms facilitating the use of 3D-printing needs to be considered, in particular production platforms which offer a complete service for designers to market their designs.

---

32 Nicole D Berkowitz, 'Strict Liability for Individuals? The impact of 3-D printing on Products Liability Law' (2014) 92 Washington University Law Review 1019. She develops this argument in the context of product liability (tort) rather than sales law.

33 Nicole D Berkowitz, 'Strict Liability for Individuals? The impact of 3-D printing on Products Liability Law' (2014) 92 Washington University Law Review 1019, 1049.

34 They are: (1) seller's experience in manufacturing, selling or designing products, (2) scale of business in units and income generated, (3) ability to spread costs or obtain insurance, (4) societal desirability of the product in issue, and (5) seller's good faith. Nicole D Berkowitz, 'Strict Liability for Individuals? The impact of 3-D printing on Products Liability Law' (2014) 92 Washington University Law Review 1019, 1049.

35 See generally, Peter P Swire, 'When should "Consumers-as-Producers" have to comply with Consumer Protection Laws?' (2008) 31 Journal of Consumer Policy *473,* 473–487.

A *selling platform* generally acts as an intermediary to allow sellers to offer items on-line and for buyers to place an order. The contract for the supply of the item will be between the buyer and the seller. From a buyer's perspective, the main legal question is whether the buyer's consumer rights are engaged, and, as discussed above, this will only be the case where the seller falls within the legal definition of seller or trader.

However, many selling platforms are more than just mere conduits: often, they provide facilities to support transactions, e.g., by offering means to receive and process payments, and also by offering dispute resolution mechanisms if either party has cause for complaint.[36] In practical terms, this means that they are more actively involved in the transaction than, e.g., a business organising a car-boot sale. This raises the question whether there ought to be some degree of liability on a selling platform if there is a problem with the goods supplied. Such liability could be concurrent with that of the seller,[37] it could be a fall-back liability if the seller does not perform his obligations and refuses to put things rights, or it could be limited to liability for those aspects which are within the control of the platform, such as problems created by order or payment processing. It is an open question whether there ought to be specific regulation of the role of selling platforms, particularly with regard to the liability of the platform towards a consumer buyer if there is a failure by the seller to deliver goods, or to provide a remedy when goods are not in conformity.

The situation is more complex still when one turns to *production platforms*. As explained above, such platforms combine the role of a 3D-printing service which allows a designer to have their design turned into a 3D-printed item with the possibility of marketing and selling items made from their design to third parties. The challenging aspect here is that this is an emerging business model and a greater understanding of the precise nature of the respective obligations undertaken by the various parties in this context is needed. A production platform could be handling all of the stages involved in creating the finished item, processing orders and payment, and despatching the finished item to a buyer.[38] A buyer will access the platform, identify an item he wishes to purchase and place an

36 Etsy has a so-called 'Buyer Case Resolution' procedure, for example. See <https://www.etsy.com/uk/help/article/4521> accessed 29 October 2015.

37 This could be developed by analogy with connected lender liability available e.g., under s 75 of the Consumer Credit Act 1974 in the United Kingdom.

38 This is what shapeways.com does, for example.

order directly with the platform, which then produces the item based on the design contained in the CAD-file uploaded onto the platform by the designer. On some platforms, items can be viewed both by type and by designer, which adds to the potential confusion as to whether the platform or the designer is the contractual seller.

As mentioned above, a key question therefore is what sort of arrangement is in place on any given production platform. There are two basic ways of analysing this situation: (i) there is a contract between the consumer buyer and the platform as trader. The platform is the sole contracting party with the consumer. The platform essentially operates as a licensee of the designer to produce and sell the item, and the designer will receive a royalty payment as a percentage of the overall price every time an item based on the design is ordered; (ii) there is a contract between the consumer buyer and the designer, with the platform effectively sub-contracted to the designer to process orders and 3D-print the item. The costs incurred by the platform would be deducted from the overall price paid by the consumer and the remainder paid to the designer as profit.

Deciding which analysis is the better one will vary from platform to platform and depend on how its terms and conditions define the relationship between designer and platform, and platform and consumer. So the particular business model adopted by any particular platform will determine whether the first or second analysis is appropriate. If a particular platform operates in line with the first type of arrangement, then consumer law would apply to the contract between platform and consumer. However, it the conclusion is that it is the second type, then additional questions (already discussed) become relevant, in particular the need to determine whether the designer is a hobbyist or a business/trader, and the extent to which the platform could be directly liable to the consumer, for what, and on what basis.

VI. Summary

It is evident from the discussion thus far that there are potentially quite complicated questions that arise when it comes to 3D-printing. However, it is also clear that none of these issues are unique to 3D-printing: questions about the regulation of digital content and the role of online platforms are of broader relevance, as is the difficulty of finding an appropriate way of distinguishing B2C from P2P transaction.

The following section considers the extent to which existing EU law already manages to deal with these issues, and to highlight areas where further action might be needed, whether by clarification of current law or the introduction of new legislation.

1. 3D-printing and current EU law

This section will consider current EU-Law with regard to the five key legal issues discussed in the previous section.

a) Sales Law and 3D printed products

As explained above, when it comes to simple contract of sale between a trader and a consumer, the fact that the goods are made using a 3D-printing process has no bearing on the trader's liability towards the consumer in respect of the trader's obligations under Art 2(1) of the Consumer Sales Directive (99/44/EC) to deliver goods which are in conformity with the contract. The criteria for the presumption of conformity in Art 2(2) apply in the same way as they would to goods made by other manufacturing means. If the item is not in conformity with the contract, the remedies in Art 3 will apply, which means that the consumer has the initial choice between repair and replacement, subject to the proviso that either must be possible and not disproportionate compared to the other.

The application of these provisions in the context of 3D-printed goods potentially raises a number of questions. Assume that the consumer has bought an item which has been 3D-printed and is not in conformity with the contract. The consumer now has the right to choose between repair and replacement. However, with most non-conformities that might arise with 3D-products, one might expect that repair will not be possible. This is because the 3D printing process creates the object in a single continuous process, so it will often not be possible to repair any flaws. Instead, replacement (i.e., re-printing) would seem to be the more appropriate option. However, this will require the trader to identify the likely cause of the non-conformity. As discussed earlier, the cause of that non-conformity could be the manufacturing process, the material used or the CAD-file itself. If the trader has sole control over that process, then he can attempt to make any necessary corrections (e.g., by checking the CAD-file, or the material used for the printing process). If the item was obtained from a manufacturer, then the trader has to request another item from that manufacturer.[39] Either way, the printing process will have to be repeated with adjustments made either to physical ingredients or to the CAD-file.

This remedy has to be provided free of charge, but process will create additional costs for the trader. As explained above, the cost of printing each item is the same, so the cost of making the non-conforming item will have been wasted expenditure. The trader might be tempted to argue that replacing a 3D-printed item imposes disproportionate costs on him. Although Art 3(3) of the Consumer Sales Directive does provide for instances when a trader can refuse to provide a remedy on the basis of disproportionality, this would only be possible if the remedy requested 'imposes costs on the seller which, in comparison with the alternative remedy, are unreasonable' In *Weber and Putz*,[40] the CJEU confirmed that replacement could only be regarded as disproportionate on the basis of a comparison with the cost of repair, which means that the high cost of replacing a 3D-printed item cannot be assessed as a stand-alone question. However, in that case, the CJEU also identified that there is a limitation on the trader's obligation to provide a remedy free of charge with regard to the overall costs of having to uninstall goods which were not in conformity with the contract. On this issue, the CJEU held that the consumer's right to have the costs of removing the non-conforming goods and installing the replacement reimbursed by the trader would be limited to requiring the seller to pay a proportionate amount, because Article 3

> 'aims to establish a fair balance between the interests of the consumer and the [trader], by guaranteeing the consumer, as the weak party to the contract, complete and effective protection from faulty performance by the [trader] of his contractual obligations, while enabling account to be taken of economic considerations advanced by the [trader].'[41]

---

39 Art 4 of the Consumer Sales Directive contains a provision allowing a seller to "pass-back" liability to whoever in the distribution chain is responsible for a non-conformity, but this provision lacks bite because it defers to national law to set the conditions for this.

40 Joined cases C–65/09 *Weber v Wittmer* and C–87/09 *Putz v Medianess Electronics* [2011] ECR I–5257.

41 Para [75].

However, any reduction to a proportionate amount should not 'result in the consumer's right to reimbursement of those costs being effectively rendered devoid of substance'.[42] Although this ruling was concerned with a different question (the significant cost of uninstalling non-conforming goods and installing their replacement), the CJEU has opened the door to arguments that a trader might be able to cite the very high costs of providing a remedy as a reason for not having to bear the full financial burden of this.

In the context of replacing goods using 3D-printing, a trader could argue that the high unit cost of making the replacement creates such a high financial burden that he should not be required to bear the full cost. It seems doubtful whether such an argument would ultimately be successful, but the specific cost of 3D-printing means that it would require careful consideration in light of *Weber and Putz*. Although a consumer is entitled to receive conforming goods, account has to be taken of 'economic considerations' raised by the trader. So this is one aspect where the law is potentially uncertain – not because of the legal rules in the Consumer Sales Directive itself, but because of the interpretation adopted by the CJEU in *Weber and Putz*.

If neither repair nor replacement can be provided, however, then the consumer is entitled to request a price reduction or ultimately rescission of the contract. If the non-conformity is not minor (cf. Art 3(6)), then rescission might well be the most appropriate remedy in the case of non-conforming 3D-printed goods where a replacement is not provided.

b) Digital Content and Conformity

If the non-conformity is the result of a problem with the CAD-file (either because the design itself is unsuitable, or because of some other flaw), then there may be instances when a consumer might need to bring a claim against the supplier of the CAD-file. This leads to the question whether there are conformity rules and remedies available in respect of digital content.

The rules of the Consumer Sales Directive would not be applicable, because Art 1(2)(b) defines goods as 'any tangible movable item' and

42 Para [76].

therefore only physical items. Existing EU legislation therefore does not provide any rules applicable to the supply of digital content.

In contrast, the proposal for a Common European Sales Law[43] (now withdrawn) did contain a number of specific provisions dealing with both conformity and remedies in respect of digital content. Article 2(j) CESL defined digital content as 'data which are produced and supplied in digital form, whether or not according to the buyer's specifications, including video, audio, picture or written digital content, digital games, software and digital content which makes it possible to personalise existing hardware or software'. This definition would cover a CAD-file used for 3D-printing. However, there are exclusions from that definition, and of particular relevance is paragraph (vi) which excludes 'the creation of new digital content and the amendment of existing digital content by consumers or any other interaction with the creations of other users'. It would seem that open-source CAD-files (which are often subject to amendment by various users) would not have been covered by this definition. On the other hand, a CAD-file made available for download free of charge would have been covered if the file was not intended to be modified by other users.

A CAD-file acquired by a consumer in return for paying a price or some other form of consideration, as well as a file made available for downloading only, would have been subject to the CESL's conformity requirements in Arts.99-103. The approach taken in CESL was to apply these provisions both to goods and to digital content. The only specific reference to digital content is found in Art 100 CESL, which sets out the criteria for establishing conformity. Article 100(g) mentions 'such qualities and performance capabilities as the buyer may expect. When determining what the consumer may expect of the digital content regard is to be had to whether or not the digital content was supplied in exchange for the payment of a price'. Art 102 CESL would have dealt with freedom from unfounded third-party rights, including intellectual property rights. With regard to remedies, Art 106 CESL would have applied the full range of remedies to both goods and digital content, although Art 107 CESL would have excluded most of the remedies where the consumer did not pay a price for the acquisition of the digital content. In that situation, the remedies would have been limited to 'loss or damage caused to the buyer's

43 European Commission, *Proposal for a Regulation of the European Parliament and of the Council on a Common European Sales Law* (COM (2011) 635 final.

property, including hardware, software and data, by the lack of conformity of the supplied digital content, except for any gain of which the buyer has been deprived by that damage' (Art 107 CESL).

In comparison, the United Kingdom's Consumer Rights Act contains specific provisions on conformity and remedies with regard to digital content.[44] The conformity provisions mirror those applicable in respect of goods, i.e., digital content has to be of satisfactory quality,[45] fit for a particular purpose,[46] and be as described.[47] There remedies are similar (although not identical) to those for non-conforming goods: there is an initial choice between repair and replacement of the digital content, with a second-stage remedy of price reduction (up to the full value of the price paid).[48] Damages for additional losses can also be recovered.[49]

One important question is how possible remedies for non-conforming digital content would work when it comes to a CAD-file for a 3D-printed product which is not in conformity. There are two aspects to this: first, there is the need to provide a CAD-file which is in conformity with the contract. Depending on the nature of the non-conformity, this could be achieved through 'repair', i.e., modifications to the design and the coding in the file, or through 'replacement', i.e., creating an entirely new CAD-file for the item in question.

Secondly, there is the item which has already been 3D-printed and which is also not in conformity because of the problem with the CAD-file. The assumption is that it cannot be repaired and that a second attempt needs to be undertaken using the repaired or replaced CAD-file. This means that there will be additional costs for the consumer for the second attempt, either in terms of materials if printed at home, or the cost of asking a 3D-printing service to produce the item. Thus, a consumer in this situation will have incurred quite specific financial loss as a consequence of the non-conforming digital content, which would be recoverable by way of damages.[50]

---

44 See also Christian Twigg-Flesner, Rick Canavan, Hector MacQueen and John Adams, *Atiyah's sale of goods* (13th edition, Pearson 2016) ch 22.

45 s 34.

46 s 35.

47 s 36.

48 ss 42–44.

49 s 42(6)/(7)(a).

50 The UK's Consumer Rights Act 2015 s 46 deals with damage to a "device" caused by digital content, but this would not be a basis on which a consumer could claim

c) 3D-printing Services

The second legal issue is the extent to which commercial 3D-printing services could be held liable for any non-conformities in the finished item. As explained above, the consumer will provide the 3D-printing service with the CAD-file, and the service will then produce the physical item. The key question is whether the liability of the 3D-printing service should be the same as that of any other service provider, or whether there should be strict liability for a non-conformity in the finished item akin to that imposed on a seller of goods.

On one possible analysis, the Consumer Sales Directive might be applicable to the activities of a 3D-printing service. Although the Directive does not contain a full definition of 'contract of sale', Art 1(4) states that 'contracts for the supply of consumer goods to be manufactured or produced shall also be deemed contracts of sale for the purpose of this Directive.' A contract for a 3D-printing service to convert a CAD-file supplied by a consumer into a finished item could be regarded as a contract for 'goods to be manufactured', which would make it a contract of sale within this extended meaning. The provisions on conformity and remedies from the Directive would apply, and a consumer could hold a 3D-printing service liable for any non-conformity in the goods in the same way as a trader who sold the physical item to the consumer.

However, the 3D-printing service only has control over the 3D-printing equipment and materials used for printing, but has had no influence over the information contained in the CAD-file. The file has been supplied by the consumer, who may have bought the file separately, downloaded it from an open-source website, or designed the item on his computer using standard CAD software. If the non-conformity is found to have been caused by the CAD-file, then it would seem inappropriate to still hold the trader providing the 3D-printing service liable for this. In the Directive, the potential inequity is acknowledged in Art 2(3), which provides that 'there shall be deemed not to be a lack of conformity … if the lack of conformity has its origin in materials supplied by the consumer'.

As worded, this provision deals with the situation where a consumer has materials to be turned into a finished item, such as fabric to be used

---

to be entitled to have an item 3D-printed based on a non-conforming CAD-file to be entitled to repair of the item or compensation for the damage.

for making a suit. If, after making the suit, there is a problem with it because of a flaw in the fabric, the tailor will not be liable for the non-conformity on the basis of Art 2(3). The question is whether this derogation could also be applied to the CAD-file supplied by a consumer to the 3D-printing service. It might be thought that the word 'material' only covers tangible material, rather than something intangible such as a CAD-file. The question of whether the derogation in Art 2(3) extends to designs is not new,[51] and whilst it may be arguable that the word 'materials' should be given an extended meaning to cover anything which a consumer has provided to the trader to make the finished item, it might be objected that this would unduly stretch the meaning of the word 'materials'. However, the underlying policy not to impose strict liability for non-conformities in this situation remains sound, and so a clarification to the wording of the derogation in Art 2(3) would be appropriate and necessary to cover designs supplied by a consumer.

It is therefore possible to argue that current EU law provides a solution which adequately balances the interests of the consumer and the trader. However, this depends on how broadly the wider definition of sale in Art 1(4) is interpreted, particularly with regard to a contract where the consumer supplies the *design* rather than (some of) the materials to be turned into the finished item,[52] and also on the extent to which Art 2(3) can be interpreted to exclude from the 3D-printing service provider's liability any instances where the non-conformity is due to the design/

51 See Christian Twigg-Flesner and Robert Bradgate, 'The E.C. Directive on Certain Aspects of the Sale of Consumer Goods and Associated Guarantees - All Talk and No Do?' (2002) 2 Web Journal of Current Legal Issues <http://www.bailii.org/uk/other/journals/WebJCLI/2000/issue2/flesner2.html> accessed 27 October 2015. The authors note that English cases have held that in this type of case, although the contract may be one of sale, the seller is not liable (*Cammell Laird & Co v Manganese Bronze & Brass Co Ltd* [1934] AC 402 (HL)). However, it may be arguable that the trader is or should be under a duty of care to warn the consumer if the design is defective.

52 By way of comparison, note the approach in Art 3 of the UN Convention on the International Sale of Goods 1980. Although the wording of that Article differs from the corresponding provisions in the Consumer Sales Directive, it is nevertheless helpful to note that the provision of plans or a design by a buyer did not make this a service contract: see *UNCITRAL Digest of Case Law on the United Nations Convention on Contracts for the International Sale of Goods* (UNICTRAL 2012) 21, and Peter Schlechtriem and Petra Butler, *UN Law on International Sales* (Springer 2009), 23–4.

CAD-file itself. If the outcome this analysis suggests is acceptable, then it might be appropriate to clarify the law by holding a 3D-service provider strictly liable for non-conformities in the 3D-printed item except where these are caused by the CAD-file supplied by the consumer.

d) The threshold from hobbyist to businesses/trader

The next issue is the lack of clarity as to whether a consumer buyer is dealing with a trader or another private individual offering a few 3D-printed items, or just a CAD-file, for sale as a hobby (i.e., a 'hobbyist'). There are two elements to this: the first is that the consumer might not be able to tell from the way goods are offered for sale whether this is done by a trader or a hobbyist, and the second is that the person offering the goods might themselves not be aware whether they have crossed the line from being a hobbyist offering the occasional item or CAD-file for sale to a trader for whom this is a business activity.

There are familiar definitions of seller/trader in existing EU legislation. For example, Art 1(2)(c) of the Consumer Sales Directive defines 'seller' as 'any natural or legal person who, under a contract, sells consumer goods in the course of his trade, business or profession', and Art 2(2) of the Consumer Rights Directive defines 'trader' in a slightly wider sense as 'any natural person or any legal person … who is acting … for purposes relating to his trade, business, craft or profession …'. The difficulty is in identifying when an activity which might have started out as a hobby takes on the character of a trade, business, craft or profession, and therefore turns the hobbyist into a trader. Although both the CJEU[53] and EU legislation[54] have had to consider when a person ceases to be regarded as a consumer in circumstances where a contract is for goods which are used for both private and professional purposes, there is no clear guidance on when a person crosses the threshold from being a private individual to being a trader.

As discussed above, there are a number of possible additional criteria which could be deployed to identify when the threshold is crossed, and clarification of current law is needed.

53 C–464/01 *Johann Gruber v BayWa AG* [2005] ECR I–439.

54 Europeant Parilament and Council Directive 2011/83/EU of 25 October 2011 on consumer rights [2011] OJ L 304/64 (Consumer Rights Directive) Recital 17.

e) On-line platforms for selling/producing 3-D prints

The final issue to be considered is how on-line platforms involved in the sale and production of CAD-files and 3D-printed products should be treated. It was explained above that a principal distinction can be made between 'selling platforms' (such as etsy or eBay), and 'production platforms' (such as shapeways). At the present time, there is no EU Law in place which addresses the issues raised by these platforms. There is provision in Arts.12-14 of the E-Commerce Directive (2000/31/EC), under which the liability of intermediaries in the context of e-commerce is very limited.[55] It is therefore necessary to explore more fully the potential role of these on-line platforms and the extent to which their liability should be reviewed.[56] The various policy options were discussed earlier.

2. Conclusions

3D-printing is going to become an important new method of production with potentially wide-ranging applications. Consumer can already purchase a range of products made using this method. The novelty lies in the combination of computer-aided design, which is now open to anyone with reasonable IT skills, with a new way of converting designs into finished items. This has some implications for (consumer) contract law, although, as the discussion in this paper has demonstrated, these are significant beyond the narrow context of 3D-printing. Thus, greater clarity is needed to be able to identify the dividing line between a hobbyist and a trader. More thought needs to be given to rules on the conformity of digital content and remedies in respect of non-conforming digital content, including consequential losses. The latter might be dealt with under established principles on damages, foreseeability and remoteness, but it might be necessary to consider whether their application would always lead to a reasonable outcome. Also, the use of open-source design and multi-party

55 Cf C–324/09 *L'Oréal SA and Others v eBay International AG and Others* [2011] ECR I–6011.

56 The European Commission's consultation on the Regulatory environment for platforms, online intermediaries, data and cloud computing and the collaborative economy, <https://ec.europa.eu/eusurvey/runner/Platforms/> accessed 29 October 2015, does not specifically raise these issues.

involvement in developing and refining designs raises a new challenge (although one for which Tort Law might be better suited to develop a response).

However, the most difficult, but equally important, question is what sort of legal response is needed to the increasing use of online platforms, both selling and production platforms. In particular, there is the question of the extent to which such platforms should be held directly liable towards a person buying goods from such a platform if a seller fails to deliver goods, or if goods are not in conformity. As noted, a liability model based on concurrent or residual liability might be an appropriate solution, but further investigation into the business models adopted by such platforms is needed.

3D Printing: The Limits of Contract and Challenges for Tort

*Geraint Howells / Chris Willett**

I. Introduction

3D printing offers great potential for democratising the production process. Almost anyone can become a producer either of products they have designed themselves, or by using code purchased from third parties directly or through sharing platforms. They can use printers in their own home or take their code along to outlets that offer 3D printing services. Defects in the final product can arise from the original design, the code, the printer, the use of the printer or the materials used. These all create problems in terms of identifying where the problem arose. There may also be issues as to the interaction between the code, printer, materials and the persons using them – all issues that affect how liability should be allocated.

All this challenges traditional liability rules. A familiar refrain in the digital legal world is that the regulatory problems and solutions amount simply to 'old wine in new bottles'.[1] That could be the case here. For example, there is nothing new about the debate as to whether computer codes are products. Design codes for 3D printing may simply be a further example of this familiar dilemma. Likewise the issue of who is a 'producer' (for the purposes of liability under the Product Liability Directive) or is selling in the course of a business (in sales law) might simply involve application of traditional criteria.

The nature of 3D printing might be reason to, at the very least, review the traditional approach. This approach has often been based on assumptions which the new model might challenge. Thus we might wish to exempt small time sellers from consumer law rules, as they cannot be expected to trouble themselves to be familiar with rules, given their small scale production, and will be unlikely to have the resources or infrastruc-

---

* Geraint Howells is Professor of Commercial Law at the City University of Hong Kong. Chris Willett is Professor of Commercial Law at the University of Essex.

1 Christopher Reed, *Internet Law* (2nd ed., CUP 2004).

ture to manage risks. The democratisation of printing means many of the 'real' producers may not have the attributes of those parties the law traditional allocates responsibility to (e.g. if these producers are not really commercial). However, our view might be different if, instead of traditional home-made produce like marmalade, the small production run of 3D printers includes heart valves, firearms or even cars?[2] Indeed, does the rationale for treating code as a product become even stronger if consumers come to see 3D printing as an everyday device, so that when they buy the code, they view themselves as effectively buying the product?[3] More radically does the nature of the new production process require a rethinking of the fundamental rules? Should one look to a new style of liability? Typically this might focus on the commercial operators, but there may be a variety of commercial operators, performing various functions – designer of code, designer of printer, operator of commercial printer, supplier of materials etc.- and it may be hard to justify making them liable for the faults of third parties that they have no control over. The liability of the sharing sites bringing these parties together is equally a matter of topical debate.

In his paper Chrstian Twigg-Flesner outlines the limits of contract law in dealing with 3D printing.[4] There are intriguing questions waiting to an answered in this regard, but our suspicion is that front-line sellers may be less likely to be liable in this new world of 3D printing. The result of this may be that tort law is required to step in as the primary source of liability. Our paper seeks to contribute to the debate on this, by considering what special challenges there are for traditional strict product liability rationales.[5] This democratic production revolution challenges us to think afresh about liability. Here we present some initial reflections and tentative ideas,

2 Admittedly the law can overlay special rules for particular products before they can be released onto market.

3 Comparisons might be made here with how large numbers of people now download music, rather than buying a CD.

4 See Christian Twigg-Flesner, in this volume, 35.

5 For other early thoughts on this, see Nora Freeman Engstrom, '3D Printing and Product Liability: Identifying the Obstacles' (2013) 162 [35] University of Pennsylvania Law Review Online 35; Lucas S Osborn, 'Regulating Three-Dimensional Printing: The Converging Worlds Of Bits And Atoms' (2014) 51 San Diego Law Review 553; Preeta Reddy, 'The Legal Dimension of 3D Printing: Analyzing Secondary Liability in Additive Layer Manufacturing' (2014) XVI The Columbia Science and Technology Law Review 222, 222–247.

but we certainly see this as just a small contribution to a process of encouraging debate.

II. Traditional primary role for contract law: front-line seller liability

In a 'normal' market, contract law is normally seen as having the primary role to play, in providing redress to consumers when they buy defective products. Where injury is suffered, strict (tort based) product liability may be an alternative, but buyers will still typically turn to their seller, if he is liable for consequential losses. Under the Sales Directive,[6] sellers under a contract of sale, are responsible for delivering to the consumer goods 'which are in conformity with the contract of sale'.[7] Goods are presumed to be in conformity if they meet certain key requirements in relation to compliance with description and with the way they appeared in any sample or model; fitness for any particular purpose which the consumer made known to and accepted by the seller at the time of conclusion of the contract; fitness for the purposes for which goods of the type are normally used; and demonstrating the quality and performance that is normal in goods of this type and which can reasonably be expected, given the nature of the goods and any public statements on their specific characteristics made by the seller, the producer or his representative, especially in advertising or on labelling.[8] If the goods do not conform in some such way, the seller is liable to the consumer, and the consumer becomes entitled to repair or replacement of the goods, and in certain circumstances, to price reduction or rescission of the contract.[9]

Further, however, although it is not provided for in the Sales Directive, many Member States will make some provision for consumers to claim damages for the breach of contract. This might be used as an alternative to one of the remedies from the Directive (e.g. the consumer obtains repair or replacement from a third party and claims the cost of this in damages from

6 European Parliament and Council Directive 99/44/EC of 25 May 1999 on certain aspects of the sale of consumer goods and associated guarantees [1999] OJ L171/12 (Consumer Sales Directive) (and also under most national systems even before implementation of the Directive-see David Oughton and Chris Willett, 'Quality Regulation in European Private Law' (2002) 25 JCP 299, 299–328).

7 Art 2 (1).

8 Art 2 (2).

9 Art 3.

the original seller), and, of course, damages can in many systems compensate for damage to property, injury or other consequential losses caused by the non-conformity. This enables an injured buyer to turn to their seller for compensation for an injury, rather than having to turn to the producer.

Even though the law imposes strict tort based liability on the producer, the seller may be more accessible in practice, and these conformity standards in the Sales Directive (upon which the seller's liability turns) are also 'strict liability' standards. There is no mention of the seller liability being based on whether he exercised such reasonable care as would ensure compliance with the description, quality and fitness standards. There is no mention of any sort of 'defence' based on establishing reasonable care, a lack of fault, negligence or anything of this nature. Indeed, it will very often be the case that the seller has not been at fault in any way, that he has exercised what would be considered to be reasonable care in selecting the goods, storing them, etc., and that any defect would not have been detectable by any reasonable care that could have been exercised by the seller. None of this matters. If the goods do not conform to the contract in the ways described, there is a breach of contract, and the seller must provide the remedies provided for in the Sales Directive. As indicated, the damages remedy is often also available. Now, in some systems, some degree of negligence must be shown in order for damages to be available, but in other systems, no negligence is needed.[10]

These strict liability conformity standards and remedies are, as indicated, imposed on the 'seller', who is defined as:

'any natural or legal person who, under a contract, sells consumer goods in the course of his trade, business or profession.'[11]

So, the front-line seller strict liability model applies only to someone who can be said to have a trade, business or profession, and to be selling in the course of this trade, business or profession. One might rationalise this in terms of the idea that if someone is a sufficiently regular and professional seller, then, he should have the resources to provide these conformity guarantees and provide the appropriate remedies if the goods do not conform, despite there being no fault on his part.[12] As we shall now

---

10 Compare, e.g., Germany and the UK.

11 Art 2(c).

12 Cases like C–537/13 [2015] ECR I–nyr interpret the 'acting for purposes relating to trade, business or profession' concept from the Unfair Terms Directive, as covering a lawyer who provides legal services for a fee. So, if we have someone

suggest, it may be that the 'democratised' nature of the 3D printing market is such that this traditional justification for strict front-line seller liability, does not exist nearly as routinely as it does in a 'normal' product market.

III. Democratising production: retreat of contract? tort must step up?

Suppose X buys a printer from a shop, uses the printer to make things at home and sells them to friends, neighbours or others, who are injured or whose property is damaged. Alternatively, suppose X goes to a shop that has a printer, gets the shop to print things out, and then X sells these things to friends, neighbours or others, who are injured or whose property is damaged. The question then arises: is a 'hobby producer/seller', such as X, a regular/profitable enough seller to be treated as acting 'in the course of his trade, business or profession', and therefore to be responsible in relation to the conformity standards and remedies under the Sales Directive? The answer, surely, is that it will depend on the particular facts of the case, *but* that there are likely to be a great deal of people in X's situation who are not regular and/or profitable enough sellers to fall into this category. It is also important to point out that, there might certainly be many such people who would at least be very surprised if they were placed in this category. The law should certainly be very cautious about allowing such people to fall unwittingly under legal obligations, especially as they will be unlikely to have given any thought as to how to manage this risk (e.g. by the acquisition of expertise and/or insurance).

Of course, there has always been the hobby seller, the law has always faced the difficulty of where to draw the line. How much profit should there be? How regular should be the sales? How relevant should it be whether the seller displays other business patterns of behaviour (advertising, marketing etc.)? There have always been plenty of people in various sectors whose activities raise tricky borderline questions in these respects- small businesses selling, for example, second–hand cars, factory workers making 'foreigner' machine parts etc. for neighbours, collectors

---

who is qualified to perform a particular activity, as here, this is covered at least be this definition in the UTD. This case says nothing of regularity of such transactions, but would that be the logical way of determining business status, where no formal professional qualification is involved? This is at least an important element in the UK law approach (Stevenson v Rogers (1999) 1 All ER 613).

selling off (perhaps regularly) parts of their collection (of stamps, for example) etc. More recently, the popularity of e-bay and other on-line auctions, has meant that there are many more, probably tens of thousands more, home/hobby sellers. This poses a challenge in terms of deciding when such sellers are selling for business purposes.[13] If they are not, then they will not be liable strictly in contract law.

How is 3DP any different? First, it is a question of numbers. The 3DP revolution may add hundreds of thousands to the hobby seller community, and a proportion of these will not be selling for business purposes. But this does not just increase very significantly, the numbers of consumers that will not obtain a remedy in contract, it increases hugely the numbers *in relation to which we might reasonably expect that there should be some form of liability-and if this cannot be in contract, then it must be in tort*. A second point relates to what is being sold. In the above examples what is being sold is very often second hand. It will have been some time since it was made and distributed by a producer. The chances are that any defects that it possesses now, have nothing to do with the producer. So, we would not expect to be able to attach strict product liability to the producer. In the 3DP context, however, the product causing the injury or damage to property will be new. In such circumstances, we would typically expect that there should at least sometimes be some form of strict tort based liability if contract law cannot help. The question then is what possibilities there are to impose such liability. This must either be tort liability imposed on our hypothetical X (see above), who has either produced the thing and sold it, or has had the thing produced by someone else (a shop) and then sold it; and/or it must be tort liability imposed on someone further up the chain-whether the printing shop, the maker of the printer, someone responsible for its upkeep, the supplier of a code that makes the printer perform its tasks, the supplier of the materials that are used to make the final product etc.

13 Martin Morgan-Taylor and Chris Willett, 'The Quality Obligation and Online Marketplaces' (2005) July Journal of Contract Law 155, 155–171; Christine Riefa, *Consumer Protection and Online Auction Platforms* (Ashgate 2015) ch 2.

IV. Strict and Negligence Based Liability in Tort

Normally tort steps in when there is a break in the contractual chain, e.g. family or friends did not buy the product under a contract (and therefore have no contractual rights), but have been affected by the product and need a tort remedy; or where the buyer of the product, who does have contractual rights, finds that the party against whom he has these rights, has become insolvent; or where, like in our example, there may be no contractual rights because of the private status of the seller.

In the latter part of 20th century, most western legal systems (e.g. EU Product Liability Directive) developed non fault (i.e. non negligence) based strict liability in tort.[14] One general rationale for this has been that, while the law should not discourage production by over-regulating, those that advertise to consumers, sell to them, and profit from a mass market, must be incentivised to produce safe products by taking a fair share of the risk of defects. Indeed, for some, the act of marketing a product for profit is a justification in itself for making that person liable for its defects regardless of fault.[15] Sometimes this is linked to a deep pocket theory-the idea that those marketing for profit often have the resources to compensate when defects arise, but, of course, not all traders are wealthy conglomerates. Wealthy or not, one justification for imposing strict liability might well be that traders can be expected to have reflected on the need for insurance cover. But, whether the act of supply alone is enough to justify liability is debateable. Some supporters of strict liability would add other rationales, such as internalising the costs of the product so its price reflects its full costs.[16] However, other commentators see a far more limited role for strict liability, perhaps only seeing it as a proxy for negligence, when there is difficulty in proving negligence. In the US this has led to a

14 E.g. Council Directive 85/374/EEC of 25 July 1985 on the approximation of the laws, regulations and administrative provisions of the Member States concerning liability for defective products [1985] OJ L210/29 (Product Liability Directive) and Geraint Howells, *Comparative Product Liability* (Dartmouth 1993).

15 Tony Honoré, 'Responsibility and Luck: The Moral Basis of Strict Liability' (1988) 104 LQR 530 and Jane Stapleton, *Product Liability* (Butterworths 1994) 185.

16 Guido Calabresi 'Some Thoughts on Risk Distribution and the Law of Torts' (1961) 70 Yale LJ 499.

'retreat', so that true strict liability is now only applied in the case of manufacturing defects.[17]

The core focus of a strict product liability action is whether the product that has caused the loss is defective (whether it contained a 'defect', i.e. whether it was not as 'safe as a person is entitled to expect').[18] In other words, the focus is on the state of the product. As in the case of strict liability in contract, it is the state of the product that determines whether there is liability. The defendant's *input* does not matter. It does not matter that the defendant has not been negligent, that he has exercised reasonable care. All that matters is the final condition of the product. In contrast, in the case of negligence, it is precisely the input that matters. The defendant is only liable if the defect is due to the defendant having not exercised reasonable care. What is reasonable care then becomes a matter of considering what is normal practice in the sector in question, and performing a cost-benefit type analysis. Given what is normal in the sector, and given the costs of doing what the defendant did, could he have done more to prevent this defect arising, or did he do all that could have been expected?[19]

This is of course the theory, when it comes to the difference between strict liability and negligence in practice, however, courts often slip into negligence style analysis, when purportedly applying a strict liability standard. The 'expectation' of consumers (supposedly an expectation primarily focussed on the state of the product) can all too easily be read as only being an expectation that a producer takes reasonable care, and to the extent that a 'risk-benefit' analysis is allowed, the framing of the debate can resemble negligence. Indeed, once state of the art and development risks questions are included, the difference between strict liability and negligence might even end up being limited to one based on different burdens of proof.

---

17 George L Priest 'Strict Products Liability: The Original Intent' (1989) 10 Cardozo L Rev 2301.

18 Arts 1 & 6(1).

19 E.g. in the UK the famous 'Bolam test' from Bolam v Friern Hosoital Management Committee (1957) 1 WLR 582, but see how the approach now emphasises that there will be negligence where normal practice has been followed, but this normal practice is not logical, or is not based on a professional assessment of the risks and benefits of the conduct in question: Bolitho v City and Hackney Health Authority (1997) 4 All ER 771, 778–779, Lord Browne-Wilkinson.

This blurring of the lines between strict liability and negligence perhaps emphasises the need first to be convinced on the rationale for imposing strict liability and then to apply a framework that delivers against those principles. In this paper we shall focus on the extent to which liability can arise under strict product liability options and the issues that these options give rise to. We make this our focus as we are after all, considering whether there is an alternative to the normal *strict* liability contract route, so it is most logical to look at the route which would offer the most conceptual similarity to this, i.e. a strict liability tort route. We leave to one side a negligence based action, as this is generally more routinely available in most countries than is a strict liability action. It is not such a priority to analyse negligence options, as they probably do not pose as many difficult fundamental policy questions as strict liability. In short, it is easier to justify imposing liability based on negligence, given the higher degree of culpability involved.[20] The important policy question is whether a strict liability regime can be defended.

V. Issues where there may be a defect in a printer or in materials, supplied by a producer

This section considers the situation where the source of the problem in the final product supplied by X, may well be a defect in a printer or in materials supplied by a traditional producer of such things. It is suggested that, even in this situation, the 3DP context may raise distinctive questions and/or cause distinctive difficulties.

---

20 But note that the first set of difficulties discussed below-whether there should be liability for quality defects, problems in establishing defects and causation, and difficulties with the development risks concept-probably all apply in the case of negligence liability, just as they do in the case of strict liability. However, in the case of a negligence action, the issue in relation to defects, discussed below, would not only be whether the thing was defective when it left the defendant, but whether the defendant could be shown to have been negligent (this perhaps being particularly challenging due to the time lapses that may be involved).

1. Quality defects

There is often no tort remedy for pure quality defects-whether damages, cure, price reduction or refund. Under the Product Liability Directive, there is liability for 'damage' caused by a defective product.[21] 'Damage' is defined as:

(a) damage caused by death or by personal injuries;
(b) damage to, or destruction of, any item of property other than the defective product itself'.

So, while there is a damages claim to cover death and personal injury and damage caused by the defective product to *other* property,[22] there is no damages claim (and there is no right to a cure remedy to put the problems right), if the product is simply of poor quality, or self-destructs, or indeed even if the product is dangerously defective, but has not caused any actual injury yet.[23]

This approach is justified partly on the grounds that quality is a matter of contractual expectation, and therefore recovery for pure economic (quality) losses is within the province of contract law. Closely associated is the idea that allowing recovery of economic loss in tort, would 'open the floodgates' of liability, given the range of potential claimants there would be.[24]

The question has been raised on several occasions as to whether producers of goods should (along with sellers) be liable for the quality of goods.[25] Any such scheme (examples of which do exist in the Member States[26]) might be conceptualised as an extension of contractual sales law

---

21 Art 1.

22 E.g. defective washing machine floods floor, defective boiler blows up and destroys house.

23 This sort of approach reflects the general reluctance to award pure economic loss in the tort of negligence, e.g. in UK, Murphy v Brentwood DC (1990) 2 All ER 908.

24 See, famously, Justice Cardozo in Ultramares Corp Touche (1932) 174 N.E 441.

25 See Chris Willett, 'Direct Producer Liability' in Geraint Howells and Reiner Schulze, *Modernising and Harmonising Consumer Contract Law* (2009 Sellier) 189, 189–212; and Martin Ebers, André Janssen and Olaf Meyer (eds), *European Perspectives on Producers' Liability* (Sellier 2009).

26 See Martin Ebers, André Janssen and Olaf Meyer (ed), *European Perspectives on Producers' Liability*, (Sellier 2009).

or a new form of tortious liability, but it is in any event akin to tort; at least in the sense that it would involve imposing responsibility where there is no contract in the traditional, genuinely consensual sense.

The question here is whether in the 3D context, there is a particularly strong policy case for allowing some sort of pure economic loss claim in tort, or at least some form of 'quality based' claim by the party who buys a poor quality item, against the producer of a printer or of materials, where it is a defect in this printer or materials that is the reason that the item finally produced is defective.

Essentially, the case for this would be that here (unlike in general goods cases) the unavailability of a contract remedy for pure quality defects will be much more routine. This is for the reasons that we have outlined above, i.e. that there may be large numbers of sellers of 3D printed products, who end up not being characterised as business sellers, so that, in this market, there may be many buyers who do not have the strict liability contract remedy that is normal in other sectors. At least with general goods, *most* buyers will get a remedy for pure quality defects.[27] So, perhaps it is less necessary to allow for some economic loss or quality based claim against the producer. But, if there is very often not a contract remedy in the 3DP context, perhaps there should be a routine economic loss or quality based claim, at least against mass producers of the printers or materials that are responsible. One way to achieve this would be by an extension (applicable only to 3DP) of the concept of 'damage' in the Product Liability Directive, to cover pure economic loss. However, this can be rather messy. It would be hard to pin down exactly when any new form of liability would arise. Drafting a clause that included 3D printers alone might be technically difficult and soon become redundant as technology advanced. Equally material producers may not be aware of the extent they might be held liable for economic loss given their lack of control over what their materials are sued for.

27 It will only be exceptionally that consumers do not have a strict liability contract remedy, e.g. where the seller has become insolvent.

2. *Proving causation and defects-particularly problematic?*

Again suppose the seemingly simple case, where it may be that it is a defect in a printer or in materials supplied by a traditional producer that is the source of the problem in the final product. In such cases, the democratisation of production in the 3DP market could cause particular problems in relation to proving the existence of a defect, and in proving causation. There may often be a more diverse and fragmented production process here than in traditional product distribution. Different parties may be involved in manufacturing the printer, designing codes, supplying materials and performing the printing. This interaction could make it particularly difficult to establish that there is a defect in one or more items that were supplied at some earlier stage; and it could also make it particularly difficult to prove that any defect that can be established, was actually the cause of any injury or other loss that has later occurred.

Suppose a final product produced by 3D printing methods injures or causes damage to property. It could be harder than normal to establish where, if anywhere, is the source of the defect, because production is a more multi stage (and possibly multi-party) process than is traditional. Is it the printer, the code, the materials, actions of the buyer/seller etc. that caused the harm? In particular, one can imagine debates as to whether the source of the harm was the printer or the way in which the home user or shop printed out the item.

Under the Product Liability Directive, the defect must have existed at the time the product was put into circulation by the producer.[28] This is also the point in time at which defectiveness is assessed.[29] Indeed, it is specifically provided that a 'product shall not be considered defective for the sole reason that a better product is subsequently put into circulation'.[30] A difficulty in proving that there was a defect at the point when the printer, code, materials etc., were supplied, is that, in the 3DP market, it may often be that the thing that we are trying to establish is defective, has been in circulation for longer than is typical in the case of traditional products. Even in the case of a traditional product, it is made, then supplied, perhaps to a wholesaler, then perhaps a shop, then it is sold to a consumer. There may be quite a period of time between initial production/supply and the product

28 Art 7(b).
29 Art 6(1).
30 Art 6(2).

causing an injury. It passes through the hands of these various parties, perhaps taking a while to be sold on, and perhaps taking some time to injure the consumer even after he has bought it. However, with 3DP, there is another stage in the time-line. The printer, code or materials, are made, and distributed down to shop level in the way described above. But *then* the shop prints out a further (the actual final) product for a customer, or the shop sells a printer to a customer, who prints out the actual final product at home. The product may then be sold on to the final buyer. So, if what is trying to be established is not that the actual product is defective, but rather that some product (printer, materials or code),is defective because it caused the actual product to be defective, these things (printer, materials, code etc.) may have been around for quite a long time, before they were used to make the final product. So, even if it can be established that the printer, materials or code was not working properly when used to make the final product, it is far from obvious that it was defective when it was first produced. Apart from anything else, it may be perfectly plausible to say that the current defective condition of the printer or materials is down to no more than natural wear and tear and, if anyone is to be held legally responsible, it may be someone further down the chain than the initial producer. The Product Liability Directive also has a ten year long stop limitation period and this might even have expired (at some future date) by the time the actual product that causes injury is produced.[31]

Then, suppose that it is shown that there was a defect in the printer, materials or code, at the time these were first put into circulation. It must also be established that this defect is the cause of the injury, or other loss, that has been suffered by the end-user. But this could be far from easy in this multi stage, multi-party distribution chain. Perhaps the real cause was the way the printer was used by the shop, or by the home user. Perhaps it was the indications/guidance given by such a shop and/or by others as to how to use the printer or the thing to be produced by the printer. Perhaps, the problem was at the home of the person who did the printing and sold it to a neighbour. Maybe this person's dog, cat or child may have interfered with/bumped into etc. the printer, before or during the time it was doing the job. Perhaps, e.g. in a case where it is shown that the printer is defective, it is also shown that the code and the materials are defective. Is one of these dominant in causal terms, or do they all play a material role? Also

31 Art 10.

to what extent can the chain of causation be broken by the failure of the final producer to inspect the product. If the product is obviously defective, or at least defective in some way that could reasonably be discovered, would the failure of this final producer to be alert break the chain of causation?

We are not suggesting that there are not hard and complex issues around establishing defectiveness (or fault) and/or causation elsewhere in tort law, especially, e.g. in medical and industrial liability cases; but it is arguable that 3DP is particularly challenging in that the very nature of the market, with its many stages and parties, seems highly likely to cause these sorts of problems. The issue is almost systemic.

These problems may be hard enough for lawyers to overcome, but it is surely desirable that legal regimes should be as accessible as possible, such as to enable consumers and businesses to resolve their disputes without using courts. This is a generally desirable goal in terms of efficiency and justice. However, it also in line with the EU legal policy position on ADR etc.[32] Now, if legal concepts are hard to apply by lawyers, they will be even harder to apply by ADR bodies, who have less expertise than courts; and they will be harder again to apply by consumers and businesses. Then, there is the point that it is often the consumer who will in practice lose out here, due to the power imbalance. For a start the consumer has the burden of proof. This will be especially hard for consumers, being in a weaker position in terms of knowledge, resources etc. It is difficult enough for a consumer to assert himself in the face of a producer who not only says that the product he supplied was not defective, or that if it was defective, there was a break in the chain of causation: 'it is well tested, it was fine when it left us, it must have been how you used it, it was your pre-existing condition that really caused your injury'. What lines of research is a consumer to take, what demands to make, what questions to ask, to assert himself in the face of these 'defences'? It is even harder, if, *in addition to these defences*, a producer can say: '...and another thing, it must have been the code supplied by X, or the materials supplied by Y, or the way it was printed by shop Z, or the way it was printed by your neighbour before he sold it to you'. Further, the producer

32 See, e.g., Directive 2013/11/EU of the European Parliament and of the Council of 21 May 2013 on alternative dispute resolution for consumer disputes and amending Regulation (EC) No 2006/2004 and Directive 2009/22/EC (Directive on consumer ADR) [1999] OJ L 165/63.

may say, 'Your neighbour should have quality controlled the final product that was produced by the printer'.

3. *Solution to the Defects/Causation Problems?*

The Product Liability Directive does not spell out how to understand or apply causation. Is this for the Member States (if 3D printing raises particular difficulties)? Is it something that CJEU would be prepared to give guidance on? Another question is whether there should be some kind of legal/technical requirement for the printer to 'remember' all its activities, and those of the user, so it is easier to establish whether the printer or code is defective, or whether the problem lies elsewhere? But this only solves the problem of whether there was some form of defect in the printer or the code, not whether the later actions or omissions of others have broken the chain of causation.

4. *Proving defectiveness*

The Product Liability Directive provides the following definition of defectiveness in Article 6(1):

> '1. A product is defective when it does not provide the safety which a person is entitled to expect, taking all circumstances into account, including:
> (a) the presentation of the product;
> (b) the use to which it could reasonably be expected that the product would be put;
> (c) the time when the product was put into circulation.
>
> 2. A product shall not be considered defective for the sole reason that a better product is subsequently put into circulation'.

We have already discussed the temporal aspects of the Directive to some extent. Here we will consider what expectations people are entitled to have. Without going into the whole jurisprudence, a few key points can be raised for discussion. The products produced by a small scale (or even a home) producer should not be judged by a lower standard just because of their form of production. Early moves to exclude artisan products from the scope of the Directive had been resisted and that would seem to rule out any special exception. Of course it may be inherent in the material used that consumers should have lower expectations than in the case of some alternative products. In the end, however, the issue is whether the products meet minimum safety requirements, taking into account factors such as any instructions and warnings. There is a specific defence if the product was neither manufactured for sale or any form of distribution for economic purpose, nor manufactured or distributed by him in the course of his business.[33] This seems narrower than the similar control in contract law, as any sale or economic distribution will still give rise to liability, even if made by someone who is not a traditional business. Many home producers may well therefore be subject to liability under the Product Liability Directive. This might also cover designers of code to produce products, subject to code being a product within the definition. Of course, this shows how difficult it is is to draw a clear line between the 'traditional' producers that this section is focussed on primarily, and other producers.

Is it fair for this line to become blurred? Should there be strict liability for defective code supplied by a 'hobby producer' in his/her bedroom. Perhaps initially this might involve no more than casual and occasional production, perhaps, for little or no profit? It is, at first sight, hard to justify any more than negligence based liability. There is no mass production, little profit/ability to absorb losses. Contract law requires an assessment that trade has become sufficiently widespread that the profits justify strict liability, or at least that the risks should be within the trader's sphere of risk i.e. the one time hobbyist has become the better loss bearer than the ultimate (injured) consumer. The Product Liability Directive seems stricter. Can the nature of harm (physical) justify such liability?

Producers of printers, code and those offering 3D printing services might argue that the law should treat them favourably to promote innovation. Obviously services will in any event fall outside the scope of strict *product* liability. But even within the scope of strict product liability, the drafters of the Product Liability Directive did not allow any exceptions for high risk industries. Each new wave of innovation seems to bring some arguments for special pleading. Of course, the concept of defect provides plenty of scope for flexible application based on reasonable expectations given the presentation of the product. In addition, for the vast majority of Member States additional producer protection is given by the development risks defence.

---

33 Art 6(c).

5. *The Development Risks Defence-particularly problematic?*

The Directive provides that:

> 'The producer shall not be liable as a result of this Directive if he proves:... (e) that the state of scientific and technical knowledge at the time when he put the product into circulation was not such as to enable the existence of the defect to be discovered.'[34]

Normally, this is about showing that the producer could not have known that there were risks of a certain type when the product was put into circulation. For example, whilst we all *now* know about a risk, the producer could not have known then that this drug would have these side effects etc.

Are there *more* opportunities for this argument in the 3DP context, simply because we have added more things and people to the process? For example, there may be an opportunity for the producer to argue that, e.g., scientific and technical knowledge, at the time he put a printer on the market, was not such as to enable him to know that this printer can interact with codes or materials in a particular way. Or could it be argued that a material when used by a printer will have different qualities than when used in other production processes? It is unlikely that the test will be very generous to such producers. The burden of proof is on them and the courts have been willing to find the defence is lost once there is a sniff of a risk[35] i.e. any level of awareness even if the risk cannot be reduced.[36]

VI. More fundamental questions about rationales for strict liability

If the problem is the printer and/or the computer codes supplied comprised in the printer, this being a printer supplied by a traditional mass producer, then this is clearly supply of a defective product and normal strict liability applies (and can be justified as for products generally). The problems in these cases are the above ones about proving defects, proving causation etc.

---

34 Art 7(e).

35 [36] Case C–300/95 *Commission v UK* [1997] ECR I–2649.

36 See non-application of the defence to manufacturing defects: German Supreme Court, 'Mineral Water Bottle case' [1995] NJW 2162.

But, does the democratisation of the production process draw in players who do not fit the traditional 'profile' for rationalising/justifying strict product liability? What happens to the following scenarios?

1. In-shop printing

Suppose X goes with design code and materials to a business (shop) that does the printing, which produces a product that X supplies to Y, and which causes injury, but no defect can be proved in relation to the code or the materials. Here is the shop manufacturing a product, thereby being a producer, who is strictly liable to Y? Or is X the producer and the shop just a service provider? Even if the shop is indeed a service provider, can it also be a producer?

Whatever is the technical legal answer to these questions, what result do we want from a policy perspective in this situation? Should the shop only be held liable on proof of negligence, as the shop has limited knowledge of the materials, code etc., supplied by the consumer making the outcome rather speculative?

Alternatively, should the shop be held strictly liable, especially given that it could be very hard to show negligence, e.g. where the shop shows that they do regular checks on the machine? Would they be expected also to take responsibility for the code and/or materials, even if provided by hobby producer? If it was decided that shops should be liable, would this be under the Product Liability Directive-by adding them as potential defendants? If so, how would they be classified? Are they producers, because they affect the qualities of the product?[37] Or would this be a new category of quasi-supplier, but with primary liability? How can they be distinguished from other parties who do sub-contracted work for producers?

2. Defective Code

Suppose the problem lies in defective code supplied by a third party mass producer of such things (i.e. a code inserted after the printer has been

37 Cf the Directive 2001/95/EC of the European Parliament and of the Council of 3 December 2001 on general product safety [2001] OJ L 11/4.

supplied by its producer)? Do we only impose negligence based liability, on the basis of a similar argument to that raised above in relation to a service, i.e. that the outcome is too speculative?

Or do we impose strict liability, on the basis of the similarity to goods (mass production, loss bearing ability etc.), and the trajectory towards treating digital content like goods in contract law?[38] If so, would we need to clarify whether or not, e.g. the Product Liability Directive definition of 'product' includes digital content.[39]

What about defective code supplied by 'hobby producer' in his/her bedroom? Perhaps there is no more than casual and occasional production. If there is little or no profit it may be at first sight, hard to justify any more than negligence based liability (no mass production, little profit/ability to absorb losses)? Is it a case of deciding when production become sufficiently widespread/profits sufficient, to justify strict liability- i.e. when does the hobby producer become the better loss bearer than the ultimate (injured) consumer?

But, in deciding on when someone crosses the threshold here (when production is sufficiently regular, widespread, profit-oriented etc., to be 'in the course of a business'), should it be easier for the hobbyist here to cross the threshold and be treated as a business supplier for tort liability purposes? The argument for this might be that with contract liability, comes obligations to cure, reduce price, and pay damages for pure economic losses that are consequent upon pure quality defects. But should the hobby code producer not perhaps expect to be strictly liable in tort, even without much regularity or profit, at least for the injury he or she causes by circulating codes in the market? On the other hand, damages may be a lot higher in tort, which could be a reason for *not* making the hobby code producer liable unless negligence is shown. A further question is how all this could or should be influenced by insurance practice, e.g. could insurance be sold with each printer/use of printer, and might this weaken the argument for imposing strict liability on hobby producers? Of course, another dimension here is the extent to which the debate around strict liability should be affected by whether the products that can be made by the code are (i) inherently dangerous (guns, knives etc.), (ii) potentially

---

38 E.g. new UK Consumer Rights Act 2015, Chapter 3, setting strict liability standards, reflecting those applicable to goods.

39 Karin Alheit, 'The applicability of the EU Product Liability Directive to software' (2001) 34 Comparative and International Law Journal of Southern Africa 188.

dangerous (mechanical, electrical products and parts thereof), or (iii) inherently safe (ornaments, fluffy toys). One might argue that the case for strict liability is strongest in the case of (i) and (ii), and weakest in the case of (iii).

VII. Solving the Problems by other Means-Network Liability

We have raised several issues about how 3D printing challenges the traditional framework of the Product Liability Directive, which channels liability to the producer. Perhaps the assumptions behind such liability do not apply well to the 3D printing context. Even if hobby producers are potentially liable, they may not have the resources to cover large claims-imagine a student produces a code for a product that causes mass damages. Little might be possible where individuals simply use materials, products and services on the market, but where commercial operators come into play, there might be more scope for network liability. For instance, a commercial 3D printing operation might be given responsibility for checking the quality for products produced. Equally sites that seek to bring designers of code into contact with producers might be subject to some obligations. This is a new area. Business models are just being established. We are just starting to suspect some of the issues that may arise. We need to work out what role the law has and what role can be played by other forms of governance e.g. voluntary assumption of responsibility. It will be important to assess how the insurance market can evolve to allow business to cover their risks. We are well aware this paper does little more than place some of the issues on the table for discussion. We intend to reflect on how legal principles can assist us in developing a framework that meets the business needs of an innovative sector and adequately protects consumers. We would encourage others to reflect on these issues and join in the debate. The very fluidity of the market allows for policy to direct it and policy-makers need to find the right balance between innovation and protection. We have concentrated on tort law, but we also need to consider product safety regulation. We want society to embrace the possibilities of new technology but only in ways which enhance welfare.

Share Economy & Internet Platforms

Regulation of Share Economy: A Consistently Changing Environment

Larry A. DiMatteo[*]

I. Introduction

The share economy continues to evolve and present potential legal issues for regulatory and private law. American law on the subject is fragmented between federal and state regulatory authorities, as well as by private law, mainly tort, property, and contract law found in the independent common laws of each state. The types of regulations include government regulation, self-regulation (private), and non-regulation. At times the regulatory regimes overlap. For example, a particularly punitive contract clause can be held to be unconscionable under contract law by a state court. One such clause is a 'gag clause', which prohibits consumers from posting negative reviews and testimonials online relating to a manufacturer or seller's products. The American Federal Trade Commission (FTC) has ruled that such gag provisions used by Florida-based marketers of a line of weight-loss supplements that allegedly made baseless claims for their products was an unfair trade practice. The benefit of the FTC action, instead of a state judicial decision, is that it has national effect.

This chapter will review a few of the many issues and problems presented by the share economy and some of the initial legal-regulative responses found in the United States. The areas of the share economy that will be focused upon include: transportation services, legal services, social media, advertising, fraud, and mass collaborations. In the end, the analysis cautions against a rush to regulate. The experience in the United States has been that despite the seeming novelty of technological change often existing regulatory structures have been found to be sufficient.

The share economy is a fundamentally different business model that has the potential to create innumerable benefits for society. Regulators will

---

* Larry A DiMatteo is Professor of Contract Law & Legal Studies at the University of Florida.

always be confronted with new products, technologies, and business practices that fall within their jurisdiction but do not fit comfortably within their existing regulatory frameworks. In the face of economic and regulatory disruption, regulators should be flexible and willing to collaborate with stakeholders to develop dynamic performance standards and self-regulatory regimes as an initial response. Although, the need for targeted new regulations will become apparent over time.

1. What is the share economy?

The share or collaborative economy's technological mirror is what has been called Web 2.0, which focuses on Websites that emphasize user-generated content (UGC) that includes any form of content such as blogs, wikis, discussion forums, posts, chats, tweets, podcasting, pins, digital images, video, audio files, advertisements and other forms of media that is created by users of an online system or service. Modern technology has enabled the collaborative economy due to its usability (ease of use and learnability) and interoperability (the capability of different programs to exchange data via a common set of exchange formats).

The 'tag cloud'[1] for Web 2.0 is based upon metadata or tags that are assigned to a website by the creator of the website in order to be found when online searches are made. But, there is also tagging through folksonomy, which is a system in which users apply public tags to online items, typically to aid them in re-finding those items. This can give rise to a classification system based on those tags and their frequencies of use. This practice is also known as collaborative tagging, social classification, social indexing, and social tagging. The larger the word in the tag cloud the more often it is frequented or linked to the search word, which in the case of Web 2.0 include: participation, standardization, usability, economy, design, convergence, remixability, blogs, joy of use, sharing, Wikis, folksonomy, data driven, economy, accessibility, podcasts, user-

1 A tag cloud is a visual representation of text data, typically used to depict keyword metadata or tags on websites, or to visualize free form text.

centered, collaboration, social software, affiliation, and so forth.[2] This set of scattered words is the essence of what is called the share economy.

2. Share Economy as Disruptive Economic Force

The share economy is primarily a positive development from the perspective of consumers, users, and the free market. It is a disruptive force that allows for the sharing of underutilized assets, from spaces to skills to things, for monetary gain on a scale that would not be achievable without modern technology. This system facilitates localized production, cooperation, and the proliferation of microbusinesses, which allows consumer needs to be met by a large cross-section of society. This ease of access is made possible by platform companies, which are the businesses that broker the transactions.

Economists refer to collaborative consumption strategies as 'disruptive' because the extremely low cost of online transactions can displace established business models. Neighbors who can lend each other rarely used power tools and ladders won't have to rent or buy those items. Businesses using crowdfunding won't need to borrow the money at higher interest rates from a bank. 'Crowdsourcing' has allowed some companies to replace employees and suppliers with an undefined, generally large group of individuals via an open call on the Internet. Crowdsourcing has proven to be a viable means of production and has proliferated rapidly since it provides access to capital, new ideas, and talent by leveraging the low-cost, global, open, and distributive power of the Internet.

3. Do we need new regulations for the share economy?

In its infancy the share, peer to peer, or bit economy was viewed through an idealized lens. It was the technological means to connect people with similar needs, matching providers with customers, and to work on collaborative projects. But, as sharing companies have proliferated through creation of 'apps' some sharing concepts crossed the line between the

2 'Tag Cloud' for Web 2.0: Creative Commons (Vectorised and linked version by Luca Cremonini, 25 December 2006; Original by Markus Angermeier, 2 January 2007).

private and the public. One app searched for open parking spaces on city streets and then auctioned them off. In Los Angeles, the app was banned as improperly privatizing a public asset.

The idealism of the sharing economy is coming up against profit-driven tendencies, resulting in a questioning by political and legal authorities. Is the share economy amoral by totally embracing unregulated freedom? If so, some form of regulation will be needed. The regulation will come in two forms: government legislation or regulations and through the court system. As to the former, a further question is whether new laws are needed or are structures already in place to regulate the share economy? In the US, a regulatory apparatus recently put in place is the Consumer Financial Protection Bureau (CFPB) established in 2012 in the wake of the 2008 Financial Crisis as a core eliminate of the Dodd-Frank Bank Reform and Consumer Protection Act.[3] The CFPB's purpose is to protect consumers in financial transactions with bank and non-bank institutions. However, its mandate is vague and broad, and has been set up in way to make it independent of political pressures. It is a potential model for an EU-wide consumer regulatory agency that would issue regulations when needed without further legislative authorization. It is suggested that the organizational structure of the CFPB be studied as a part of a broad, omnibus type of EU Regulation aimed at regulating digital content and the share economy.

The other initial response to the share economy has come through the courts through private litigation. This may be all that is necessary in the way of regulation or it may need to be followed by government regulation. As in the early days of the Internet era, there was much debate as to whether this new technology required new law. There was the feeling on one side of the debate that current law was not sufficient to control this new form of unfettered communicative freedom. But, in the end, the existing legal structures were flexible enough to be applied. The constructs of contract, privacy, trespass and property were made applicable to most legal issues posed by the information age.

---

3 *Dodd–Frank Wall Street Reform and Consumer Protection Act*, P.L. 111-203, 124 Stat. 1955 (21 July 2010).

II. Regulating the Share Economy

There are three approaches to regulating the share economy—regulation, self-regulation, and non-regulation. Regulation here means the intrusion of public regulatory authorities into the private market. Self-regulation is seen as the delegation of the duty to regulate to private parties and their associations, prime examples are the learned professions (legal, accounting, medical). Any regulation of the share economy must be weighed against its power to produce public goods and overall societal benefits, and to innovate. Non-regulation does not necessarily mean the non-existence of regulation. However, the policing of bad behavior in a non-legal sense are left primarily to the market. Corporate social responsibility codes, industry standards, proper e-etiquette are examples of market-based regulation.

The notion of regulatory lag should be understood and play a role in the decision of when to regulate. It also goes to the question of how to regulate, such as through local, state or federal regulatory levels. With the continuous innovation of digital products and business models via the Internet there will always be a regulatory lag. In this case, regulatory lag is a good thing since it gives time for private entities, associations, and electronic platforms to analyze new innovations and respond to unexpected obstacles, problems, and abuses. It also gives regulatory authorities time to determine if the current law and regulatory schemes are sufficient or whether new regulations are necessary. In the share economy, government intervention in some cases has occurred at the local government level and to some degree at the state government level. Often regulatory lag will be greatest at the federal level.

The share economy applies to many different types of products and services, some of which are transmitted purely through the Internet, as apps on Smart phones, or, as in the case of Uber (transportation services) there may be additional proprietary electronic devices or information provided by the service provider. Given the nature of the share economy, large omnibus laws are not a good fit. Instead, targeted laws dealing with sub-sector specific problems is the best means of regulation. Although it is conceivable that an independent government regulatory agency could be established that could issue regulations as needed. In some cases, local ordinances or state laws will prove to be a sufficient and rational regulatory approach. In the case of Airbnb (vacation home rentals) this may be the case because of the particularities of different residential communities.

In other cases, the ubiquitousness of a problem requires a federal, if not an international, regulatory approach.

Given the endless variety of goods and services, the ubiquity of the provider-user online interface, and the rapidity of the innovation of new products and services in the share economy, three filters will be used to provide some order in covering the legal and regulatory implications of this new marketplace. First, there is a need to disaggregate the share economy into sub-sectors. Second, the legal problems and gaps found in a given sub-sector will need to be found. Third, an assessment will be needed of the proper and most efficient mix of regulatory schemes that can be applied to fix the problems and gaps.

III. Sub-Sector Analysis

The analysis of the share economy is best approached from a legal or business-oriented approach. The first approach would: (1) segment broad areas of law, such as privacy and security, fraud, competition, employment and labor, and marketing and advertising law, (2) analyze the structure of the sub-sector to see which of the legal areas seems most relevant, and (3) tailor specific regulations that serve to prevent abuse in these legal areas in the given sub-sector. The second approach would be to first segment the share economy into sub-sectors, such as transportation, real property, personal property, collective works sharing, and then tailor regulations for the different sub-sectors. In the end, the first approach is more appropriate for purposes of creating an omnibus law to cover an entire sector of the economy. A mapping or matrix of the share economy and related legal issues is helpful in assessing regulatory gaps. Figure 1 is a meager attempt at creating such a matrix.

Figure 1: Matrix of Issues—United States

Issues	**Type Of Sharing**	**Current Regulation**	**Need for New Regulation**	**Type of Regulation**
Privacy	Personal Information & Big Data	Self-Regulation: privacy policies (EU Directives)	Yes	Government
Marketing	Social Media; Electronic Word of Mouth	Self-Regulation	Yes	Government/ Self-Regulation
Social Entrepreneurship	Core Purpose is promoting a shared socially beneficial outcome	Self-regulation	No	Self-Regulation
Contract Formation	All Types	Contract Law	No	Judicial/Ad hoc Regulation (existing regulatory agencies)
Contract Disputes	All Types	Private Arbitration Rules or Civil Procedure	Online Dispute Resolution	Private initially; enabling regulations for online resolution
Online Defamation	Reviews, Testimonials, Chat Rooms, Bulletin Boards	Tort Law	None, except jurisdictional issues	Judicial
Securities Law	Pump & Dump	Government	No	Government
Fraud	All Types	Tort Law	Yes	Judicial/ Government
Financing	Crowdfunding	Self-Regulation	No	Self-Regulation
Legal Services	Lawsourcing	Self-Regulation	No	Self-Regulation
Independent Contractor Status	Agency	Employment Law	No	Judicial
Workers' Rights	Collective Bargaining	Government/ Judicial	No	Government/ Judicial
Security/ Criminal	Fraud; Theft, Espionage	Government/ Judicial	No	Government/ Judicial
Taxation	Internet Sales	Government	Debatable	Yet to be determined

Each sub-sector presents a unique mix of technology, digital content, and business models. The sub-sector analyses studied here are: (1) Transportation Services (Uber; Lyft); (2) Home Rental Services (Airbnb); (3) Social Media, Advertising, Fraud; and (4) Legalsourcing (legal information and research).

1. Transportation Services

There has been a decades-long trend towards replacing (or attempting to replace) employees with independent contractors. The *Times* attributes stagnating wages to this 'gig economy', acknowledging that other forces, including the decline of unions and globalization, as contributing factors. As of 2014, independent contractors occupied 18% of all jobs held in the United States.[4] Some people choose to be self-employed consultants so that they can work flexible hours and work from home. But it's hard to find a silver lining here for ordinary workers. Some can succeed as independent contractors, but their wages tend to be low and they have no job security. The connected car or ride sharing services provided by such companies as Uber and Lyft has been attacked by their characterization of their drivers as independent contractors.

a) Uber-Lyft and Employment Law

On June 3, 2015, the California Labor Commissioner's Office ruled that Uber drivers were employees deserving of workplace protections. In *Berwick v. Uber Technologies*,[5] Uber argued that it was merely an electronic platform and its 'Users' (drivers) were independent contractors that used the platform to connect with other users, those needing a ride. Uber argues that its contract establishes and independent contractor relationship because the drivers are entitled to accept, reject, and select among the requests received via the service. But, the Labor Commissioner looked at

4 Noam Scheiber, 'Growth in the 'Gig Economy' Fuels Work Force Anxieties' *New York Times*, (New York 12 July 2015) <http://www.nytimes.com/2015/07/13/business/rising-economic-insecurity-tied-to-decades-long-trend-in-employment-practices.html?_r=0> accessed 1 December 2015.

5 Case No. 11–46739, Labor Commissioner State of California (3 June 2015).

other provisions of the Uber contract and business model to demonstrate that it exercised the type of control over its drivers that is common in the employment relationship. The contract provided that: (1) you must perform the request in accordance with the User's specifications; (2) you agree that you shall maintain a vehicle that is a model approved by the Company; (3) you acknowledge that there is no tipping for any transportation that you provide; (4) you agree that, in the Company's sole discretion, a user's Cancellation Fee may be waived, in which case you will have no entitlement to any such fee; (5) Company will issue identification and password keys to the Transportation Provider to access the service; and (6) the Device (iPhone) is at all times the property of the Company and must be returned to the company. The California Supreme Court previously listed factors to be used in making the employment determination,[6] which when applied to the Uber business model shows that Uber is not a neutral technological platform, but controlled every aspect of the transport service operation. The Labor Commission ruled that the Uber employees were entitled to have expenses paid in the operation of their personal cars including 56 cents per mile (IRS Mileage rate) and toll charges.

The California decision is supported by § 220(2) of the *Restatement (Second) of Agency*, which focuses on the extent of control the employer exercises over the details of the work, such as, (a) the extent of control which, by the agreement, the master may exercise over the details of the work; (b) whether the one employed is engaged in a distinct business; (c) whether, in the locality, the work is usually done under the direction of the employer or without supervision; (d) whether the employer or the workman supplies the instrumentalities, tools, and the place of work for the person doing the work; (e) whether or not the work is a part of the regular business of the employer; and (f) whether the principal is or is not in business. The California labor commission found that an Uber driver is not an independent contractor but an employee—a decision that, if upheld, could reshape this type of share economy business model. The decision, however, is not binding precedent since it only applies to the single complaint.

6 *In S.G. Borello & Sons v. Department of Industrial Relations*, 48 Cal 3d 341 (1989).

The larger picture is that Uber has come to symbolize the share economy and other companies have used its business model.[7] There are two avenues of response for this sharing model as it relates to the employee-independent contractor distinction. First, the so-called 'platform' can re-adjust its business model and conform to employment regulations. Second, sharing companies can give up some of the control they exert over the individuals who use their platforms. Either response, however, may result in the platforms losing their competitive advantage over traditional companies.

Two class action cases, in 2013, were brought against Uber and Lyft by its drivers: *O'Connor v. Uber Technologies, Inc.*,[8] and *Cotter v. Lyft, Inc.*[9] While recognizing that the right to control is the principal test for employee classification, the court in the Lyft case noted that a finding of employee status does not require that the company retain the right to control every last detail; employee status may still exist even when a certain amount of freedom is inherent in the work.

Prior to the Uber and Lyft cases, *Air Couriers International v. Employment Development Department*[10] held that delivery drivers were employees rather than independent contractors. This was despite the fact that the drivers: (1) decided when and how long to work; (2) worked other jobs while driving; (3) were not required to accept every job, but instead rejected jobs for a variety of reasons and were not required to give reasons for doing so; (4) did not suffer repercussions for rejecting jobs; (5) were paid by the job, and were able to negotiate higher rates on some jobs for a variety of reasons; (6) supplied their own vehicles, supplies, and equipment when delivering; (7) were not required to wear uniforms; and (8) received no formal training. California courts support a broad definition of employment with a presumption that anyone providing services to another is an employee. The court in *JKH Enterprises, Inc. v. Department of Industrial Relations*[11] held that special delivery drivers were employees for purposes of the state's workers' compensation statute despite the facts

7 Geofrey Fowler, 'There's an Uber for Everything Now' *Wall Street Journal* (New York 5 May 2015) <http://www.wsj.com/articles/theres-an-uber-for-everything-now-1430845789> accessed 1 December 2015.

8 2015 WL 1069092 (N.D. Cal. Mar. 11, 2015).

9 2015 WL 1062407 (N.D. Cal. Mar. 11, 2015).

10 150 Cal. App. 4th 923, 59 Cal. Rptr. 3d 37 (Cal. Ct. App. 2007).

11 142 Cal. App. 4th 1046, 48 Cal. Rptr. 3d 563 (Cal. Ct. App. 2006).

(as noted by the *Cotter v. Lyft*) that the drivers called in to a JKH dispatcher to say when they were available to deliver packages, were free to decline to perform a particular delivery, and performed delivery services for other companies.[12]

The control factor in the economic reality test focuses on the extent to which the worker is dependent upon the employer for his or her livelihood, under the argument that the more dependent the worker is the less independent he or she is. However, with the rise of the share economy, workers are much less dependent on the intermediary employer, yet the employer still exercises a significant degree of control. The nature of work exemplified by the share economy requires a classification test that focuses not on the dependence of the workers on the employer, but the dependence of the employer on the workers. If the enterprise arranging all of these individualized tasks and services is dependent on the service providers for its existence, then those service providers should be considered employees of the enterprise.

b) Uber-Lyft and Standard Term Contracts

A number of Uber and Lyft contract clauses have been attacked at the state and federal levels. The Uber contract contained the following clause: 'YOU ACKNOWLEDGE AND AGREE THAT YOU aRE WAIVING THE RIGHT TO PARTICIPATE AS A PLAINTIFF OR CLASS MEMBER IN ANY PURPORTED CLASS ACTION OR REPRESENTATIVE PROCEEDING.' The courts in *Mohamed v. Uber* and *Gillette v. Uber* held that the arbitration clause, which contained a class-action waiver, was unconscionable under California law.

On September 11, 2015, the Federal Communications Commission (FCC) issued a Citation and Order against Lyft for violating the Telephone Consumer Protection Act (TCPA),[13] which requires a company to obtain the consent of an individual before sending phone messages or text messages for marketing purposes. Lyft required customers to 'Agree to the Terms of Service' (TOS) before being able to obtain the service. In the

12 *Cotter*, 2015 WL 1062407, at *11, citing, *Air Couriers*, 150 Cal. App. 4th at 926–28, 59 Cal. Rptr. 3d at 38–39).

13 Federal Communications Commission DA 15-997, *In the Matter of Lyft, Inc.* (Adopted 11 September 2015).

TOS was a provision stating the customer consented to receiving autodialed calls and texts: 'By becoming a User, you expressly consent and agree to accept and receive communications from us, including via e-mail, text message, and call notifications to the cellular telephone number you provided to us. By consenting to being contacted by Lyft, you understand and agree that you may receive communications generated by automatic telephone dialing systems and/or which will deliver prerecorded messages sent by or on behalf of Lyft, its affiliated companies and/or Drivers. IF YOU WISH TO OPT-OUT OF PROMOTIONAL EMAILS, TEXT MESSAGES, OR OTHER COMMUNICATIONS, YOU MAY OPT-OUT BY FOLLOWING THE UNSUBSCRIBE OPTIONS PROVIDED TO YOU. Standard text messaging charges applied by your cell phone carrier will apply to text messages we send. You acknowledge that opting out of receiving text messages or other communications may impact your use of the Lyft Platform or the Services.'

The FCC investigation discovered that no such 'unsubscribe option' actually existed. There was no easy way to find the unsubscribe option and consumers had to navigate Lyft's website to find the opt-out page. If they did manage to find it, if they opted out, they couldn't use the service. The FCC ruled that a default opt-in unless you opt-out, which is not really an opt-out since it leads to a termination of services is not consent under the TCPA. Other provisions of the Lyft User Contract are equally onerous and should be regulated. Examples of such provisions include: (1) a modification of agreement clause giving Lyft the right to modify the terms and conditions of this Agreement at any time, effective upon posting the amended terms on this site, and without notice (placing a duty on the user to periodically review the agreement); (2) Lyft is given the right to use the user's information and to receive a non-exclusive, worldwide, perpetual, irrevocable, royalty-free, sub-licensable right and license to exercise the copyright, publicity, and database rights related to that information; (3) Lyft is also given the right to access user's social networking sites (SNS) accounts and allow Lyft to store any content that the user has stored including 'without limitation any friend, mutual friends, contacts or following lists' (SNS Content); and (4) Lyft is protected by an assortment of disclaimers including, Lyft Platform is provided on an 'as is' basis and without any warranty or condition, express, implied or statutory, Lyft does not warrant that any defects in the Lyft Platform will be corrected, or that the Lyft Platform is free of viruses, Lyft has no control over the quality or safety of the transportation services provided, Lyft does not warrant that its users are over the age of eighteen, and Lyft does not warrant the privacy of personal information that it transfers to third parties.

Despite the regulatory interventions, illustrated by the California cases and actions of the FCC, shared transportation services remain largely unregulated. In fact, the Lyft contract lists only the following state and local laws in its disclosure provision, most of them related to insurance and lien law regulations: (1) *California*: prohibited from providing services at some airports and must carry $1 million in liability insurance, (2) *Colorado*: must notify lienholders of automobiles being used for transportation services; (3) *Pennsylvania*: must notify insurance carrier to determine if any impact on insurance policy; (4) *Portland*: must certify that driver has been licensed to drive for a minimum of two years; (5) *Seattle and Kings County*: must provide background check results, driver history and social security number for the purpose of obtaining a for-hire license; (6) *Virginia*: driver must certify that automobile is not a salvage, non-repairable or rebuilt vehicle, and must notify any lienholders; and (7) *Washington State*: insurance policy requirements and required notification of lienholders.

2. House Rental Services (Airbnb)

Airbnb is a house renting or sharing platform that allows travelers to rent someone's apartment or home for their vacation or business needs. This San Francisco startup has gained much attention and market value, and is seen as a model for the collaborative consumption-peer economy. However, this business model allows Airbnb and their 'hosts' to avoid paying taxes and the need to obtain business licenses. Since the taxes and licenses required by hotels are mostly regulated at the local level, this type of collaborative business may be best regulated at that level. The City of Santa Monica, California, recently passed an ordinance that prohibits property owners and residents from renting out their places unless they remain on the property themselves and banned eighty percent of Airbnb's Santa Monica listings. The regulation states the rationale and public purpose of the regulation of house renting:

> Santa Monica's primary housing goals include preserving its housing stock and preserving the quality and character of its existing single and multi-family residential neighborhoods. The City must preserve its available housing stock and the character and charm which result, in part, from cultural,

> ethnic, and economic diversity of its resident population; the City affords a diverse array of visitor-serving short term rentals, including, hotels, motels, bed and breakfasts, vacation rentals and home sharing, not all of which are currently authorized by local law; operations of vacation rentals, where residents rent-out entire units to visitors and are not present during the visitors' stays are detrimental to the community's welfare; the presence of such visitors within the City's residential neighborhoods can sometimes disrupt the residential character of the neighborhoods; with the recent advent of the so called *sharing economy*, there is a longstanding practice of 'home-sharing,' whereby residents host visitors in their homes, for compensation, while the resident host remains present throughout the visitors' stay; home-sharing does not create the same adverse impacts as unsupervised vacation rentals because, among other things, the resident hosts are present to regulate their guests' behavior; existing law authorizes the City to collect Transient Occupancy Taxes (TOTs) for vacation rentals and home-sharing activities; and existing law obligates both the hosts and rental agencies or hosting platforms to collect and remit TOTs to the City.

The Ordinance provides the following regulations. First, Home-Sharing shall be authorized as long as the host obtains a City Business License, collects and remit TOT (taxes) and such use complies with the Zoning Ordinance. Second, the Hosting Platform shall be responsible for collecting all applicable TOTs and must disclose to the City on a regular basis each of its Home Sharing and Vacation Rentals located in the City. Third, any person violating this Ordinance is subject to a fine not exceeding two hundred fifty dollars; or a misdemeanor, which shall be punishable by a fine not exceeding five hundred dollars, or by imprisonment in the County Jail for a period not exceeding six months or both; and any interested person may seek an injunction or other relief to prevent or remedy violations of this Ordinance. A new San Francisco law allows only permanent residents to offer short-term rentals, establishes a new city registry for hosts, mandates the collection of the hotel tax, limits entire-home rentals to 90 days per year, and requires each listing to carry $500,000 in liability insurance.

3. Social Media, Advertising, and Fraud

Collaborative authorships or works created online present issues of ownership and copyright. Practical issues and problems 'arise when copyright law and content monetizers encounter a work (or perhaps more accurately, a series of interdependent works) with an unprecedented number of people who could ostensibly assert authorship over some element of the content.'[14] One commentator has proposed the creation of share-commerce license in which collaborators are treated as a class rather than as individuals.[15]

a) Mass Collaborations and Fanfiction: User-generated content (UGC),

Fanfiction is the popular name given to a large class of derivative works that routinely arise under these circumstances: (1) the underlying work is (a) prepared commercially and (b) protected by copyright, while (2) the derivative work (a) does not generate profit, (b) is unauthorized by the copyright holder, and (c) is digitally self-published. The recognition of a share-commerce license addresses the issue of copyright in mass collaborations. First, it addresses the primary commercial interest of flexibility with regard to monetization. The share-commerce license allows anyone who wants to profit to do so, including the initial producer, but not without paying some portion back into the collective. At the same time, it allows amateurs or hobbyists to continue to contribute without fear of either the project or their individual ideas being capitalized without some recognition. At the same time, a share-commerce license system allows the monetizing production to keep the majority of its profits while compensating individual achievement. Second, the share-commerce license is simple and easy to adopt; all contributors in order to participate agree to be governed by the license.[16] Such a license scheme would preempt the possibility of a small minority of contributors obstructing the creative efforts of others

b) Electronic Word-of-Mouth (eWOM)

Electronic word-of-mouth (eWOM) has become a powerful social and advertising instrument. It is the use of user-generated content (UGC),

14 Elisabeth S Aultman, 'Authorship Atomized: Modeling Ownership in Participatory Media Productions' (2014) 36 Hastings Comm. & Ent. L. J. 383, 389.
15 Elisabeth S Aultman, 'Authorship Atomized: Modeling Ownership in Participatory Media Productions' (2014) 36 Hastings Comm. & Ent. L. J. 383, 389.
16 Elisabeth S Aultman, 'Authorship Atomized: Modeling Ownership in Participatory Media Productions' (2014) 36 Hastings Comm. & Ent. L. J. 383, 389.

primarily on social media sites, to promote a product, service or a government action. By creating 'buzz' using social media sites, a person or persons utilize eWOM; statements users share over the Internet about a service, event, company, product, or brand. As the message spreads, it becomes more reputable because it appears it is coming from trusted acquaintances rather than from a company or brand. This is the modern 'earned media' as opposed to the older form of advertising known as 'paid media'.

On the other hand, it can be used as a weapon against competitors and government action. A successful strategy has been to pay or incentivize persons or consumers to provide eWOM, though postings on various sites. For example, persons may be paid to post disparaging reviews of competitors, such as posting negative reviews on TripAdvisor on competitor hotels. At best, this can be called 'disguised UGC' when in reality it is an unfair trade practice or fraud.[17]

The ease of such illicit schemes is made possible by the existence of a litany of 'review platforms' for every conceivable product or service. The abuse of these 'neutral' websites clearly calls for regulation, but not necessarily new laws. For example, the US enacted the Federal Trade Commission Act in 1914, which states that: 'Unfair methods of competition in or affecting commerce, and unfair or deceptive acts or practices in or affecting commerce are hereby declared unlawful.'[18] The Federal Trade Commission published in 1975, 'Guides Concerning Use of Endorsement and Testimonials in Advertising', with updates in 1980 and 2009. The 2009 update warned of concerns about reviews and statements posted on social media that endorse a product or service. It noted that 'truth in advertising' is vital in all forms of media including social networking sites and blogs. The European Union passed the *Unfair Commercial Practices Directive*, which requires the prohibition of the use of editorial content in the media to promote a product where a trader has paid for the promotion without making that clear and falsely representing the reviewer as a consumer.

The FTC Guidelines states that if a person joins a network marketing program under which she periodically receives various products about

17 Steven J Stanton, Jennifer Cordon Thor and John Kim, 'Legal and Ethical Perspectives on Electronic Word of Mouth Marketing' (9 May 2015) (manuscript on file).

18 15 U.S.C. § 45 (2014).

which she can write reviews, the person must disclose any connection between the herself as endorser and the seller-marketer of the product or service.[19] It requires the manufacturer-seller, when they provide the incentive to the consumer-reviewer to inform the consumer-reviewer that she has a duty to disclose the connection and the manufacturer-seller has a duty to monitor the consumer-reviewer to make sure that the necessary disclosure is made.

Unfortunately, enforcement of the FTC Guidelines has been difficult and the FTC has not gone after very many violators. *In the Matter of Reverb Communications, Inc.*, Reverb employees posted public reviews in gaming applications in the iTunes store without disclosing that they were employees; *In the Matter of Legacy Learning Systems, Inc.* the FTC pursued a company that manufactures and markets instructional DVDs and used sales affiliates that earned commissions on sales of the DVDs to post positive reviews. Thus, this is an area that requires stronger regulations and more enforcement actions.

4. Legalsourcing

'Crowdsourcing' is the process of obtaining needed funding, services, ideas, or content by soliciting contributions from a large group of people, and especially from an online community, rather than from traditional employees or suppliers. Given its unique ability to efficiently source talent and resources, crowdsourcing has become a disruptive innovation. This type of innovation assists in 'creating a new market by applying a new set of values that help to displace industry incumbents who control an existing market.'[20] The issue, however, is whether this disruption ultimately is in the best interests of consumers and society.

A popular form of crowdsourcing is 'crowdfunding' in which people raise money for many different purposes by seeking financing from an online community, usually by compiling large numbers of small donations, investments, or loans. This section will review the application of the

19 16 CFR, Part 255.5.
20 See Jordan Furlong, 'Lawyers and Social Media: Can Legal Advice Be Crowdsourced?' (2012) 38 ABA Law Practice 5.

crowdsourcing model to legal services called 'legalsourcing'.[21] Legalsourcing possesses the potential to have a significant and disruptive impact on the legal services sector. The following is a review of some examples or specific applications, as well as general applications of legalsourcing, as discussed in a paper by David Orozco entitled: 'The Use of Legal Crowdsourcing or Lawsourcing to Achieve Legal, Regulatory, and Policy Objectives.'

As noted above, crowdsourcing has been commonly used to raise funds. A party with insufficient means to support a lawsuit can post a call for funding online. The prospective plaintiff can describe the merits of the case and ask for 'loans' if it is a commercial case or donations if it is a public interest case. The solicitor may be able to provide a lien to secure the loans. The 2001 Revision of Article 9 of the Uniform Commercial Code recognized interests in commercial tort litigation as collateral. In Spain, an online community offered funds and information via a Twitter hashtag campaign that targeted a former bank executive who allegedly engaged in fraudulent behavior.[22]

In order to avoid non-meritorious infringement by patent trolls, crowdsourcing of prior art literature searches among the technical and scientific community can provide the information needed to fend off such claims. A company called Article One Partners engages in the business of crowdsourcing prior art literature searches among the technical and scientific community. The clients of Article One Partners are able to use the information to invalidate patent infringement claims that have been asserted against them.

Online platforms act as intermediaries or clearinghouses for legal information between consumers and lawyers (for a fee). For example, Rocket Lawyer specializes in the area of start-up and technology firms looking for cost-effective legal solutions in areas such as contract review, incorporation issues, and intellectual property. LawPivot collects a fee from the users of its platform (those seeking legal information). Lawyers are not paid, but get the opportunity to obtain high growth clients and build a

---

21 David Orozco, 'The Use of Legal Crowdsourcing or Lawsourcing to Achieve Legal, Regulatory, and Policy Objectives' (2016) 53 [1] American Business Law Journal 1

22 See Ter Garica, 'Spanish 15M Movement Takes a Big Bank to Court' (20 June 2012), available at <http://wagingnonviolence.org/feature/spanish-15m-movement-takes-a-big-bank-to-court> accessed 30 November 2015.

reputation based upon LawPivot's 'ranking algorithm'.[23] Casetext has entered the legal research market dominated by Lexis-Nexis and Westlaw. Casetext provides an online platform for providing the public with free access to legal research linked to an online legal community. The core aspect of their model is to crowdsource legal commentary on cases and legal annotations, which are the central value offered by Lexis-Nexis and Westlaw. Casetext's revenue model is based on charging fees for premium features.

These types of online legal services pose numerous legal and ethical questions, such as, whether these platforms constitute the unlicensed practice of law. The legal profession regulates the delivery of legal services in order to ensure the competency of the services, but also to benefit incumbent legal service providers by creating barriers to entry. There are existing regulations that may apply to Q & A Platforms like LawPivot. Most states prohibit or regulate attorney referral services; other just prohibit fee splitting. However, LawPivot only collects fees from customers not attorneys and the crowdsourcing model routes legal information requests to numerous attorneys who then directly contact the customer.

The problems posed by LawPivot and similar platforms include the prescreening of attorneys, which may be characterized as illegal referral services; lawyers benefiting from the marketability of the platform, which may violate some state laws; and some sites directly dispense legal forms and advice on how to complete the forms, such as Legal Zoom, which has been considered to be an unauthorized practice law.

The legality of Q & A websites may hinge on the interpretation of the US Supreme Court's decision in *Bates v. State Bar*.[24] The case involved the legality of state laws prohibiting pharmaceutical advertising. The Supreme Court held that: 'The First Amendment right to receive information and ideas, and that freedom of speech necessarily protects the right to receive [this information].'[25] The Supreme Court extended this to legal advertising by striking state laws prohibiting attorney advertising.

---

23 See Ter Garica, 'Spanish 15M Movement Takes a Big Bank to Court' (June 20, 2012), available at <http://wagingnonviolence.org/feature/spanish-15m-movement-takes-a-big-bank-to-court> accessed 30 November 2015 at 13–14.

24 433 U.S. 350, 376-77 (1977).

25 *Virginia State Board of Pharmacy v. Virginia Citizens Consumer Council, Inc.*, 425 U.S. 748, 757 (1976).

Attorney's using Q & A Platforms to obtain business could argue that regulations limiting the use of such platforms violate the Supreme Court rulings.[26] Any new regulations should recognize the legality of Q & A platforms, but place restrictions on their usage including (1) prohibiting attorneys from paying fees for use of the website, (2) require the platform to perform due diligence in pre-screening attorneys, and (3) prohibiting the direct dissemination of legal advice by the sites.

IV. Regulatory Response

Los Angeles and San Francisco are suing Uber for fraud for deliberately misleading consumers about the level of background checks it conducts on potential drivers. Uber is also dealing with litigation over whether their drivers in California are employees or contract workers. This distinction is important for the entire on-demand economy. The share economy's 'on-demand' workers are essentially operating with no legal rights, take all the risks, and work long hours for minimal compensation. One response would be the enactment of a US federal law or EU Individual Worker Directive that clarifies the status of workers in the share economy as employees and when it is appropriate to recognize independent contractor status.

Much that happens within the collaborative or share economy is beneficial to society and should not be subject to government regulation unless a clear pattern of abuse is demonstrated. Preferably, share companies or platforms will create industry guidelines for those that wish to be identified as share economy companies: 'While technology may be the modus operandi, the soul of a true sharing economy company lies in its morality' and that morality should lead to the creation of online mechanisms (platforms) that set standards and the means by which companies can be designated as a sharing company.

Questions from the Münster Workshop

Two questions raised in Münster dealt with the issue of competition law and digital content. The first issue seems to be one comfortably covered

26 David Orozco, 'The Use of Legal Crowdsourcing or Lawsourcing to Achieve Legal, Regulatory, and Policy Objectives' (2016) 53 [1] American Business Law Journal 1.

by existing EU competition law. The types of businesses created online or facilitated by the Internet can be monitored for market share, collusion, tying arrangements, and so forth in the same way as businesses in the traditional economy. The second issue deals with the liability of providers and websites for illicit content, such as pornography and hate speech. The answer in the United States, mainly due to the pervasive role played by freedom of speech rights under the First Amendment to the US Constitution, has been to provide Internet providers an exemption from liability for the content placed on their service. In exchange for this exemption, providers are obligated to remove offensive material once notified of its existence and to provide information to the government and courts to uncover the identity of the offending party.

Share Economy and the Consumer Concept

*Rafael Illescas Ortiz**

I. Overview

The focus of the following is on the disruption, disruptive electronic technologies and their consequences on the legal system, mostly on private law, civil and commercial law, national and European law. To begin, it is to be noted that the law on electronic commerce was essentially founded at the end of the 20th century on four basic principles: functional equivalency, non-alteration of pre-existing law, technological neutrality, and very good faith. Freedom of contract of course plays a key role in the creation of legislative rules for this area of law.

However, amongst these principles it is clear that the non-alteration of pre-existing law has of course suffered increased erosion over the past 25 years. The main cause of this attrition lies in the continuous technological innovations and the necessity to clarify the legal status and approaches to the issues that may arise. The solutions may not always be found in traditional approaches applied to commercial and industrial processes, therefore new and up-to-date responses are needed which may result in alterations to pre-existing approaches.

The topic of share economy and the consumer concept reflects two aspects of contemporary developments. Whereas the notion of the consumer is no longer in its infancy, the same cannot be said for share economy. As the alternative expression 'peer-to-peer'[1] economy suggests, the consumer may not be concluding a contract with a business but rather

---

* Rafael Illescas Ortiz is Emeritus Professor of Commercial Law at Carlos III University of Madrid. The following text is an edited transcript of the presentation given at the conference on which this volume is based.

1 The EU Commission has introduced new terminology on the issue. In this way the Commission follows a habitual practice in this field, the promotion of a different terminology to the one employed in USA. "Collaborative economy" is the European-born term designating the peer-to-peer economy or share economy. I prefer for the time being to keep with the original terminology used in the country in which the economic innovation took place first time.

with another 'consumer'. Accordingly, one can question whether under such circumstances the acquiring party may or may not require protection vis-à-vis its contract partner.

II. Share Economy

The concept of share economy 'is based on people (the peers) choosing to participate in a platform because a company has made the process cheap and straightforward'[2]. It involves 'a new breed of business models their entrepreneurs are creating based on the power of online marketplaces'[3]. Whereas the former description emphasises the personal elements of the new kind of contractual interaction, the latter focuses on the media that facilitate the interaction between the parties.

The result of both conceptualisations is quite simple: in fact, in many cases the company need not necessarily exist because the peers are simply accessing an application that takes them to a virtual place or an e-marketplace. One can observe the inverse situation in cases of negative consumer participation, namely where the consumers decide their self-exclusion of an operating e-mechanism of information or advertising operating an ad hoc application. Accordingly, there are two diverse kinds of applications or programs that should be identified: inclusionary and exclusionary. The former permits the active participation in the exchange of goods and services facilitated by the application or company. The latter, however, permits isolation from commercial initiatives promoted by third parties by erecting a form of electronic barrier.

Three or four main cases of share economy can be chosen in order to consider the effects of the innovation on pre-existing consumer law. With regard to the inclusionary model, one should consider three relevant application-companies: (i) the well-known peer-to-peer marketplace for interchange of material goods, e-Bay[4]; (ii) the somewhat notorious (in Europe)

---

2 Robin Chase, *Peers Inc: How People and Platforms Are Inventing the Collaborative Economy and Reinventing Capitalism* (Public Affairs 2015).

3 Jonathan Moules, 'How a Peruvian start-up remodelled a US cosmetics concept' *Financial Times* (London, September 2015) <http://www.ft.com/intl/cms/s/2/c0541856-4ce9-11e5-b558-8a9722977189.html#axzz3tAg4bhtL> accessed 2 December 2015.

4 <http://www.ebay@com> accessed 1 December 2015.

car-sharing platform for urban carriage of persons, Uber[5] and (iii) the increasingly popular site for sharing or renting holiday accommodation, Airbnb[6]. For the negative side of the share economy or auto-exclusionary sense, one can note, inter alia, the greatly used applications blocking, at the will of the peer, inserted into e-pages and websites (Peace[7], Purify[8] and Crystal[9] as the most common): 'ad-blockers' is the common label for this kind of application. The ad-blockers are of particular relevance for the Internet as they have the capacity to exclude one of the functions thereof, namely as an advertising platform. Using ad-blockers therefore reduces the function of the Internet to non-commercial communications. Consequently, in respect of an economy – conventional, shared or collaborative – it is important to note that Internet users can choose their own commercial or non-commercial activities.

The effective operation of any of the two new kinds of applications is different yet complementary: the inclusionary applications concerning goods or services allow for consumer's needs to be satisfied not by an established professional or trader but instead by another consumer enjoying excess of capacity and making it available to his peers. This function is achieved through the use of intermediaries providing the relevant applications or through reciprocal participation at e-marketplaces. The exclusionary applications prevent the user from to be reached by advertising messages directed to consumers on a non-discriminatory basis through electronic media.

The results of the interaction between both kinds of applications are complementary: the peers ignore advertising messages and satisfy their needs outside the commercial mainstream encompassing offers and messages. They refer to the e-marketplaces – it is irrelevant whether these marketplaces are the product of a simple application or a large or small incorporate business; similarly, it is also irrelevant if they operate from a computer or a smartphone application.

---

5 <https://www.uber@com> accessed 1 December 2015.
6 <http://www.airbnb@com> accessed 1 December 2015.
7 For the time been removed from the offering places.
8 <https://www.purify-app.com> accessed 1 December 2015.
9 < http://crystalapp.co/> accessed 1 December 2015.

III. The New Situation and Associated Question Marks

The described new situation can imply some legal consequences. The aforementioned innovations in electronic operations and contracts probably generate innovative facts non previously considered by early consumer legislation. This mostly concerns two different fields: (i) the consideration of the new realities by the consumer protection rules currently in force and (ii) the new profiles within the notion of the consumer which are to be sanctioned in order to extend the coverage. In this respect, one is to consider whether the legal policy favours an extension of the scope to encompass the new realities.

IV. Coverage of Consumer Protection Rules

Determining the coverage of consumer protection rules requires an answer to the questions surrounding the status of the parties: are both parties consumers? If only one party qualifies a consumer, which party is it? What is the status of the counterparty? If no party or both parties fulfil the requirements for a consumer – and trader, respectively – one is likely facing a 'peer-to-peer' (P2P) situation which differs from the business-to-consumer (B2C) situation required by consumer protection legislation. As a consequence, share economy can be located outside of the scope of consumer protection rules.

It is my view that the definitions of consumer and trader under the Consumer Rights Directive[10] do not apply to well-known instances of share economy. In fact, it is quite clear that the acquiring peer usually does not enter into a contract with a trader but rather with another peer. This relationship is dubiously covered by the Directive's provisions.

In fact, Art 1 Consumer Rights Directive declares the 'Contract concluded between consumers and traders' as its subject-matter. For this purpose, Art 2(1) defines the 'consumer' as 'any natural person who, in

---

10 Directive 2011/83/EU of the European Parliament and of the Council of 25 October 2011 on consumer rights, amending Council Directive 93/13/EEC and Directive 1999/44/EC of the European Parliament and of the Council and repealing Council Directive 85/577/EEC and Directive 97/7/EC of the European Parliament and of the Council [2011] OJ L304/64.

contracts covered by this Directive, is acting for purposes which are outside his trade, business, craft or profession'. Art 2(2) is less revealing as it defines the trader – as the consumer's contract partner – as a person 'who is acting, including through any other person acting in his name or on his behalf, for purposes relating to his trade, business, craft or profession'.

The simple contrast between the above described P2P e-commerce patterns and the rules of the Consumer Rights Directive on its scope raises significant doubts on the inclusion of the P2P trade under the Directive. As stated, more cases of P2P e-commerce are cases in which the relevant contractual link embraces two consumers – the acquirer and the provider. The contract will only fall under the Consumer Rights Directive if the relationship is between a consumer and a trader operating at an e-marketplace. However, this basis will be missing when the contractual link between both parties, qualified as consumers, is established by the intermediation not by a company but by the common operation of a mere e-application at their respective disposal.

We have thus to conclude that the coverage of the Consumer Rights Directive concerning P2P e-commerce is limited or inexistent.

V. Possible Reasons for Affording Consumer Protection in P2P Contracts.

The above provisional conclusion lies only on positivist reasons derived from the literal construction of the preliminary rules sanctioned by the Consumer Rights Directive. But additional reasons for can be identified; reasons derived from the reciprocal interests of the parties of the P2P contracts. Any decision of legal policy on the future consumer legal protection to P2P contracts should be made on the basis of these various economic reasons.

As an initial issue, it should be considered that in case of interaction of consumer parties by means of an e-application, it is not easy to determinate which party is to be granted legal protection. In fact, usually in B2C contracts the legal protection is granted to the acquiring consumer party. However, reasons can be found to grant equal protection – or a protection of differentiated concern – to the 'selling' consumer. This second party is not a trader and, even more, is 'acting for purposes which are outside his trade, business, craft or profession'. For instance, why should the consumer's withdrawal right – in terms of Arts 9–16 Consumer Rights

Directive – only be legally attributed to acquiring consumer but not to the selling consumer? This kind of question raised in a great variety of circumstances will be eliminated if similar – or zero –protection is at any event granted to the both consumer parties acting in a P2P situation. The decision on the parallel attribution or not attribution of rights to both parties remains, however, unsolved for the time being.

Moreover, other more practical reasons can be argued in favour of keeping the P2P contracts entered into by means of an e-application outside the scope of the Consumer Rights Directive: (i) the unidentified information asymmetry between the contracting parties; (ii) the reciprocal disposal by both the parties of similar business opportunity and (iii) the value price to be obtained by both the parties entering into the contract, a remarkable manifestation of the business opportunities offered by the share economy.

The information asymmetry between trader and consumer does not appear when the contract entered into is a P2P contract. Neither of the parties are experts or experienced traders in the relevant field: mostly both peers occasionally contract in each opportunity. This shared characteristic disappears when for a B2C contract: in this case the trader is a professional of the specific trading and usually a *connoisseur* of the traded products or services. The asymmetry therefore is patent and the legal protection of the consumer has solid foundations.

Secondly, in P2P contracts the agreement offers parallel business opportunities for its parties: for the seller, the disposal of an exceeding capacity or goods; for the acquiring consumer, the correlative acquisition in easy and favourable conditions. The shared economy in fact facilitates the satisfactions or needs or conveniences that only occasionally surge in the ordinary lives of non-professional contracting parties. This does not occur for one of the contractual parties in the case of B2C relationships.

One of the more conspicuous features of these shared business opportunities concerns the prices for transactions agreed on e-applications. These prices usually are much lower than on professional e-marketplaces and, even more, on open markets – electronic or physical. The main reasons for these lowers prices are twofold: the nature of the goods as typically being second-hand or surplus and the absence of an agreement on intermediaries. All these circumstances militate in favour of the continued exclusion of shared economy contracts from the scope of the Consumer Rights Directive.

VI. The Role of E-Marketplaces.

The conclusion from the above favours the exclusion of B2B contracts from the scope of application of the Consumer Rights Directive. However no firm conclusion has been made on the juridical nature of the participation of e-marketplaces and companies in the share economy.

A first approach to the issue identifies the role of e-marketplaces as being a determinative factor of the concept of share economy as an economy based upon relationships between consumers and traders; the e-marketplaces assume this second role i.e. the role of traders. That is a real possibility in view of the definition of a trader under Art 2(2) Consumer Rights Directive.

The question can be approached from a second context, in view of the seminal, quite scarce, e-Commerce Directive[11]. According to its Art 2(b) the e-marketplace can generally qualify as 'service provider' – 'any natural or legal person providing an information society service'. However, it can be more specifically identified as a 'trusted third party. The difference each classification relies on the contractual role played by each person. The service provider contracts with the recipient of the information service. The trusted third party, as indicated by its denomination, can be a mere intermediary without necessary contractual participation acting in a *de facto* manner.

Even when the e-marketplace is considered as a contractual party, his position is protected by the special rules on provider's liability in Arts 12, 13 and 14 e-Commerce Directive. These rules mean *de iure* a very limited liability in three very relevant cases: (i) non-liability by 'mere conduit' of data or offers of product and services – the service provider is not liable for the information transmitted under relevant but usual legal conditions; (ii) non-liability by 'caching'[12] and (iii) non-liability, under relevant legal

---

11 Directive 2000/31/EU of the European Parliament and of the Council of 8 June 2000 on certain legal aspects of information society services, in particular electronic commerce, in the Internal Market [2000] OJ L 178/117.

12 'Where an information society service is provided that consists of the transmission in a communication network of information provided by a recipient of the service, Member States shall ensure that the service provider is not liable for the automatic, intermediate and temporary storage of that information…' (Art 13 e-Commerce Directive).

conditions, by 'hosting' or storage by the service provider of information provided by the recipient of such information.

Accordingly, when the service provider consists of in an e-marketplace, in general, its contractual position is almost irrelevant.

VII. Provisional Conclusions.

1. For the time being, the P2P contractual relationship appears to be very different from a B2C relationship.
2. The information legally required for the B2C trader should not be the same that the required information in case of P2P.
3. The consumer parties to share economy contracts in general know, in a comprehensive way, their respective interests and accordingly the legal framework fits for the purpose of caring for their respective interest. Even more, subjection of the share economy activities to the ordinary e-commerce rules will be too cumbersome and would be to the detriment of the share economy.
4. Rules should be maintained in cases in which the share economy clearly generates a B2C relationship.

Share Economy and Consumer Protection

Caroline Meller-Hannich[*]

I. Collaborative Consumption rather than Consumer Protection?

The reversal of the schematic division between production and consumption by means of a sharing economy establishes a new relationship between actors in the economy.[1] At the beginning sharing was to meet new people, get connected, save resources or because of social and sentimental aspects.[2] The sharing economy ideal is now to expand personal opportunities, improve the quality of the goods and services on offer, reduce transaction costs and increase autonomy.[3] This leads to changes in the economic, legal and social position of the consumer. If there is now only p2p (peer-to-peer) instead of b2c (business-to-consumer) trading, is the national, European and international concept of consumer protection outdated? Is the main contribution made by the sharing economy that 'it

---

* Caroline Meller-Hannich is Professor of Law at the Martin-Luther-Universität Halle-Wittenberg for Civil Law, Civil Procedure Law and Commercial Law.

1 Jefferson-Jones, 'Airbnb and the Housing Segment of the Modern "Sharing Economy": Are Short-Term Rental Restrictions an Unconstitutional Taking?' (2015) 52 Hastings Constitutional Law Quarterly 557, 562; Pia A Albinsson and B Yasanthi Perera, 'Alternative Marketplaces in the 21st century: Building community through sharing events' (2012) 11 J Consumer Behav 303; Mareike Möhlmann, 'Collaborative consumption: determinants of satisfaction and the likelihood of using a sharing economy option again' 14 (2015) J Consumer Behav 193, 195.

2 Christian Solmecke and Bonny Lengersdorf, 'Rechtliche Probleme bei Sharing Economy, Herausforderungen an die Gesetzgebung auf dem Weg in eine geteilte Welt' (2015) 8 MMR 493, 493, 495, 497; Juna Hamari, Mimmi Sjöklint and Antti Ukkonen, 'The Sharing Economy: Why People Participate in Collaborative Consumption' [2015] ASIS&T 1, 5 et seq.

3 Caroline Meller-Hannich, 'Zu einigen rechtlichen Aspekten der "Share-Economy"' [2014] WM 2337; compare to Mareike Möhlmann, 'Collaborative consumption: determinants of satisfaction and the likelihood of using a sharing economy option again' (2015) 14 J Consumer Behav 14 (2015) 193, 194.

has overcome market imperfections without recourse to traditional forms of regulation'[4]?

In crowdfunding, the *private individual* lends or gives money to the businessman. This is the opposite of a consumer loan. Couchsurfing is like staying with friends and not at a hotel. In second-hand trading, private individuals sell to private individuals and deal in used goods. Meal- or food-sharing is intended to prevent waste and promote personal relationships. Car-sharing saves money and reduces environmental pollution. When private individuals deliver parcels for Amazon, this could indeed be considered b2c business, but actually with a *reversed* allocation of roles. And when somebody who has room in their car takes with them somebody who happens to need to go to the same place, is that not actually an act of friendship too?

A sharing economy is collaborative, participative and horizontal. It represents business models and practices aimed at equality and sharing. Subordination and exclusivity are perhaps the ideal antithesis of the sharing economy. Access over ownership, circulation of capital between individuals, open knowledge, education and data – these are the keywords with which the phenomenon of the sharing economy is usually positively associated.

The fact that this can lead to the demise of monopolies and the beginning of increased competition between private and commercial suppliers was particularly noticeable in the taxi industry, with its licences, protected prices and strictly regulated organisational specifications. This is also why the (legal) disputes with the transportation service Uber are currently being conducted so aggressively.[5]

---

4 Christopher Koopman, Matthew D Mitchell and Adam D Thierer, 'The Sharing Economy and Consumer Protection Regulation: The Case for Policy Change' (2015) 8 [2] The Journal of Business, Entrepreneurship & the Law 529.

5 Exemplary Norbert Wimmer, 'Der Fall Uber – ein Lehrstück in Sachen Sharing Economy?' [2014] MMR 713; Albert Ingold, 'Gelegenheitsverkehr oder neue Verkehrsgelegenheiten? Taxi-Apps und Ridesharing als Herausforderung für das Personenförderungsrecht' (2014) 46 NJW 3334; Rainer Grim, Special: 'Uber, Apps und andere' (2014) S3 VW 10; See also the contributions in (2015) 4 EuCML 154, 154–158.

So can we replace b2c with p2p, like Collaborative Consumption is understood on many online platforms?[6] Or is it like a 'peer' being a trader and so acting as a businessman?[7]

II. Models

Before departing from the classic businessman/consumer division, it should be looked at the individual models in more detail, divided into business sectors.

1. Housing

Collaborative housing is now a trend. It ranges from the offer of providing affordable accommodation to the offer of a sofa in your own living room, either for free or for a charge. Platforms such as Airbnb, Couchsurfing and Wimdu act solely as an intermediary between individuals. However, not every landlord is interested in transferring their right of use in this way and cities such as Paris, Berlin, New York, Barcelona and Madrid now prohibit short-term rentals as well as govern them under commercial law and/or subject them to tax or are planning to do so.[8] Meanwhile it is even in competition to the classic hotel industry.[9] This shows that here the economic and legal interests of third parties definitely carry some weight and that a range of different fields of law are affected.

---

6 Compare to Juna Hamari, Mimmi Sjöklint and Antti Ukkonen, 'The Sharing Economy: Why People Participate in Collaborative Consumption' [2015] ASIS&T 1, 4; Matthew Feeney, 'Is Ridesharing Safe?' (2015) 767 Policy Analysis 1, 2.

7 Similar to Claudia Pezler and Nora Burgard, *Co-Economy: Wertschöpfung im digitalen Zeitalter* (Springer 2014) 24.

8 Compare to Jamalia Jefferson-Jones, 'Airbnb and the Housing Segment of the Modern 'Sharing Economy': Are Short-Term Rental Restrictions an Unconstitutional Taking?' (2015) 52 Hastings Constitutional Law Quarterly' 557, 570.

9 Compare to Claudia Pezler and Nora Burgard, *Co-Economy: Wertschöpfung im digitalen Zeitalter* (Springer 2014) 38.

2. *Vehicles*

Sharing is a term used most notably in relation to car-sharing. In car-sharing, however, the car is not shared among the individual users, but is made available to each user by a central provider for a certain period of time.[10] So the users do not share among themselves, nor is the object shared; instead, the time for which it is used is shared, in that it is allocated to several people, one after another. This leads to a better parking situation because a fewer number of cars are necessary.[11] And that in turn means less consumption of oil, what is therefore a good result because it safes resources.[12]

The providers are sometimes organised as non-profit associations, or are even considered to be in the public good and operate on a not-for-profit basis.[13] However, there are also car-sharing providers organised in the form of Gesellschaften mit beschränkter Haftung [limited liability companies]. The names, which speak for themselves, range from 'Ökobil Bamberg e.V.' [literally 'Eco-Mobililty Bamberg e.V.'] and 'Dorfmobil der evangelisch-lutherischen Kirchengemeinde Martinsheim-Gnötzheim' [literally 'Village Mobility of the Evangelical Lutheran Parish of Martinsheim-Gnötzheim'] to Car2Go (the car-sharing branch of Europcar and Daimler) and DriveNow (the car-sharing branch of Sixt and BMW).

3. *Transport/logistics*

In logistics, we are mainly dealing with b2b or b2c sharing concepts in the fields of transport/transportation services (e.g. Uber), freight (e.g. freight

10 Caroline Meller-Hannich, 'Zu einigen rechtlichen Aspekten der "Share-Economy"' [2014] WM 2337, 2338.

11 Jordan M and Paul L Caron, Tax Regulation, 'Transportation Innovation, and the Sharing Economy' (2015) 82 The University of Chicago Law Review Dialogue 69, 80.

12 Jordan M and Paul L Caron, Tax Regulation, 'Transportation Innovation, and the Sharing Economy' (2015) 82 The University of Chicago Law Review Dialogue 69, 81.

13 Compare to Caroline Meller-Hannich, 'Zu einigen rechtlichen Aspekten der "Share-Economy"' [2014] WM 2337, 2339 et seq.

exchanges), CEP (courier, express and parcel) services (e.g. private individuals as distributors for Amazon) and storage (e.g. multi-user stores).[14]

Especially the concept of collaborate transportation is nothing new. Above all in form of busses and airplanes it is a really old practice.[15] For sure with the help of smartphone apps it is now more comfortable.[16]

4. *Information goods*

Vast areas of the internet are based on the principle of sharing information, texts or music. This can also be classed as collaborative consumption. This concerns education, do-it-yourself instructions, tutorials, courses, forums, let's plays and wikis, but also 'grand' affairs such as 'Bibis Beauty Palace', which places all kinds of products on its You Tube channel in an extrovert, amusing way and receives millions of hits.

5. *Consumer goods*

Collaborative consumption is ultimately the continuous circulation of goods by way of sharing, exchanging and lending, with access taking priority over ownership and the waste of resources being counteracted. This ranges from irons shared by neighbours and clothes-sharing to food- and meal-sharing. However, arguably the most well-known platform for this, 'Why own it', ceased trading in March of this year. It appears that outside of the circle of friends and the neighbourhood, everybody wants to borrow *for themselves* rather than lend to others.[17]

---

14 Anja Falkenstein, Nutzen statt Besitzen kommt in der Logistik an (2015) 49 Lebensmittelzeitung, 42.

15 Jordan M and Paul L Caron, Tax Regulation, 'Transportation Innovation, and the Sharing Economy' (2015) 82 The University of Chicago Law Review Dialogue 69, 70; Norbert Wimmer, 'Der Fall Uber – ein Lehrstück in Sachen Sharing Economy?' [2014] MMR 713, 714.

16 Jordan M and Paul L Caron, 'Tax Regulation, Transportation Innovation, and the Sharing Economy' (2015) 82 The University of Chicago Law Review Dialogue 69, 71.

17 <http://whyownit.com/blog/we-failed-warum-die-verleih-app-why-own-it-nicht-funktioniert-hat> accessed 30 October 2015.

III. Sociological and economical interpretation - sustainability and altruism vs. efficiency

Many of the models described serve the purposes of sustainability and altruism.[18] If I offer couchsurfing, my apartment is never empty; if I provide car-sharing, my car is always in use; and if I share food and meals, I counteract the throwaway society. Crowdfunding replaces bank loans and the use of gardening equipment by the entire neighbourhood means that the equipment doesn't have to be purchased several times. A sharing economy is an alternative to other forms of commercial trade. Trust is often referred to as its currency. Quality is not assessed by legal categories, but by points systems and ratings, a digital form of social control.

However, when we consider the sharing economy from a sociological perspective, we can also see that when a private individual delivers parcels when going on walks, when you accommodate strangers in your own home and when money is collected to fund projects, commercialisation and monetarisation take the place of ordinary social behaviour.[19] You can simply go on a walk, or take a GoPro or a parcel with you to deliver; the former is for recreation, the latter brings in money. The room in a student flat that is unused during the holidays can be used for friends. Or it can bring in money. A share economy is not a playground; a share economy is an *economy*. It must therefore be interpreted economically and measured against efficiency criteria. This does not mean that we need to resort to such terms as 'platform capitalism' to describe this new economy.

However, the new business models undoubtedly successfully extend to where previously unused added value is to be found. And I don't want to live in a world in which a neighbour takes money for taking delivery of my parcel or for lending me their iron, or only does so in return for my sledgehammer.

My initial conclusion would be that a sharing economy involves a wide variety of different realities and that the classification is ambivalent. There is a crucial difference between the interest in intercultural exchange that a

---

18 See footnote 1 and 2.

19 Compare to Dieter Schnaas, 'Die Gefahren der Share-Economy' [2014] WiWo < http://www.wiwo.de/politik/deutschland/tauchsieder-die-gefahren-der-share-economy/10695116.html> accessed 30 October 2015.

free place to sleep is intended to facilitate and the highly commercially successful and currently intensively discussed platform 'Airbnb'.

IV. Legal Interpretation

In any case, interests are of some economic relevance and interests in integrity are affected in a sharing economy, so we cannot assume extrajudicial facts. With that, the legal classification is to be analysed and so the importance of consumer protection law in the sharing economy.

1. Obligatory character and obligation type

It may not always be clear to the individual user that deals in a sharing economy are contracts and binding in nature. Whenever interests have a certain legal or economic relevance, for example, because the respective service (offer of accommodation, use of a car, granting of a loan) is offered in return for payment or other consideration, a contract with corresponding performance obligations should be assumed. And even services rendered free of charge or for no consideration cannot readily be assumed to be a simple act of goodwill.[20]

Take couchsurfing: Someone who primarily offers their sofa to strangers due to cultural or altruistic motives is not free from legal obligation per se, but the sofa, if it has been promised in this way, must actually be provided when the guest arrives.[21] The obligations exceed those of a good host for friends. Vice versa, the couchsurfer is obliged to act with care; after all, they are entrusted with valuable items. Overall, couchsurfing free of charge is a loan in this respect. Similarly, providing food, clothing or other used items free of charge cannot automatically be assumed to be a simple act of goodwill. In many cases, this would be considered a gift: pledging the offer of a lift would, in case of doubt, constitute a contract (errand) because it usually has clear economic relevance that somebody would like to go from one place to another specific

20 Caroline Meller-Hannich, 'Zu einigen rechtlichen Aspekten der "Share-Economy"' [2014] WM 2337, 2339.

21 Caroline Meller-Hannich, 'Zu einigen rechtlichen Aspekten der "Share-Economy"' [2014] WM 2337, 2339.

place at a specific time. Food- or meal-sharing usually constitutes a gift too. In the free-of-charge agreements for gifts and loans, however, the level of liability and guarantee in favour of the giver of the gift or the lender are modified.

Sometimes, which type of agreement exists and what legal consequences this has for liability are not otherwise so easy to determine. In any case, the 'sharing' agreement type is not recognised by European or national law.

A good example of this is car-sharing. When the General Terms and Conditions of some suppliers mention a 'right to drive' and a 'customer agreement', this does not mean that they constitute a service agreement or social contract. Car-sharing is leasing. This is not changed by the fact that membership is usually necessary to participate in car-sharing. In this case, rentals are simply made to members only. Even if the legal relationship is shaped by profit sharing, this still constitutes leasing. *Usage* is paid for, while the fixed costs of insurance, maintenance, parking, tax, etc. lie with the provider. You do not *share* a car, but different lessees are allowed to use a car one after another in return for payment.

Couchsurfing in return for payment also constitutes leasing. This means that assigning the home to a third party is not allowed if your own landlord is not in agreement.[22]

On the other hand, in the case of transportation services like Uber, a car is not rented; instead, a transportation service is sold, which constitutes a contract for work.

Besides the fields of law previously mentioned, the law of the works contract and services arises in logistics, particularly - in the event of the social dependency and lack of independence of the activity - employment law (incl. protection against dismissal, working time legislation, maternity protection, holiday legislation, etc.). A court in California recently admitted a class action by drivers against Uber, with which they wanted to attain the status of employees.[23]

---

22 Hans-Jürgen Bieber, '540 Gebrauchsüberlassung an Dritte' in Franz Jürgen Säcker, Roland Rixecker and Hartmut Oetker (eds) *Münchener Kommentar zum BGB,* vol 3 (6th edn, C.H. Beck 2012) para 3.

23 Compare exemplary Davey Alba, 'Judge: California Drivers Can Go Class-Action to Sue Uber' <http://www.wired.com/2015/09/judge-california-drivers-can-go-class-action-sue-uber> accessed 30 October 30 2015.

Regardless of this, there exists, of course, liability in the event that legally protected rights are violated.

2. *Consumer protection law, particularly mandatory law, information obligations and rights of withdrawal*

Consumer protection law applies to all b2c contracts, i.e. information obligations in credit agreements, e-commerce and distance selling, for example; rights of withdrawal in the case of distance selling and credit agreements and contracts concluded outside of business premises, mandatory protection regulations in sales law. The regulations of the Consumer Rights Directive, the Sale of Consumer Goods Directive, etc. also apply. It may be labelled co-consumption or private selling, it may lack notice of rights of withdrawal and risk transfer regulations may not be observed: As soon as a supplier pursues a commercial or independent professional goal by making an offer, supplementary mandatory law applies in favour of a consumer, the transfer of risk is precluded, there is a reversal of the burden of proof and, in the event of warranties, special information obligations apply.[24] It is even more important that in the case of Internet transactions, the standards of distance selling law and the obligations of electronic business transactions usually apply. This results in an increase in information obligations, the so-called 'button-solution' and above all: The consumer can terminate the contract by withdrawal. Consumer law already applies - contrary to widespread misunderstanding, such as in 'Ebayer circles' - when the seller acts on a permanent, planed basis, whereby even a minimum level of organisation and trading as a secondary occupation constitute this. 'Innocent' co-consumption thus becomes a b2c transaction.

3. *Liability of intermediary platform*

Finally the liability of the platform operator has to be examined. The platforms and organisers of the sharing economy like to refer to themselves as mere intermediaries between the sharers. It is a common feature of all business models in the sharing economy that the foundation for matching

24 Caroline Meller-Hannich, 'Zu einigen rechtlichen Aspekten der "Share-Economy"' [2014] WM 2337, 2342.

up the sharer is the Internet. Using websites, particularly platforms, and via apps, 'peers' are connected with each other. 'Uber does not own any of its own cars, Alibaba does not have any of its own warehouses and Facebook does not own any content.'[25] In actual fact, the platforms have pushed in between the supplier and consumer and profit from this, but allegedly do not have any responsibility.[26] However, we have definitely seen that a car-sharing provider is a lessor. And the provider of a couchsurfing platform is an agent. In the case of couchsurfing via a platform, a loan brokerage agreement is established between the payer and the intermediary. The liability for information and clarification in a brokerage agreement has not yet borne fruit in the sharing economy. In principle, it is acknowledged that a broker's clarification and advisory obligations also include reviewing the particulars of the economic circumstances of the prospective business partner. So this also applies to brokerage via an Internet platform. Therefore, the liability of the platforms cannot be precluded. This is also the message of the consultation of the European Commission which will look at the role of online platforms and the possibilities and potential issues raised by the rise of the collaborative economy.[27]

V. Conclusions

A sharing economy separates itself from the schematic division between production and consumption. The Internet plays a crucial role in this, in that its intermediary and contact platforms actually place agents in a new and more equal relationship to each other in the economy.[28] In a sharing economy, there is, without doubt, the informed, autonomous, environmen-

25 Tom Goodwin, 'The battle is for the customer interface' <http://techcrunch.com/2015/03/03/in-the-age-of-disintermediation-the-battle-is-all-for-the-customer-interface/#.o06tt9:0sCd> accessed 30 October 2015.

26 Compare to Norbert Wimmer and Mari Weiß, 'Taxi-Apps zwischen Vermittlertätigkeit und Personenbeförderung, Die verwaltungsgerichtliche Entscheidungspraxis zu den Uber-Angeboten' [2015] MMR 80, 84: Platforms are responsible agents.

27 <https://ec.europa.eu/eusurvey/runner/Platforms/> accessed December 16, 2015.

28 Jefferson-Jones, 'Airbnb and the Housing Segment of the Modern "Sharing Economy": Are Short-Term Rental Restrictions an Unconstitutional Taking?' (2015) 52 Hastings Constitutional Law Quarterly 557, 562.

tally-aware consumer, who pursues their interests and needs through contact, exchanging and sharing with like-minded, p2p or c2c. Sustainable consumption can be supported and promoted by conscious consumer behaviour. Food waste and a throwaway society can be avoided.[29] New opportunities are created for marketing otherwise non-commercialised activities and items. This does not mean, however, that the concept of consumer protection drafted by the law of the European Union is outdated. Just as often, the classic image of the consumer agreement, i.e. the b2c transaction with its information obligations under mandatory law and opportunities for withdrawal, hides behind the sharing models.[30] When purchasing via a sharing economy, when granting credit via crowdfunding and when mediating transportation services via an app, the law that applies is no different to the law that applies to other sales agreements, consumer loans, transportation agreements, services and contracts for work.[31] The informed consumer, who must, however, also be protected in his autonomy, is not obsolete in a sharing economy. Governmental regulatory functions are still required. Many of the legal issues relating to a share economy can be resolved by categories that the law already contains, which must, however, be filled with new life and content.[32] This does not destroy the opportunities associated with a sharing economy, but utilises and manages them in such a way that the rights of third-parties, the general public and weaker market participants are protected.

---

29 Caroline Meller-Hannich, 'Zu einigen rechtlichen Aspekten der "Share-Economy"' [2014] WM 2337, 2344.

30 Caroline Meller-Hannich, 'Zu einigen rechtlichen Aspekten der "Share-Economy"' [2014] WM 2337, 2344.

31 Compare to Norbert Wimmer, 'Der Fall Uber – ein Lehrstück in Sachen Sharing Economy?' [2014] MMR 713, 714 : The legally framework has to be checked, if it`s viable for the future; different to Justus Haucap, 'Die Chancen der Sharing Economy und ihre möglichen Risiken und Nebenwirkungen' (2015) 2 ZBW 91, 95, who means the modulation of existing regulations is necessary; Christian Solmecke and Bonny Lengersdorf, 'Rechtliche Probleme bei Sharing Economy, Herausforderungen an die Gesetzgebung auf dem Weg in eine geteilte Welt' (2015) 8 MMR 493: There are no corresponding regulations right now.

32 Caroline Meller-Hannich, 'Zu einigen rechtlichen Aspekten der "Share-Economy"' [2014] WM 2337, 2345.

VI. Outlook

Finally, one has to think about possible regulatory approaches for the future. Firstly, the introduction of value thresholds should be considered. In the case of crowd-investing this has already occurred. In accordance with the Kleinanlegerschutzgesetz [German Retail Investors Protection Act] of July of this year[33], there are detailed specific obligations for investors and issuers depending on the issue volume and investment limit.[34] So value thresholds are also an appropriate method, for example, when determining from which size accommodation for persons should be subject to legal regulations, such as those relating to hygiene. Internet platforms' insurance obligations could also be made dependent on value thresholds. This is more difficult in the case of certificates, taxes, licences and permits. Here, the type of activity seems more meaningful than the value. For example, bans on short-term rentals control the selling-out of popular cities to tourists. At least, this seems like an excessive encroachment on property rights. On the other hand, the introduction of tax can be considered. That private sub-letting - in contrast to commercial - should not require permission, as recently claimed by the Chairman of the Federal Consumer Protection Association in Germany, Klaus Müller[35], is something that should be watched highly sceptical. Even re-letting within limits should be subject to request from the landlord. Here, we definitely have criteria that still leave opportunities for the purely private provision of housing. So shared use simply for a visit does not constitute a subtenancy anyway. Even on eBay, a 'power seller' is also a trader and not a consumer - so no new law is required for this. Here, the opposition to other views, which hold that European legislation is not yet ready for a shared world, is represented. The rules are there. Some more will be established on the basis of the above mentioned (3.) consultation process. With regard to the Proposals for Directives of the European Parliament and of the Council 'on certain aspects concerning contracts for the supply of

---

33 Bundesgesetzblatt (2015) I 1114 of 3 July 2015.

34 Jean-Pierre Bußalb <https://www.bafin.de/SharedDocs/Veroeffentlichungen/DE/Fachartikel/2015/fa_bj_1501_kleinanlegerschutzgesetz.html> accessed December 16, 2015.

35 <http://www.vzbv.de/content/deutscher-verbrauchertag-2015> accessed 16 December 2015.

digital content'[36] and 'concerning contracts for the online and other distance sales of goods'[37] it is to mention that the proposals intend to be seen in the context of the approach related to the role of platforms.[38] However, the black market for rentals and illegal employment, the exploitation of workers, the formation of monopolies and bogus self-employment are not a problem specific to a sharing economy. The rules just have to be applied and implemented - and, in some classic business models from the time before the sharing economy, there may already be too many rules – that is admittedly a slightly provocative note.

---

36 COM(2015) 634 final of 12 December 2015.

37 COM(2015) 635 final of 12 December 2015.

38 'Consistency with other Union policies': COM(2015) 635 final, 5; COM(2015) 634 final, 4.

Internet of Things

Profiling and Targeting Consumers in the Internet of Things – A New Challenge for Consumer Law

Natali Helberger[*]

I. Introduction

> 'The door refused to open. It said, "Five cents, please."
> He searched his pockets. No more coins; nothing. "I'll pay you tomorrow," he told the door. Again he tried the knob. Again it remained locked tight. "What I pay you," he informed it, "is in the nature of a gratuity; I don't have to pay you."
> "I think otherwise," the door said. "Look in the purchase contract you signed when you bought this conapt."
> ... From the drawer beside the sink Joe Chip got a stainless steel knife; with it he began systematically to unscrew the bolt assembly of his apt's money-gulping door.
> "I'll sue you," the door said as the first screw fell out.
> Joe Chip said, "I've never been sued by a door. But I guess I can live through it."'[1]

Having a legal debate with a smart door sounds very much like a vision from a hopefully very hypothetical future – like the one the science fiction author Philip K. Dick described in his novel. And yet, today, almost 50 years after Dick has first published Ubik, this future does not sound that hypothetical or even far away anymore. This chapter will argue that there is a role for consumer law to make sure that we do not have to have conversations like these with our doors, toasters or other smart appliances in the Internet of Things (IoT).

One of the promises of IoT is that everyday appliances, like doors, toasters and fridges will become smart, have some computer-implemented intelligence of their own and are able to communicate. The Internet of Things, sometimes also referred to as the Internet of Objects is 'about attaching varying amounts of identity, interaction and inference to

---

* Natali Helberger is Professor of Information Law at the Institute for Information Law (IViR) at the University of Amsterdam.

1 Philip Dick, *Ubik* (Doubleday, 1969) 80–81.

objects'.[2] 'Smart things' or devices are equipped with the ability to collect and process data and interact with other smart things, users but also traders and third parties (such as insurance companies, governments or advertisers). Smart devices are able to take on new functionalities, run applications and provide a platform for (tailored) services and (commercial) communications. Examples are the by now almost proverbial smart fridge that can connect to the local supermarket; smart watches and other fitness devices that monitor users' vital body functions; bottles that notice when they have been opened;[3] smart meters that measure and adjust energy consumption; or smart doors that set the conditions for access, as in the quote above. Insofar, the Internet of Things can revolutionise many aspects of consumers' daily life, but also the very way consumers purchase and use products and services, and engage in their dealings with traders.

Take the example of a smart watch. Equipped with all kinds of sensors, smart watches can track a consumer's steps, the distance walked, the stairs climbed, the calories burned, the routes walked, but also the consumer's heart rate, body temperature, sleep pattern and many others. This information can enable not only companies such as Fitbit, Microsoft or Apple to offer consumers coaching services and (personalised) health and fitness advice. The collected user and usage information can also be shared with insurance companies to adjust the insurance fee;[4] social networks to share personal achievements with friends; advertisers to market new diets or self-awareness services; or governments to monitor the overall fitness of the population. In addition, the smart watch can be directly connected to the smart scale or the smart phone, and maybe soon to the smart fridge or smart cross trainer.

This also means that through the purchase of a smart watch, the consumer does not only acquire a watch. The watch itself is only a tiny part of an entire service universe, and this service univere is at least in parts based on the collection of highly individualised data. Thanks to the continuous collection and processing of that information, apps and value-

---

2 Connect Advisory Forum, *Internet of Things: The Next Revolution. A Strategic Reflection About A European Approach to the IoT* (European Commission 2014).

3 <http://www.cnet.com/news/smart-whisky-bottle-knows-when-someones-been-in-your-stash/> accessed on 15 November 2015.

4 ATKearney, *The Internet of Things: Opportunities for Insurers* (ATKearney 2014).

added services can be targeted to the needs and preferences of individual consumers.

The question that this chapter will address is what this shift from buying a simple watch to a smart watch, or more generally from buying 'things' to 'smart things' means for consumers and consumer protection law and policy. In so doing, the chapter will focus in particular on the aspect of profiling and targeting in the Internet of Things. Profiling and targeting is a topic that is more commonly associated with data protection law and privacy. This chapter will demonstrate that consumer law, too, will have to play an important role in protecting the legitimate interests of consumers, and guaranteeing a fair balance between consumers, providers of smart things and services, advertisers, insurance companies and other parties.

II. Profiling and targeting consumers in the Internet of Things

The IoT can not only revolutionise the life and experience of consumers. It certainly also revolutionises the way companies can learn about who their consumers are, communicate and interact with these customers. According to an estimate by Cisco, by 2020 fifty billion devices will be connected to the internet. This would translate roughly into 6.58 connected devices per person.[5] The result will be an exceptionally fine-mazed mesh of sensors that surround consumers and can measure any aspect of the consumers' life. Through the ability to turn that information into data, and to combine this data with data available elsewhere, companies will be able to gain completely new, real-time and hyper-personal insights into individual consumers' preferences and behaviours.

Unlike data that is collected about user's online behaviour, the data that smart things collect will have its own quality. Such data is potentially far more situational as it is collected by things that surround consumers and are used by consumers in 'real-life' situations. The data is potentially more complete, as at least some smart things can collect that data 24/7. And the data can be more easily assigned to a concrete person if the device in question is used primarily by one person (e.g. in the case of a

5 Cisco, *The Internet of Things. How the next evolution of the Internet is changing everything* (Cisco 2011).

smart watch or a smart phone), whereas computers and portables are potentially used by an entire household. For these reasons, the data collected by smart things is also potentially very useful for manufacturers, service providers but also third parties, such as advertisers, insurance companies or health care providers.

It is not difficult to imagine all the new opportunities to use that information to target consumers individually and provide them with services and products that are specifically tailored to their individual needs and preferences. Profiling and targeting consumers signifies a shift from previous modes of mass communication (advertisements that were 'broadcast' to an anonymous mass of consumers) and the mass production of products and services to far more tailored and personalised ways of engaging with customers. And while profiling and targeting is not a development that is restricted to the Internet of Things, the Internet of Things certainly offers particular attractive opportunities for profiling and targeting. Many devices will possess some form of interface and means to communicate with individual consumers, either via the device itself or via connected devices such as smart phones and computers. Consumers can thus be targeted far more specifically and immediately in particular situations, in specific locations or at particular times of the day. And based on the particularly detailed and situational information that can be collected about users and the way they use and interact with smart devices, apps, services and advertisements can be targeted and customised with even greater precision and timing.

A recent study by Cognizant, for example, identified the ability to profile and target consumers in the Internet of Things as one of the key trends in the future development and the application of IoT for businesses. Based on the insights from interviews with 200 companies that develop smart products and services, Cognizant found that '[p]roduct data increasingly underpins finer-grained product personalization and richer customer experiences. Smart products reveal insights for remaking how products are built, priced and sold – directly and through channel partners.'[6] Almost a third (28%) of the respondents indicated that they would use the data collected from smart products to personalise products and services .[7]

---

6 Cognizant, *The Rise of the Smart Product Economy* (Cognizant 2015) 3.

7 Preceded by automated customer service (40%), the analysis of product use (39%), sharing the information with suppliers to collaborate on products (32%) and the

The same study also observed that, as a direct consequence, IoT will dramatically change the customer-manufacturer relationship, and introduce far more direct, personalised relationships between manufacturers, service providers and consumers.[8] In other words: consumers do not simply buy a product (such as a smart watch). Buying that product is only the beginning of an intimate and potentially long and dynamic relationship with the manufacturer or a network of traders and third parties that profile consumers' behaviour and target them with personalised services. Insofar, IoT can affect the features and characteristics of products and services, as well as the dynamics between traders and consumers.

These dynamic interactions between traders and consumers can take the form of, for instance, personalised advertising, also referred to as 'behavioural targeting' or 'Interest based advertising'. Commercial messages are tailored to individual consumers, based e.g. on their online behaviour or virtual profiles. It is possible to dynamically adjust prices to certain groups of consumers, individual consumers but also the situation of individual consumers (e.g. airline ticket prices that go up after a consumer has searched repeatedly for a particular ticket, or charging Mac users higher prices than PC users).[9] Not only prices, but also terms and conditions can be personalised, also in the IoT. Car and health insurance companies, for example, are experimenting with personalised insurance conditions and 'Pay as you drive' or 'Usage based insurance' models.[10] One step further is the use of data analytics and personalised services to actively influence or even change consumer behaviour through personalised nudges.[11]

---

analysis of a products' life cycle (29%), Cognizant, *The Rise of the Smart Product Economy* (Cognizant 2015) 8.

8 Cognizant, *The Rise of the Smart Product Economy* (Cognizant 2015) 7.

9 <http://www.cnet.com/news/mac-users-pay-more-than-pc-users-says-orbitz/> accessed on 15 November 2015.

10 <http://www.heise.de/newsticker/meldung/Auch-Allianz-plant-Kfz-Tarife-mit-ueberwachtem-Fahrverhalten-2679007.html> or <http://uk.businessinsider.com/how-the-internet-of-things-is-transforming-the-insurance-industry-2015-7?r=US&IR=T> accessed on 15 November 2015.

11 ATKearney, *The Internet of Things: Opportunities for Insurers* (ATKearney 2014); Cass R Sunstein, *Impersonal Default Rules vs Active Choices vs Personalized Default Rules: A Triptych* (2012) Available at SSRN: <http://ssrn.com/abstract=2171343> or <http://dx.doi.org/10.2139/ssrn.217134> accessed on 30 November 2015.

III. New challenges for consumer law

It probably goes without saying that the massive collection and combination of all sorts of data raises concerns about privacy and the fair processing of personal data and data security. Insofar, when talking about IoT and consumer concerns, data protection and data security are commonly the most prominently discussed concerns.[12] An aspect that has received lesser attention so far are the implications of profiling and targeting in IoT for consumer protection and the application of consumer law, and here in particular the rules about consumer information, contract law and unfair commercial practices.

Profiling and targeting in IoT affects the way products and services are marketed and advertised, the conditions that are offered, the calculation of prices, and even the question of whether certain consumer (profile)s are offered access to certain services at all (see section II). These are issues that touch upon acknowledged principles of consumer protection, such as the requirement that consumers are sufficiently informed, the protection of consumers from unfair practices and the maintenance of autonomous choice as a basic consumer right. The following section will identify a number of implications from the IoT, and from profiling and targeting in the IoT in particular, for the relationship between consumers and traders, and some of the challenges that flow from this for the application of existing consumer law. It would go far beyond the scope of this contribution to give a complete account of all implications from profiling and targeting in the IoT for consumers. Instead, the next section will focus on three aspects: the shift from off-the shelf to 'hyper personal' products and services (section III 1.); the new deal: give data to get service (section III 2.) and the issue of digital market manipulation (section III 3.).

---

12 Rolf H Weber, 'Internet of Things: Privacy issues revisited' [2015] Computer Law & Security Review 618, 618–627; Frederik Zuiderveen-Borgesius, *Improving privacy protection in the area of behavioural targeting* (Kluwer Law International 2015); Art 29 Data Protection Working Party, *Opinion 02/2013 on apps on smart devices* (Art 29 Data Protection Working Party, 27 February 2013); European Parliament, 'Big Data and smart devices and their impact on privacy. Study for the LIBE Committee' (September 2015); European Data Protection Supervisor, *Preliminary Opinion of the European Data Protection Supervisor. Privacy and competitiveness in the age of big data: The interplay between data protection, competition law and consumer protection in the Digital Economy* (March 2014).

1. From off-the shelf to 'hyper personal' products and services

One important implication from IoT, and more specifically from profiling and targeting in the IoT is that consumers no longer simply purchase an 'off the shelf product'. Due to the inbuilt intelligence, products can and will become hyper personal, or as some call it 'hyper-relevant' products. This also means that the functionality of a product is no longer only in the product itself. Instead, the functionality is the result of a complicated web of interrelated apps and services and, ultimately, of the input of the consumer herself. Corresponding to the heterogeneity of the consumer base, each personalised product, or rather 'product-service package' is potentially different, and its characteristics can change dynamically over time. What will this mean for the level of consumer protection, and the application of consumer law?

One possible implication will be that many smart devices will fall under a combination of consumer sales law and contract law, but also that consumers, when purchasing and operating a smart device will engage in transactions (be it for money or data) with a variety of players, not all of whom will be known to the consumer. The arising, complex issues of liability and contractual relationships will be treated in another chapter in this book.

Another implication is that each smart product or rather, 'smart product package', will be different, depending on the level of customisation, subscription to value-added services, etc. This may sound trivial but seeing that, as Winn has argued, standardisation is one, if not the earliest form of consumer protection,[13] buying smart products will take on an entirely new complexity for consumers. Unlike in situations in which consumers purchase a 'normal dumb' fridge or watch, consumers as well as judges will need to assess smart products not so much as a thing but rather as a platform for value added services, similar to a (mini)computer.

A maybe still somewhat hypothetical but not uninteresting question is to what extent personal relevance and quality of personalisation can become a part of the assessment of the product, and if so, what would that mean for the standard of reasonable expectations as a benchmark? Could I return a smart whisky bottle because it does not give me the serving tips

---

13 Jane Winn, 'Information Technology Standards as a Form of Consumer Protection Law' in Jane Winn (ed), *Consumer Protection in the Age of the 'Information Economy'* (Ashgate 2006) 99, 99–120.

that I like? Or the smart meter because it does not help me to save energy optimally? Personal relevance as quality benchmark of smart devices seems like a notoriously difficult to handle yardstick, not only from the perspective of consumers and providers, but also from the perspective of judges.

2. A new deal: 'give data to get service'

One important reason why things in the IoT are smart is that their functionality feeds on a constant flow of usage and user data. In order to be able to provide consumers with real-time feedback on their performance, on the temperature and energy consumption in the house or on the state of maintenance of one's car, devices need to be able to collect and communicate data to the manufacturer or provider of the service. In other words, in order to get functionality consumers need to give data. This also means that consumers no longer simply buy a product in exchange for money. 'Paying with your data' will often become part of the deal when buying a smart watch or a smart device. This is data that can be used to enhance the functionality of the service, but also for all other kinds of purposes, such as marketing, profiling, re-adjusting terms and conditions, or reselling and sharing the data. As such, the data can become a commercial asset in its own right. And if some value-added services or apps in the IoT are offered 'for free' this is usually not because of the wish 'to do good' but because the IoT offers such excellent opportunities to collect very personal and very accurate data about users and usage.

There is a growing awareness among policy makers as well as academics that data can become a valuable resource and even a commercial asset in its own right.[14] Only recently, Chancellor Angela Merkel called on German consumers to be less protective about their personal data for the sake of the German economy: „Unser Verhältnis zu Daten ist in vielen Fällen zu stark vom Schutzgedanken geprägt (...) und vielleicht noch nicht ausreichend von dem Gedanken, dass man mithilfe von Daten

14 Commission, 'Communication from the Commission to the European Parliament, the Council, the European Economic and Social Committee and the Committee of the Regions. Towards a thriving data-driven economy' COM(2014) 442 final; World Economic Forum, *Personal Data: The Emergence of a New Asset Class* (World Economic Forum 2011).

interessante Produkte entwickeln kann. Mit einer falschen Gewichtung entsteht aber auch die Sorge, dass durch Digitalisierung einerseits Arbeitsplätze wegfallen und auf der anderen Seite nicht genügend neue Arbeitsplätze entstehen. Deshalb muss das 'Data Mining' (...) die Erhebung und der Umgang mit großen Datenmengen, etwas werden, das sozusagen ein Hoffnungssignal sendet."[15]

In other words, data can turn into a form of (additional) remuneration that consumers are required to pay for services.[16] The European Consumer Commissioner Meglena Kuneva has said already in March 2009: 'Personal data is the new oil of the Internet and the new currency of the digital world.'[17] 'Paying with your data' is an often heard common-place in debates about the new advances of data analytics and the data-driven economy. Services such as Handshake[18] or Datacoup[19] offer brokering services for consumers who want to sell their personal data. And, yet, under European consumer law, the legal implications of the 'paying with your data' analogy, and how consumer law can contribute to make sure that 'give data to get service' is actually a fair deal are not yet well-understood.

a) Informing consumers about the non-monetary price they pay

Notwithstanding the question of whether it is sensible at all to consider data a price that the consumer pays, it can be stated that *if* the sharing of (personal) data would be part of the 'price' consumers pay for receiving value-added services in the Internet of Things, established consumer law

---

15 Angela Merkel, *Rede von Bundeskanzlerin Merkel zur Eröffnung des Zentrums für Forschung und Vorausentwicklung der Robert Bosch GmbH am 14. Oktober 2015* (Die Bundesregierung 14 October 2015).

16 Chris Hoofnagle and Jane Whittington, 'Free: accounting for the costs of the Internet's most popular price' [2014] University of California Law Review 606, 606–670; Katherine Strandburg, 'Free Fall: The Online Market's Consumer Preference Disconnect' [2013] The University of Chicago Legal Forum 95, 95–172; Natali Helberger, Lucie Guibault, Marco Loos, Chantal Mak, Lodewijk Pessers and Bart Van der Sloot, *Digital Consumers and the Law. Towards a Cohesive European Framework* (Kluwer Law International 2013).

17 Meglena Kuneva, *Roundtable on Online Data Collection, Targeting and Profiling* (European Commission 2009).

18 <http://handshake.uk.com/hs/index.html> accessed on 15 November 2015.

19 <https://datacoup.com/> accessed on 15 November 2015.

principles require that they are informed about this fact. Providing consumers with the information they need to be able to make informed choices has always held a prominent position in European consumer law. According to Arts 5(1)(c) and 6(1)(e) of the Consumer Rights Directive, consumers need to be informed in advance about 'the total price of the goods or services inclusive of taxes.' Though the notion of price is still commonly interpreted in a sense to refer to the exchange of money, arguably this is bound to change to the extent that in an online environment with its changing business models, contracts are increasingly being performed also on the basis of non-monetary exchanges, such as data, but possibly even social capital or attention. One major difficulty in that context is assessing the value of data as a currency. One of the clear advantages of money is that it provides a fairly standardised and transparent way of describing value. It would go beyond the scope of this article to describe the difficulties of attaching concrete value to data.[20] The Consumer Rights Directive foresees in the situation that the price itself cannot be calculated because of the nature of the goods or services,[21] but not in the situation that the price cannot be easily specified because of the nature of the price. Insofar, the Consumer Rights Directive still lacks the necessary instruments to deal with non-monetary forms of remuneration.[22] Having said that, an interesting and often overlooked fact is that with the Consumer Rights Directive, consumer law now at least contains an obligation to inform consumers explicitly about the fact that tracking is taking

20 See insofar Chris Hoofnagle and Jane Whittington, 'Free: accounting for the costs of the Internet's most popular price' [2014] University of California Law Review 606, 606–670; Katherine Strandburg, 'Free Fall: The Online Market's Consumer Preference Disconnect' [2013] The University of Chicago Legal Forum 95, 95–172.

21 In which case consumers shall be informed about 'the manner in which the price is to be calculated as well as, where applicable, all additional freight, delivery or postal charges', Arts 5 (1) (c) and 6 (1)(e) of the Consumer Rights Directive.

22 Note from the author: The EC Proposal for a Directive of the European Parliament and of the Council on certain aspects concerning contracts for the supply of digital content (COM(2015)634 final (European Commission, 9.12.2015) could bring some welcome changes in this respect. Because, as mentioned in the introduction to this book, the proposal has been published after the research for this book has been concluded, these changes and their possible implications will be explored in a future contribution.

place, but also, specifically, that communications are personalised.[23] It is also worth noticing that these are obligations that go beyond the level of protection that is offered under data protection law.

Unfair commercial practice law might go further in demanding that consumers are adequately informed, also about non-monetary 'prices' to be paid, or rather: the return-services they are asked to perform (sharing data). An important role of the rules about unfair commercial practices is to create the conditions so that consumers can take better informed decisions on the basis of accurate and well-presented information.[24] Unfair commercial practice law could matter for the given context in at least two different ways. First, one could argue that the material information traders are required to disclose in accordance with Arts 6 and 7 of the Unfair Commercial Practices Directive includes information on the price, and that in a digital environment the notion of 'price' must be interpreted broadly, including non-monetary forms of exchanges, such as data, but also attention, intellectual property rights to user generated content, etc. This interpretation is further supported by the qualification in Art 7(2) Unfair Commercial Practice Directive, namely that a misleading omission can have taken place if a trader fails to identify the commercial intent of the commercial practice (if not already apparent from the context). In particular with the 'give data to get service'-deals mentioned above, an underlying and not always sufficiently transparent fact is that the data collected via smart devices will often not only be used to improve the service, etc. but also to monetise that data, share it with advertisers, etc. It is no secret that part of the particular attractiveness of the IoT for the consumer services and products sector is the wealth of information, and potentially very profitable information that can subsequently be commercialised in various manners (re-selling, using for advertising and marketing, etc.). Unfair commercial practice law seems to suggest that the use of data not only to provide the service but to extract extra commercial

23 Arts 5(1)(g), 6(1)(r) and Recital 19 of the Consumer Rights Directive and Commission, 'DG Justice Guidance Document concerning Directive 2011/83/EU of the European Parliament and of the Council of 25 October 2011 on consumer rights' (June 2014).

24 James Nefh, 'Misleading and unfair advertising' in Geraint Howells, Ian Ramsay, Thomas Wilhelmsson and David Kraft (eds), *Handbook of Research on International Consumer Law* (Edward Elgar Publishing 2010) 107, 107.

value from that data, and doing so without telling the consumer, can constitute an unfair commercial practice.

The critical question in that context is of course whether the consumer needs that information to take an informed transactional decision, and whether (not) having that information would cause her to take a transactional decision she would not have taken otherwise.[25] This is a difficult and ideally also an empirical question. Much will depend on who the 'average consumer' is in the profiling and targeting context. Is that the enlightened, critical digital consumer who is reasonably media literate, aware of the fact that data is streaming and for whom considerations of privacy and information security are important enough to not buy a product or subscribe to a service if her privacy and fair dealings with personal (Big) data is not guaranteed? Or is this a consumer who is primarily interested in the product she is buying, and does not muse about the technical and organisation background as long as the watch (or any other smart device) does what it is supposed to do? We will come back to this question later.

Second, and maybe of even greater practical relevance is No. 20 of the Annex to the Unfair Commercial Practices Directive, i.e. the black list of unfair commercial practices: "Describing a product as 'gratis', 'free', 'without charge' or similar if the consumer has to pay anything other than the unavoidable cost of responding to the commercial practice and collecting or paying for delivery of the item." Unlike under Arts 6 and 7, for the application of No. 20 of the Annex it is not relevant if the practice actually has an effect on the consumer's choice and decision to perform a transaction or not. Arguably, the provision is broad enough to also cover the payment of non-monetary forms of remuneration, seeing the lack of a direct reference to notions such as 'money' or 'price'. This interpretation seems to be confirmed by the European Commission itself which, in its

25 It is worth noting that the argument that the exchange of data for service would not constitute a "transactional decision" in the sense of the Unfair Commercial Practice Directive because that exchange would not affect a consumers "economic interest" is difficult to accept in an environment in which data is openly described as "the new currency" of a data-driven economy. Here, protecting the privacy and personal data of consumers is clearly not only a matter of "taste and decency" only but also a matter of economic interests that should fall under the ambit of the directive (in favour of a broad interpretation of economic interest also Thomas Wilhelmsson, 'Scope of the Directive' in Geraint Howells, Hans-W Micklitz and Thomas Wilhelmsson (eds), *European Fair Trading Law* (Ashgate 2006) 49, 58.

guidance on the application of the Unfair Commercial Practice Directive, stated that: 'This provision is based on the idea that consumers expect a 'free' claim to be exactly that, meaning they receive something for nothing: no money or other consideration has to be given in exchange.'[26]

And there are valid reasons to choose such a broader interpretation that also covers the 'give data to get service'-deals mentioned above. One is, as already mentioned, that personal data will often have a very real economic value to either the provider of a service or application, or third parties, such as advertisers. Insofar, principles of fairness seem to suggest that consumers should be informed about this, or at least not mislead about the fact that they get services 'for free'. A broad interpretation also avoids a situation that consumers are misled about the fact that they do not owe a service in return, namely the sharing data. Finally, applying No. 20 to also include non-monetary forms of remuneration would have the added benefit of increasing awareness of the economic value of data for both, consumers as well as traders. It could be an important means to re-establish the balance between consumers and traders in a digital, data-driven environment.

b) About the fairness of 'give data to get service'-deals

Another question is to what extent 'give data to get service'-deals should be a matter for scrutiny under unfair contract terms regulation. The objective of contract law and the Directive about Unfair Terms in Consumer Contracts[27] is to promote fairness and the balancing of rights and obligations, especially in situations in which the consumer is in a weaker negotiation position (such as in the case of standard form contracts). Even if one does not consider data as (part of the) price that consumers commit to pay or even denies a typical 'economic' interest, still contract law can have a role to play. As Wilhelmsson and Willet explain convincingly, fairness rules in contract law can also be used to support other societal

26 Commission, 'Commission Staff Working Document. Guidance on the Implementation/application of Directive 2005/29/EC on Unfair Commercial Practices' (2009).

27 Council Directive 93/13/EEC of 5 April 1993 on unfair terms in consumer contracts [1993] OJ L95/29.

policies or entitlements from fundamental rights.[28] Fundamental rights, too, can have a role in the weighting process, even though, as Collins points out, it might be necessary to translate e.g. the constitutional conception of privacy into a concept that fits better the realities of a relationship between private actors (rather than the state-citizen relationship).[29] So, if the Unfair Terms in Consumer Contracts Directive declares that a contractual clause 'shall be regarded as unfair if, contrary to the requirement of good faith, it causes a significant imbalance in the parties' rights and obligations arising under the contract, to the detriment of the consumer' (Art 3(1) Unfair Terms in Consumer Contracts Directive), that provision is arguably open to a broader interpretation. In other words, it could leave room to consider also other than the 'typical' consumer interests. Such, possibly more digital consumer-specific interests could include interests of privacy and the protection of personal data, freedom of expression and protection from the chilling effects that surveillance might have.[30]

For example, if an insurance company does make the amount of the insurance fee dependent on the willingness to agree to tracking and data sharing, or if providers of smart meters reserve the right to share the collected data with third parties, such as advertisers or environmental agencies, could that create a significant imbalance in the parties' rights and obligations? Particularly when taking into account that the sharing of energy consumption information with advertisers is not necessarily in the interest of consumers? Receiving targeted advertising may not be the

28 Thomas Wilhelmsson and Chris Willet, 'Unfair terms and standard form contracts' in Geraint Howells, David Kraft, Ian Ramsay, and Thomas Wilhelmsson (eds), *Handbook of Research on International Consumer Law* (Edward Elgar 2010) 158, 159–160. This is not the place to discuss the general positions on contract law on whether fairness considerations or considerations of party autonomy should serve as a point of departure. While in some countries there seems to be a focus on fairness considerations in others, particularly in common law countries, party autonomy may trump, Thomas Wilhelmsson and Chris Willet, 'Unfair terms and standard form contracts' in Geraint Howells, David Kraft, Ian Ramsay, and Thomas Wilhelmsson (eds), *Handbook of Research on International Consumer Law* (Edward Elgar 2010) 158, 159–160.

29 Hugh Collins, 'Utility and Rights in Common Law Reasoning: Rebalancing Private Law Through Constitutionalization' (2007) 9 SSRWE Electronical Journal 1, 19.

30 See more generally on the threat of interference and possible implications for freedom of expression, *Altuğ Taner Akçam v. Turkey* App no 27520/07 (ECtHR, 25 October 2011) para 81.

primary purpose why consumers would buy a smart watch. And for some consumers, notably the less affluent, such a deal could create additional pressure to forsake their privacy in favour of a better deal.[31] Under such circumstances, does the obligation to share data that is collected by smart devices pose an undue burden for the consumer?

Relevant factors to consider in that assessment[32] could be e.g. the extent to which consumers are able to safeguard their own interests and bargain for fair deals, including the level of transparency provided;[33] the reasonable expectations of consumers but also the availability of choice in the form of either alternative or competing offers; the overall (substantive) fairness, but also the compatibility of certain terms and conditions with other rights and freedoms of consumers, such as the right to privacy. Wilhelmsson and Willet, for example, mentioned as an example of particularly problematic terms those that 'impact the private sphere of life and cause losses that consumers may find [...] particularly difficult to absorb.'[34] Applied to the given case this could mean that terms that require consumers to share information not only with the provider of an app or service but with third parties that may or may not be affiliated with that party could be potentially unfair. Examples could be situations in which consumers would as a consequence lose control of that data and could not prevent its abuse, or if the obligation would run counter to the

---

31 Which was also one of the reasons why in the Netherlands, the insurance company Achmea has been recently nominated for the 'Big Brother Award', an annual award that is 'won' by the person or entity with the biggest privacy sins.

32 Which can also depend on the country in question, compare Thomas Wilhelmsson and Chris Willet, 'Unfair terms and standard form contracts' in Geraint Howells, Ian Ramsay and Thomas Wilhelmsson (eds), *Handbook of Research on International Consumer Law* (Edward Elgar 2010) 158, 159–160.

33 Chris Willett, *Freedom in Consumer Contracts: The Case of Unfair Terms* (Ashgate 2007) 17.

34 Wilhelmsson and Chris Willet, 'Unfair terms and standard form contracts' in Geraint Howells, David Kraft, Ian Ramsay, and Thomas Wilhelmsson (eds), *Handbook of Research on International Consumer Law* (Edward Elgar 2010) 158, 162. See also Willett: "An important aspect of the idea of fairness/protection of consumer interests in the context of consumer contracts seems to be the idea that consumers enter contacts in order to sustain and enhance the private sphere of life, rather than to make a profit. The terms of these contracts therefore affect the physical safety, proprietary, economic and social interests arising in, and affecting, the private sphere of life." Chris Willett, *Freedom in Consumer Contracts: The Case of Unfair Terms* (Ashgate 2007) 37.

consumers' rights under data protection law. In most cases, consumers will not even be able to understand fully the implications, seeing the complexity of the value chain and the underlying technical issues. Another reason to be particularly vigilant about 'give data to get service'-deals is the difficulty, not only for consumers, to assess the real 'costs' of this form of data sharing for consumers. As mentioned earlier, it is very difficult or even impossible to attach concrete costs to data. It is equally difficult to assess the consequences when such data is being released, and whether it may lead a second or even third life on its own (without the user directly benefiting) or is used to take any decisions that disadvantage the consumer (e.g. higher insurance fees). The difficulty of developing a concrete measurement or benchmark of when the amount of data requested is out of proportion or 'too expensive' when compared to what users get in return is of course also a challenge when applying the fair balancing test to 'give data to get service'-deals.

Relying here on market forces to determine an adequate price (as suggested, though in a different context, by Willet)[35] is little helpful, as traditional market mechanisms do not work in determining the right price or value of personal data.[36] Rather, the overall picture will need to decide, e.g. whether the data in question is sensitive or not (with the result that it merits stronger protection, e.g. under data protection law); whether it is being shared with third parties or not; the risk of privacy breaches and security threats; the amount of data being collected; as well the way and the purposes for which it is being used (e.g. to further the interests of the consumer vs. the interest of an insurance company or advertiser), but also the utility that consumers get in return. In other words, it could very well be that the fact that the consumer is required to share data is being outbalanced by the added utility that she receives from that service. Vice versa, there are situations in which the sharing of data has the potential to lead to consumer detriment, algorithmic discrimination or other forms of unfavourable decision-making. Here, the assumption of contractual unfairness lies closer at hand.

Another interesting question is to what extent certain forms of 'nudging' or personalised advertising with the goal of convincing the user

---

35 Chris Willett, *Freedom in Consumer Contracts: The Case of Unfair Terms* (Ashgate 2007) 52.

36 Katherine Strandburg, 'Free Fall: The Online Market's Consumer Preference Disconnect' [2013] The University of Chicago Legal Forum 95, 95–172.

to actually enter into the contract could have for the assessment of fairness. Thal, for example, suggests two situations in which it can be concluded that the bargaining power is not equal (which could be an indicator of contractual unfairness): the situation of monopoly power with the consequence that the other party, typically the consumer, has no choice, and a situation in which the other party is particular weak.[37] Possible sources of weakness can be, according to Thal, ignorance, necessity or, quite interestingly, trust.[38] In an age of Big Data and algorithms, a fourth possible source of weakness can arise: which is susceptibility to digital market manipulation.

3. Digital market manipulation

It was noted above that IoT facilitates the collection of detailed information about the user, and the creation of user profiles. That knowledge can be used, to improve the communication with the consumer, to target messages more effectively and customise products and services. The deepened knowledge about the user, however, can also be used to identify personal biases and weaknesses. Hanson and Kysar describe this as an entirely new source of market failure.[39] They explain: 'Rather, it is that manufactures have incentives to utilize cognitive biases actively to shape consumer perceptions throughout the product purchasing context and independently of government requirements. Advertising, promotion and price setting all become means of altering consumer risk perceptions'.[40]

Kaptein et.al referred in this context to 'persuasion profiles': 'sets of estimates of the effectiveness of particular influence strategies on individ-

---

37 Spencer Nathan Thal, 'The inequality of bargaining power doctrine: the problem of defining contractual unfairness' (1988) 8 Oxford Journal of Legal Studies 17, 29.

38 Spencer Nathan Thal, 'The inequality of bargaining power doctrine: the problem of defining contractual unfairness' (1988) 8 Oxford Journal of Legal Studies 17, 29.

39 Jon Hanson and Douglas Kysar, 'Taking Behaviouralism Seriously: Some Evidence of Market Manipulation' (1999) 112 Harvard Law Review 1420, 1564–1565; Jon Hanson and Douglas Kysar, 'Taking Behaviouralism Seriously: The Problem of Market Manipulation' (1999) 74 New York University Law Review 630, 630–749.

40 Jon Hanson and Douglas Kysar, 'Taking Behaviouralism Seriously: The Problem of Market Manipulation' (1999) 74 New York University Law Review 630.

uals, based on their past responses to these strategies'.[41] Different people respond to different triggers, and knowing these can help third parties, such as advertisers or marketers to deploy a persuasion strategy. Some people are more perceptible to recommendations by friends, others to recommendations by experts. Some prefer short texts, others long, some respond to negative, others to positive framing. Similarly, different people exhibit different biases and irrationalities. And again, data analytics, profiling and targeting allows to uncover these and exploit them to the advantage of advertisers, firms, etc.[42] If studies find that women tend to feel less attractive on Monday mornings, this is useful information for advertisers of beauty products.[43] If predictive profiling makes it possible to predict which people are likely to cancel a subscription, this is valuable information for service providers' strategies to prevent them from switching to a competitor.[44] Profiling and targeting in the IoT adds an additional dimension to this because of both the ability to collect even more detailed and situational data on the consumer, and to target the user context- and situation-specifically.

There is a very fine line between informing, nudging and outright manipulation. And one, or maybe even one of the main challenges for consumer law and policy in the context of profiling and targeting in the Internet of Things is to identify and delineate where exactly this line runs.

41 Maurits Kaptein, Dean Eckles and Janet Davis, 'Envisioning Persuasion Profiles: Challenges for Public Policy and Ethical Practice' (2011) 9/10 Interactions 66, 66; also: Maurits Kaptein, Joyca Lacroix and Privender Saini, 'Individual differences in persuadability in the health promotion domain' in Thomas Plough, Per Hasle and Harri Oinas-Kukkonen (eds) *Proceedings of 5th International Conference on Persuasive Technology: PERSUASIVE 2010* (Springer 2010) 82, 82–93.

42 Ryan Calo, 'Digital Market Manipulation' (2014) 82 The George Washington Law Review 995, 1003.

43 Rebecca J Rosen, 'Is this the Grossest Advertising Strategy of All Time?' (2013) The Atlantic <http://www.theatlantic.com/technology/archive/2013/10/is-this-the-grossest-advertising-strategy-of-all-time/280242/> accessed 10 October 2015.

44 Eric Siegel, *Predictive Analytics: The Power to Predict Who Will Click, Lie, or Die* (John Wiley & Sons 2013) 6–7.

a) The Unfair Commercial Practice Directive as point of departure for the conceptualisation of fairer marketing practices in the Iot

Much of the normative discussion about profiling and targeting consumers in the IoT, and certainly the topic of digital market manipulation, is about the need to find a proper balance between the interest of industry to engage in new forms of marketing and product development, and the autonomy and free choice of consumers. Digital market manipulation cuts right into this delicate balance, exactly because of the persuasive and pervasive potential of personalised communication. The Unfair Commercial Practice Directive will have an important role to play in providing guidance on what fair algorithmic marketing practices are, in the IoT, and beyond.

Central to the Directive's objective is the autonomy of the consumers' decision-making process, through protection against deception and unfair restrictions of consumer choices. Consumers may not be 'mislead or exposed to aggressive marketing' and any claim made by traders in the EU should be 'clear, accurate and substantiated, enabling consumers to make informed and meaningful choices'.[45] The making of autonomous, free and not unfairly manipulated choices is thus a central point of attention for the Directive. But the provisions about unfair commercial practices are particularly interesting for two additional reasons.

One is that the rules about unfair trading, including those in the Unfair Commercial Practices Directive, do not exclusively take the interests of the individual consumer as point of departure. This is interesting and relevant because profiling and targeting consumers in the IoT does not only touch upon issues of individual consumer protection. It also touches upon broader, more conceptual questions about the kind of information economy we would like to live in, and the values that should shape it. Fairness, privacy, autonomous choices may be important rights or entitlements of individual consumers/citizens, but they are also the quintessential building blocks of a free digital society. And since much of the interactions within the digital society are being privatised and commercialised, it is difficult to separate the individual from the societal perspective entirely. It appears that the provisions concerning unfair commercial practices

45 Commission, *Commission Staff Working Document. Guidance on the Implementation/application of Directive 2005/29/EC on Unfair Commercial Practices* (2009) 6.

provide at least some room to also consider broader societal implications of unfair marketing practices, even if those broader societal issues are still primarily viewed through the lens of the consumer as economic decision-maker.[46]

The other is that the protection of privacy concerns is not alien to the provisions about unfair commercial practice. From the way that the rules about unfair commercial practices, coercion and harassment have been applied to situations of doorstep selling or calling people at their homes speaks a respect for the personal autonomy and privacy of consumers.[47] That the provisions about unfair commercial or unfair trading practices can play an important role in protecting also the privacy of consumers is even more established in the US. The Federal Trade Commission, the American Consumer Protection and Fair Trade Authority, has played over the past years an important role in furthering consumer privacy. The fair trading law's rules about deception and fairness have figured prominently in this. As the US scholars Solove and Hartzog argue in a recent article, 'FTC privacy jurisprudence has become the broadest and most influential regulating force on information privacy in the United States — more so than nearly any privacy statute or any common law tort'.[48]

b) Targeting & profiling in the IoT as an aggressive practice

The rules about unfair commercial practices do not only protect the interest of the consumer in being properly informed (see insofar section III 2). They also embrace a broader understanding of fairness in commercial

---

46 Thomas Wilhelmsson, 'Scope of the Directive' in Geraint Howells, Hans-W Micklitz and Thomas Wilhelmsson (eds), *European Fair Trading Law* (Ashgate 2006) 63; Commission, *'Commission Staff Working Document. Guidance on the Implementation/application of Directive 2005/29/EC on Unfair Commercial Practices'* (2009), 37–46; Chris Willet, 'Fairness and Consumer Decision Making' (2010) 33 Journal of Consumer Policy 247, 247–273.

47 Geraint Howells, 'Aggressive Commercial Practices' in Geraint Howells, Hans-W Micklitz and Thomas Wilhelmsson (eds), *European Fair Trading Law* (Ashgate 2006) 167, 178; Geraint Howells, Hans-W Micklitz and Thomas Wilhemsson, 'Towards a better understanding of unfair commercial practices' (2009) 52 International Journal of Law and Management 69, 69–90.

48 Daniel Solove and Woodrow Hartzog, 'The FTC and the New Common Law of Privacy' (2014) Columbia Law Review 583, 583.

transactions against practices that violate more vigorously the autonomy, freedom to choose, and arguably also the privacy and dignity of consumers.[49] As Howells argues, a central element of the provisions about aggressive practices is the impairment of the consumer's freedom to choose, though, as he also points out, the line between advertising as in essence a form of persuasion, and exercising undue influence or even coercion can be very thin.[50] And yet, as vague as the notion of 'aggressive practice' is, it is easy to see its relevance for the topic at hand, and in particular for the matter of 'digital market manipulation'.

Take the example of an advertiser who, thanks to the constant transfer of personalised information learns that a consumer has just stepped from the scale three kilos heavier. The advertiser seizes the opportunity to target her with advertisement for a new, rather expensive diet coaching service that is exactly tailored to her personal level of fitness and weight. Is this insensitive but perfectly legitimate advertising or aggressive commercial practice? In order to be an aggressive practice the targeted advertising would need to comply with the three requirements of Art 8 Unfair Commercial Practice Directive (respectively the national rules implementing it): it would need to constitute a form of harassment, coercion or undue influence; it would need to (or be likely to) impair the consumers freedom of choice or conduct; and it would need to (or be likely to) cause a transaction that the consumer would otherwise have not taken.

aa) Targeted advertising as harassment, coercion or undue influence

Though it does not always seem easy to draw a clear line between harassment, coercion and undue influence, there appears to be some agreement that harassment is concerned also and particularly with commercial practices that invade the private space of the consumer.[51] Possible exam-

---

49 Geraint Howells, 'Aggressive Commercial Practices' in Geraint Howells, Hans-W Micklitz and Thomas Wilhelmsson (eds), *European Fair Trading Law* (Ashgate 2006) 167, 167–168.

50 Geraint Howells, 'Aggressive Commercial Practices' in Geraint Howells, Hans-W Micklitz and Thomas Wilhelmsson (eds), *European Fair Trading Law* (Ashgate 2006) 167, 168.

51 Geraint Howells, Hans-W Micklitz and Thomas Wilhemsson, 'Towards a better understanding of unfair commercial practices' (2009) 52 International Journal of Law and Management 69, 76.

ples are doorstep selling or phoning or emailing the consumer at her home.[52] These practices force the consumer to engage with the trader within the confines of her private sphere (home), where the consumer may be less alert and less trained to defend herself against unfair practices than e.g. within the setting of a shop. If phoning and mailing the consumer in her house can already be seen as a potentially unfair invasion of the private sphere of the consumer, arguably, sending advertising to devices that directly surround the consumer in her private sphere could, under circumstances, also be considered harassing (and provided the other conditions of Arts 8 and 9 Unfair Commercial Practice Directive fulfilled). This is even truer for communication that is delivered to devices that the consumer carries close to her body, such as reaching out to her over her smart phone or smart watch.

But it is not only the location that matters, timing matters as well (Art 9(a) Unfair Commercial Practice Directive). The Internet of Things is 24/7 and gives marketers the opportunity to target consumers at any moment of the day, including in the early hours in the privacy of one's bathroom, when the consumer has just stepped of the scale and discovered she has gained a couple of kilos.

Profiling and targeting the consumer could, under certain conditions, also amount to coercion. Obviously it is less the exercise of physical power, and more the exercise of psychological power that would be at play here. As a result of profiling and data analysis, advertisers and service providers are able to identify not only personal preferences, but also possible biases and weak spots in the consumer. This does as such give room to also play on the consumer's emotions and fears, e.g. the fear of gaining weight.

The detailed knowledge about the consumer could, finally, also place traders into a position of power, in the sense of the Directive's definition of 'undue influence'. According to Art 2(j) Unfair Commercial Practice Directive undue influence is defined as the 'exploiting a position of power in relation to a consumer so as to apply pressure, even without using or threatening to use physical force, in a way which significantly limits the consumer's ability to make an informed decision'. According to Howells this can include situations in which the trader has the power to persuade

52 Geraint Howells, 'Aggressive Commercial Practices' in Geraint Howells, Hans-W Micklitz and Thomas Wilhelmsson (eds), *European Fair Trading Law* (Ashgate 2006) 167, 179, 182.

the consumer, either because the consumer depends on the cooperation of the trader, or because the trader has at his disposal psychological tools to sway the consumer into the making of a transaction.[53] The detailed knowledge about the consumer's personal situation, her preferences, fears and biases can form a potentially effective source of persuasive potential. As has been explained above, the entire purpose of making and using persuasion profiles is to find the right 'persuasion' strategy for each consumer, based on her characteristics and persuasion potential. The difficult question is to decide where the limit lies between legitimate, albeit technologically sophisticated persuasion and the exercise of undue influence.

One important factor in this context could be the knowledge of the user of the fact that she is being persuaded, based on her persuasion profile. This is because only with such knowledge is she actually able to mobilise her defence strategy, should she wish to do so. Another important factor could be her ability to opt out of targeted messages, as a means to restore the imbalance in control power between user and trader. An interesting question would be to what extent the amount of information collected about the consumer, or the sensitivity of that information could play a role in the assessment? More generally, useful insights for the assessment could be derived from the ongoing discussion about the ethics of persuasion and nudging,[54] though it exceeds the scope of this contribution to go into more depth into this strand of analysis.

bb) Impairment of the freedom of choice

There are of course the conditions in the Unfair Commercial Practice Directive itself. The practice is only unfair if it impairs the consumer's freedom of choice or conduct and causes her to make a transaction that she

---

53 Geraint Howells, 'Aggressive Commercial Practices' in Geraint Howells, Hans-W Micklitz and Thomas Wilhelmsson (eds), *European Fair Trading Law* (Ashgate 2006) 167, 188; Reiner Schulze and Hans Schulte-Nölke, *Analysis of National Fairness Laws Aimed at Protecting Consumers in Relation to Commercial Practices* (Report Commissioned by the European Commission, DG Sanco 2003) 37.

54 Andreas Spahn, 'And Lead Us (Not) into Persuasion…? Persuasive Technology and the Ethics of Communication' (2012) Sci Eng Ethics 633, 633–650; Peter-Paul Verbeek, 'Persuasive Technology and Moral Responsibility. Toward an ethical framework for persuasive technologies' (2006) Persuasive 1, 1–15.

would have otherwise not taken. Under which conditions profiling and targeting can amount to significantly impairing (or being likely to impair) a consumer's freedom of choice or conduct will depend on the persuasive potential of the personalised message and the extent to which the practice reduces the autonomous decision making process.[55] This is a difficult and also empirical question. So far, research on the effects of personalised communications in general is still a developing area of research.[56] Answering the question will require deeper understanding of how exactly profiling and targeting affects the choices of consumers in an individual case, or: to use the wording of the Directive: 'taking account of all its features and circumstances' (Art 8 Unfair Commercial Practice Directive). For example in the case of the above mentioned example – a consumer is being targeted with diet products after she has learned from her scale that she has gained a couple of kilos, it would be necessary to better understand how deep the fear of gaining extra weight is (Is she obese or bulimic, over- or normal weighted? What is her age? Does she have a history of (unsuccessful) dieting?), how perceptive to personalisation strategies, how much the timing of the message plays a role etc. It is important to keep in mind, however, that an important purpose of targeted advertising is to be better able to effect a change of behaviour in consumers, and increase the likelihood of the consumer purchasing a product or service.

55 An interesting question in this context is to what extent the directive would apply to practices that trigger not the consumer's rationality but her automatic behaviour (such as e.g. defaults do).

56 Laura Brighta and Terry Daugherty, 'Does customization impact advertising effectiveness? An exploratory study of consumer perceptions of advertising in customized online environments' (2012) Journal of Marketing Communications 19, 19–37; Jason Jensen, Andy King and Nick Carcioppolo, 'Why are tailored messages more effective? More Effective? A Multiple Mediation Analysis of a Breast Cancer Screening Intervention' (2012) Journal of Communication 851, 851–868; Richard Petty and John Cacioppo, *Communication and persuasion: Central and peripheral routes to attitude change* (Springer 1986).

cc) Causing a transactional decision that the consumer would not have taken otherwise

This observation is also relevant for the next criterion: causing the consumer to take a transactional decision that she would not have taken otherwise. Again, much will depend on the actual persuasive potential of the personalised communication. An added difficulty in this context is that because the message has been personalised to the situation and preferences of an individual, arguably the likelihood is greater that the consumer already had an inclination for taking that particular decision, because it corresponds with her individual needs and preferences. The challenge for the consumer, in the case of individual consumer redress (to the extent that national laws foresee in this possibility), would then be to demonstrate that even though the personalised communication does communicate with individual needs and preferences, the consumer was determined not to enter into that transaction, and was only swayed because of the personalised nudge to decide differently.

c) The quantified consumer – empowered or vulnerable

Much will of course depend on who the 'average' consumer of personalised IoT products and services is. The average consumer, as the 'reasonably informed, observant and circumspect' consumer,[57] is an important benchmark for the application of the Unfair Commercial Practice Directive's provisions (Recital 18 Unfair Commercial Practice Directive). Arguably, the requirements for the average consumer in a digital environment must reflect in some way or other the greater technical and organisational complexity but also the changed nature of digital or digitally-enhanced products, and hence her ability to deal with that complexity. For example, the buyer of a smart watch will need to have a different level of media literacy, technical understanding but also understanding of the basic legal implications than the buyer of a 'normal' analogue watch. Otherwise it is difficult to understand how she can correctly assess the functioning but also the implications of her choices, for example for the privacy and safety of her personal data.

---

57 Case C–210/96 *Gut Springenheide* [1998] ECR I–4657.

This leads to the question: who is the 'average user' in the IoT? Is this the technically sophisticated, media literate consumer? The concept of the Internet of Things is inevitably connected to the notion of the quantified self – a notion, or rather a movement, coined by the editors of the tech-magazine Wired, Gary Wolf and Kevin Kelly. Quantified self, or as the movement describes itself 'self-knowledge through numbers'[58] refers to the idea that digital technologies also allow users to track themselves, thereby better get know to know their body, mind, environment and behaviour.[59] Users can also use the data they collect about themselves for self-improvement: becoming more efficient, healthier, productive and social. Insofar the Internet of Things may bring consumers one giant leap closer to the notion of informed consumer in the sense that consumers get to know themselves better, their preferences and needs.[60]

At the same time, it is also exactly this complexity of the technical environment and value chain, the lack of benchmarks of similar 'standardised' analogue products and the opacity of the underlying processes that challenge the ability of the digital consumer to navigate digital product markets in the IoT; and make her potentially more perceptive to practices such as digital market manipulation. If one defines 'vulnerability' as the 'limited ability to deal with commercial practices'[61] one may even wonder at which point digital marketing practices, and in particular if they are based on intrinsic data analysis, opaque algorithms and sophisticated forms of persuasion, turn the normally 'average' consumer into a vulnerable one. So while it may be that the quantified consumer is technologically more sophisticated and empowered, it is similarly possible that as the 'profiled consumer' she is also more credulous and defenceless against new, more sophisticated forms of personalised marketing in the Internet of Things. This could be an area that merits more legal-empirical research.

---

58 <http://quantifiedself.com/> accessed on 15 November 2015.

59 Deborah Lupton, *Self-tracking cultures: towards a sociology of personal informatics' ACM, Proceedings of the 26th Australian Computer-Human Interaction Conference: Designing Figures, the Future of Design, 2-5 December 2014* (University of Technology Sidney 2014).

60 A question for future research could be to what extent self-tracking and digitally enabled self-improvement could have on the concept of the 'informed consumer' and the idea of the consumer as an autonomous economic actor.

61 Bram Duivenvoorde, 'The protection of vulnerable consumers under the Unfair Commercial Practice Directive' (2013) 2 Journal of European Consumer and Market Law 69, 73.

IV. Conclusion

This chapter has pointed to some of the possible challenges from the Internet of Things for the 'profiled consumer'. These challenges go beyond issues of privacy and data protection – which will continue to play a prominent role. In addition, the protection of contractual fairness, adequate information and autonomous and free choices comes to the fore. Particular attention has been paid to the issues of 'free services' and 'give data to get service'-deals, as well as practices of digital market manipulation. It has been argued that unfair commercial practice law will have a prominent role in ensuring fairness in the dealings between consumers and traders in the Internet of Things.

This is not to say that consumer law, and the Unfair Commercial Practice Directive in particular, are the optimal or last answer to the consumer protection challenges from profiling and targeting consumers in the Internet of Things. The strong focus on economic interests and the fact that societal interests are primarily viewed through the lens of a consumer who is about to take an economic transaction; the fact that economic transactions are still primarily considered transactions for money, not data; the requirement of an effect of a commercial practice on a consumer's transactional decision, which is limited helpful in situations in which consumers are largely ignorant or do not feel they have a choice and take the decision anyway; and the fact that the Directive describes which practices are unfair, rather than giving guidance on what fair media practices are – these are just some of the limitations that the application of consumer law, and unfair commercial practice law, to the Internet of Things encounters.

And yet, consumer law and the provisions about unfair practices can provide a new and inspiring perspective for thinking about the protection of the 'profiled consumer' in the Internet of Things. They could form the point of departure for a broader discussion on what fair marketing practices are in the context of profiling and targeting, in and beyond the Internet of Things. They could even contribute to the protection of consumers' privacy. Insofar, this chapter has also touched upon the question of how data protection law, privacy and consumer law could complement each other, and pointed to some relevant questions for further research.

Contractual Duties and Allocation of Liability in Automated Digital Contracts

*Rolf H. Weber**

I. Introduction

1. Context of Increased Role of Digital Contracts

In May 2015, the European Commission published the Communication 'A Digital Single Market Strategy for Europe'.[1] With this Strategy the Commission intends to make better use of the great opportunities offered by digital economies and to generate additional growth. The Strategy is built on three pillars, namely (i) improving the access for consumers and businesses to online goods and services across Europe, (ii) creating the right conditions for digital networks to flourish, and (iii) maximizing the growth potential of the European digital economy.[2] As a consequence, the main objective consists in the building of a data economy.[3]

The legal framework for digital contracts must be seen as important element of a digital single market. Therefore, the Commission is addressing the cross-border e-commerce rules increasing consumers' and businesses' trust as well as the reinforcement of trust and security in digital services and the handling of personal data.[4] Hereinafter, this contribution will analyze the issues of contractual duties and the allocation of

---

* Rolf H Weber is Professor of Law at the University of Zurich. This contribution has benefitted from the very valuable support of his research Assistant Dominic N Staiger and from discussions in the newly incorporated Center for Information Technology, Society, and Law at the University of Zurich.

1 A Digital Single Market Strategy (DSMS) for Europe, Communication of 6 May 2015, COM (2015) 192 final.

2 A Digital Single Market Strategy (DSMS) for Europe, Communication of 6 May 2015, COM (2015) 192 final, 3–4.

3 A Digital Single Market Strategy (DSMS) for Europe, Communication of 6 May 2015, COM (2015) 192 final, 14–15.

4 A Digital Single Market Strategy (DSMS) for Europe, Communication of 6 May 2015, COM (2015) 192 final, 4–5, 12–13.

liability in the light of the newest EU-initiatives related to the digital economy.

2. Digital Contracts – Notion and Features

Since the evolution of the internet and electronic commerce the concept of digital contracts significantly altered the way in which business is conducted online. The definition of a digital contract evolved over time starting with a simple online purchase to today's wholly cryptographic contracts including self-executing properties. This automatization in contract conclusion is based on 'outside' data from a reliable source triggering the execution process.

At the initial stage of the internet's commercial exploration national laws had to be amended to cater for electronic contract formation and the particularities of such transactions. The subsequently in 2000 enacted E-Commerce Directive[5] aimed at resolving some of the issues that had evolved in the EU. However, with the increased technological developments and a rise in consumer awareness new challenges for example in the context of the Internet of Things (IoT) have materialized.

With the IoT risks such as the involuntary disclosure of personal data, the wrongful execution of a digital contract based on third party manipulation or system errors as well as ancillary risks associated with corrupted IoT data are becoming relevant.[6] All these scenarios lead to special features in the execution of digital contracts. Thus, the contribution addresses the various risks of such contracts (partly and fully automated) and determines which party will bear the liability in different scenarios.

5 Directive 2000/31/EC of the European Parliament and of the Council of 8 June 2000 on certain legal aspects of information society services, in particular electronic commerce, in the Internal Market (E-Commerce Directive) [2000] OJ L 178/1.

6 Tyson Macaulay, 'Data Quality in the Internet of Things' available at <https://blogs.mcafee.com/business/data-quality-in-the-internet-of-things/> accessed 30 November 2015.

3. *Forms and Appearances of Digital Contracts*

a) Different Degrees of Automatization

Digital contracts are agreements entered into by two or more parties over an electronic communication line; these agreements do not exist in physical form as they are merely retained electronically by a computer system.[7] The contract formation is either carried out manually by the user of a computer system or automatically based on IoT data and a pre-established agreement to be bound by such contracts. Therefore, automated digital contracts include various levels of sophistication. However, they all have some form of an automated process as a common denominator.

A new form of contract currently emerging is a fully automated digital contract, a so-called 'smart contract'. For example, if one places a bet on a player and the TV station subsequently broadcasts that the respective player shot a goal, the code contained in the smart contract's block chain will automatically transfer the winnings into the beneficiary's account. *Richard Gendal Brown*, a leading expert on distributed ledger and consensus technologies, presented the following definition: 'A smart-contract is an event-driven program, with state, which runs on a replicated, shared ledger and which can take custody over assets on that ledger.'[8] Such a contract consists of cryptographic protocols which entail the contract parameters as well as a self-executing payment system that will deduct the amount owed under the contract from a user's bank or cyber-currency account. Despite being in the initial development stage these new systems promise a fundamental change in how contracts are formed and executed.[9]

A further anticipated development of this concept encompasses the attempt to have the digital contract and the payment reflecting real world assets in digital form. Digital assets such as Bitcoins are already used

---

7 Craig S Wright, Electronic Contracting in an Insecure World, SANS Legal Issues in Information Technology and Information Security, LEG-523, 6, available at <http://www.sans.org/reading-room/whitepapers/legal/electronic-contracting-insecure-world-2088> accessed 30 November 2015.

8 See <http://www.clearmatics.com/solution/programmable-assets/> accessed 30 November 2015.

9 See for example the Swiss company Ethereum <https://www.ethereum.org/> accessed 30 November 2015.

today. However, in the future cryptographic keys will potentially reflect real world assets and thus enable a party to securely transfer such assets by way of a smart contract.[10] Thus, the level of trust between the parties normally required for a transaction for which an intermediary generally charges assurance costs is no longer necessary as the enforcement is part of the electronic contract and cannot be altered without consent of all parties.

b) Need for an 'Oracle'

In the future, IoT data will enable the independent verification of contract parameters. For example GPS data of a package which is delivered to a specific GPS location triggers an automatic payment under the smart contract. Once the technology has evolved to a level where all assets of a person are entirely reflected by electronic means the quick and cheap execution of all types of contractual agreements including wills are enabled as the assets can be easily divided between the beneficiaries based on an electronic self-executing will.

However, the automated contract has to 'know' when to act. This requires a so-called 'oracle' which provides the factual basis for the execution of the contract. Such a source must be reliable and independent. For example the stock price of a particular exchange could qualify as a viable source of stock data.

Therefore, these contracts need an independent outside source to verify the facts that trigger their execution. The process works well when the data sought is distributed through various sources and thus can be checked easily. However, the more uncommon certain facts are the less likely it will be that there is a data source to which the contract can be linked. In these instances default options are necessary when the other party does not fulfil its obligations under the transaction by not disclosing the necessary algorithm that allows a release of the funds.[11] Mostly, such options will take the form of either a third party being able to make a determination

---

10 These digital contracts through combing the contractual terms with the capabilities of IoT devices are able to e.g. lock the electronic doors of a house when the tenant has breached his or her electronic rental agreement.

11 For a detailed technical description of such contracts see: Stefan Thomas and Evan Schwartz, 'Smart Oracles: A Simple Powerful Approach to Smart Contracts'

who is entitled to the money as otherwise after a certain time has lapsed the assets revert back to their original owner. In any case these provisions must be included in the contract at the time of formation and both parties should be aware of their effects for the business transaction.

c) Robot Device

In addition to the automated contract which is initiated by an individual, an electronic system consisting of a robot or other device may enter into a contract on behalf of its owner. Thus, the question arises as to whether the actions of such a robot are attributable to a party and whether it binds the owner or administrator.[12]

Under most civil law systems this attribution is currently hardly possible as a computer system or a robot is not a subject of law and therefore cannot enter into legally binding contracts.[13] Nevertheless, the answer to this question may change in the future with the growing number of intelligent devices assisting people in daily life.[14]

II. Design of Contractual Duties in Automated Digital Contracts

The most critical new issues related to contractual duties are the obligations in the context of the digital contract formation and execution. Therefore, the following sub-chapters concentrate on the inherent technological issues.

---

available at: <https://github.com/codius/codius/wiki/Smart-Oracles:-A-Simple,-Powerful-Approach-to-Smart-Contracts> accessed 30 November 2015.

12 To the robot devices see the contribution of Erica Palmerini and Andrea Bertolini in this volume, 225.

13 Rolf H Weber, 'Die Folgen der Nichterfüllung. Art 97–109 OR' in Max Gmür and Arthur Meier-Hayoz (eds), *Berner Kommentar zum schweizerischen Privatrecht*, Vol VI/1/5 (Stämpfli 2000) Art 101 N 39, 334.

14 Melinda F Müller, 'Roboter und Recht' 2014 AJP 595, 600.

1. Technological Features and Risks of Digital Contracts

Three main features must be present for the proper functioning of a digital contract. These include authenticity, integrity and non-repudiation.

a) Authenticity

Authenticity addresses the question whether the communication actually comes from the person the recipient thinks he or she is communicating with. Thus, especially for contractual purposes the identity of the other party must be established with a very high certainty. The onus to ensure the identity of the person one is dealing with is placed on the party claiming a fraud or other deceit.

aa) Need for Identification Systems

In order to achieve confidence in the electronic communications new identification systems have been developed, some of which can be used to communicate with government agencies to i.e. file a tax return or other official document where it is important to ensure that the party sending the document is actually the person he or she is claiming to be.[15]

These certification tools will then be accepted in court whereas otherwise the claimant would need to prove the identity of the other party. However, in reality the adoption of these certification tools is slow as they come with an initial start-up cost for the consumer and are not widely accepted as banks and other institutions are reluctant to adopt a new system.[16]

15 For example Switzerland has a new SuisseID system, available at <http://www.suisseid.ch/de> accessed 30 November 2015.

16 Patrick Bieri, 'SuisseID — die elektronische Signatur der Schweiz, Maprime', <http://www.macprime.ch/hintergrund/article/suisseid-die-elektronische-signatur-der-schweiz> accessed 30 November 2015.

bb) Legal Frameworks for Identification Issues

1) On the European level the Electronic Signatures Directive[17] has been superseded by the Regulation on Electronic Identification and Trust Services for Electronic Transactions in the Internal Market (e-IDAS)[18] which will come into force in July 2016 and will harmonize the electronic signature approval process throughout the EU. The aim of the Regulation is to facilitate a single digital market in Europe by requiring mutual recognition of electronic identification means and electronic trust services. It allows for a more advanced form of electronic signature which enables the unique identification and authentication of the signer of a document and the verification of the integrity of the signed data. Electronic verification services shall furthermore be admissible in court when certain requirements are met;[19] these include technical requirements to confirm the integrity and correctness of the data.

The Regulation distinguishes between qualified and unqualified trust services which vary in regard to the extent of their liability. Qualified services offer better security and thus a higher degree of liability in case of a breach. Furthermore, in order to increase public confidence the definition of trusted services as well as of the required supervision has been clarified.

2) In Switzerland the customer is liable for any unauthorized digital signature use unless he or she can prove that he or she has taken reasonable measures to ensure the security of the ID.[20] These measures are included in a supplementary document to the '*Signaturgesetz*' and highlight the following points: (i) the SuisseID and PIN code must be kept separately, (ii) the ID and PIN are not to be given or disclosed to third

---

17 Directive 1999/93/EC of the European Parliament and of the Council of 13 December 1999 on a Community framework for electronic signatures [1999] OJ L 13/12.

18 Regulation (EU) No 910/2014 of the European Parliament and of the Council of 23 July 2014 on electronic identification and trust services for electronic transactions in the internal market and repealing Directive 1999/93/EC [2014] OJ L 257/73.

19 Regulation (EU) No 910/2014 of the European Parliament and of the Council of 23 July 2014 on electronic identification and trust services for electronic transactions in the internal market and repealing Directive 1999/93/EC 2014] OJ L 257/73 Art 25.

20 Art 59a Obligationenrecht.

parties, (iii) the PIN is not to be easily identifiable (e.g. birth date), (iv) computers which are used with the ID must have an anti-virus software and the drivers and operating system must be up to date, (v) after using the ID it must be disconnected from the computer (vi) the ID should only be used with trusted encrypted websites.[21]

Thus, even when a SuisseID is used fraudulently and the owner cannot show that he or she took reasonable measures he or she will not be bound by the contract but only be liable for the damages incurred. However, the standard is fairly low because the reasonable measures must not be fully proven. Furthermore, the owner of the ID may seek damages from the certifying authority if it failed to ensure that adequate precautions were taken.[22]

Similarly, banks and other institutions regularly require their customers to adhere to certain security measures which form part of their contracts. Amongst others the customer must keep his or her PIN and identification card separate and he or she should not store the account information on the phone on which he or she receives the TAN (Transaction Number) for the login to the online system. All these measures aim at ensuring the security of the digital contracting the parties undertake.

3) In the US the issue of certification was addressed by the US Uniform Electronic Transactions Act 1999 (UETA) which states that a transaction is not invalid merely because an electronic record was used in its formation. Interestingly the Act focuses on the intention of the party when defining an electronic signature thus allowing for all forms of signature as long as the partie's intention is to sign a record.[23] However, this Act was only adopted by merely 22 states which is why Congress passed the US Electronic Signatures in Global and National Commerce Act 2000 (E-Sign). The E-Sign Act does not provide for the attribution and effect of an electronic record and an electronic signature. Moreover, it requires a written form for certain documents such as wills which was not part of the UETA. Thus, in some states it is possible that the UETA applies potentially allowing for digital wills whereas other states which did not implement their own law are now by default subject to E-Sign.

---

21 Matthias Ebneter, 'SuisseID und die Haftungsfrage', available at <http://www.inside-it.ch/articles/24068> accessed 30 November 2015.

22 Arts 16 and 17 ZertES.

23 UETA § 2(8).

b) Integrity

Once the identity has been established the issue is whether the communication between two parties is complete, or whether something has been lost along the way. As the communication is sent through a vast amount of servers and nods around the world it can be intercepted and altered at any point along the way. New research in the field of quantum communications will soon enable software to identity whether the data sent has been interfered with and automatically reroute the data packages through a secure channel. However, with improved security the complexity of the tools grow and thus these solutions are currently only viable for highly important financial transactions.

In the context of smart contracts the risk is very low as the contract in form of the code will be sent to the parties twice. Unless the computer of the sender or receiver is high jacked by malicious software the code will be delivered through other nodes and channels which ensure that any alteration would be detected. Furthermore, the data is encrypted with the sender's and receiver's unique code which additionally ensures the security of the information contained in the transmission.

c) Non-repudiation

As a third step the technology must enable to prove that the sender in fact sent the communication and that it has not been altered in order to bind the other party to the contract.

2. Inherent Risks in Automated Digital Contracts

The design of contractual duties is particularly important in light of the technological risks of automated digital contracts. The issues mainly arise in the context of contract formation including the need to ensure privacy and data protection throughout the contracting process. Various technological as well as legal safeguards are thus necessary in order to mitigate the risks in such contracts. A close understanding on how the technology works is, however, essential in order to be able to guard against any risks.

a) Identification in Formation Stage

Digital contracts carry an inherently greater risk than paper contracts because of their technological element. The ease of entering into such contracts is also one of their major weaknesses as without proper safeguards they can be manipulated or the data contained in them can be widely dispersed. In light of the amount of personal data as well as financial data contained in such contracts the detrimental effect third party access can have is evident.

At the formation stage of the digital contract, conclusion certification systems aim at ensuring that the parties communicating are actually the parties they hold themselves out to be. There has always been a potential for a party to fake its identity through wrong certificates or other means. However, in practice sophisticated authentication and monitoring technology ensure that the risks in this regard are minimized today.[24] As these identifying standards and systems vary across the globe they create challenges in the context of cross border contracts.

Even within the USA various states have enacted substantially differing laws on electronic identification.[25] In contrast to this legal uncertainty, the e-IDASimposes liability on any party that acts negligently in the issuance of a certification measure. The EU approach also tries to facilitate cross-border contracting by allowing foreign electronic signatures to be used which have been approved through cross border recognition procedures. Importantly when a person subscribes to an electronic signature he or she will generally be completely liable for any misappropriation that occurs with this signature even if it is stolen or lost without fault on his or her part.[26] This seems unreasonable when the liability under an electronic signature is compared with that under a credit card agreement. The user is not or only to a very limited amount liable for fraudulent credit card transactions whereas there is no limitation on the liability for the fraudulent use of one's electronic signature.

---

24 Rolf H Weber, *E-Commerce und Recht* (Schulthess 2010) 323.

25 Aashish Srivastava, *Electronic Signatures for B2B Contracts: Evidence from Australia* (Springer 2013) 55.

26 Bradford C Biddle, 'Legislating Market Winners: Signature Laws and the Electronic Commerce Market Place' (1997*)* San Diego Law Review 1225, 1236.

b) Error in Technology

Once the identity of the parties has been established there is the risk that a breakdown or error in the technology could potentially lead to a mistake in the contract or cause potentially greater effects in a smart contract scenario which results in an unenforceable contract as the code does not fulfil its intended purpose. Therefore, data and system reliability play an important role in the IoT context.

At this point the risk of corrupted IoT data on which a potential contract relies shows its greatest effect as both parties base their decision on this data without realizing that it is wrong. In most instances the corrupted data will only become apparent at the performance stage of the contract e.g. when too many goods are delivered. The issue then is one of knowledge and whether the parties have the right to rescind the contract based on mutual mistake. However, as discussed below[27], in reality these risks are mostly shifted to one party through appropriate exclusion clauses.

c) Involuntary Disclosure of Content

Furthermore, as the information contained in these contracts is being transferred through various servers around the globe, third parties can potentially gain access to the personal data as well as to other information contained in the communication. Additionally, one of the contracting parties might be subjected to a security breach which also might lead to such unwanted disclosures. This could occur if for example an employee steals the digital contracts stored on a company server. At this point not only contract laws relating to e-commerce but also data protection laws such as the EU Data Protection Directive apply to the contract.

Interestingly the E-Commerce Directive limits the liability of intermediaries in relation to transmissions[28] (communication which only passes through their systems) whereas in contrast the Data Protection Directive imposes duties and liability on them through the processor definition.[29] It

27 See Chapter 3 below.

28 E-Commerce Directive, Arts 12–15.

29 Directive 95/46/EC of the European Parliament and of the Council of 24 October 1995 on the protection of individuals with regard to the processing of personal data and on the free movement of such data [1995] OJ L 281/31.

is therefore important even for intermediary parties which only supply the platform for the digital contract to ensure that they process the data in accordance with the applicable data protection law.[30]

d) Objective of Reducing Risk through Secure Contracts

The risks of digital contracts can be significantly reduced through the use of secure technologies such as block chains or Secure Contract Containers (SeCo).[31] The SeCo ensure that the essential data as to the parties and the terms of the contract are contained in a non-changeable content layer of the digital contract which is linked to the signature block. The signature block prevents the parties from altering the contract later as once it has been digitally signed by two parties, the contract is closed to amendments. However, a new contract can be used within the same digital contract which then pushes the previous contract into the contract block used for storing previous contract versions. The log section allows parties to insert information into the contract such as receipts which allow the parties to determine the status of the contract. This is particularly useful when the contract consists of various stages according to which the buyer makes payments.

Shown in a diagram, a SeCo can have the following shape and design:

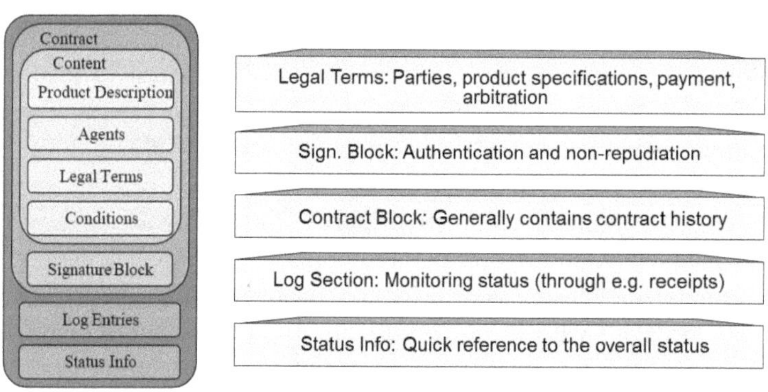

30 See Section 3.2 below.

31 Michael Gisler, Katarina Stanoevska Slabeva and Markus Greunz, 'Legal Aspects of Electronic Contracts, Infrastructures for Dynamic Business-to-Business Service Outsourcing (IDSO'00)', available at <http://ceur-ws.org/Vol-30/paper7.pdf> accessed 30 November 2015.

If only one party produces the contract, a Verification-Standard (most commonly the SHA-2 Method[32]) will ensure that the digital contract sent has not been altered as the hash values of the contract can be compared and thus any alteration would become apparent. This procedure functions by computing a hash value (number) which is based on the sender's unique key and the underlying data. The recipient can then take the received data and also use the unique code to derive the hash value of this data. If they match up, the data sent and received are the same. If this is not the case, the data has been altered during the transmission process.

3. *Specific Legal Features of Automated Digital Contracts*

a) General Principles

Digital contacts similar to other forms of contracts encompass the basic elements such as offer, acceptance and consideration. In accordance with an established legal understanding relating for example to the offering of goods or services on TV the concept of the commercial offer being a mere invitation to submit a legal offer for the displayed goods or services has generally been extended to all forms of digital contracts.[33] The basis for this interpretation is the commercial reality as otherwise the seller of a good or service can be subject to a large number of orders which it may not have the capacity to fulfil. However, exceptions remain in particular when the offering is more concrete, i.e. specific delivery dates are provided as well as immediate payment is required (Credit Card, Paypal). Thus, when being confronted with a digital contract or electronic offer one must classify the situation in accordance with how a customer would reasonably understand the advertisement – only as advertisement or as a binding offer.[34]

The offeror can send the potential customer a digital contract containing his electronic signature with an automatic expiry date at which it can no

---

32 This standard was developed by the US National Security Agency and patented but is available as an open license.

33 Rolf H Weber and Yvonne Jöhri, 'Vertragsschluss im Internet' in Rolf H Weber, Reto M Hilty and Rolf auf der Maur (eds), *Geschäftsplattform Internet* (Schulthess 2000) 43.

34 Rolf H Weber, *E-Commerce und Recht* (Schulthess 2010) 342.

longer be signed by the offeree. The offeree has the possibility to either accept by adding his electronic signature or make a counter-offer which then automatically is archived in the electronic contract's history log.

In 2000 the EU took the first step in enabling e-commerce and the digital contracts associated with such transactions by passing the E-Commerce Directive. This law places limitations on the restrictions Member States can impose on electronic commerce by requiring such laws to fall into a list of categories.[35] Furthermore, Member States must accept the conclusion of binding contracts through electronic means and ensure that no obstacles are created which would infringe on a contract's effectiveness or validity.[36]

In terms of the contract formation the Directive requires the recipient of the service to be informed about the technical steps to conclude the contract, the technical means used to identify and correct errors, the languages offered for the conclusion of the contract as well as whether the contract will be filed and accessible.[37] These rules, however, do not apply to Email exchanges.

When the contract is initiated through an automated electronic system these orders are generally attributable to the party in charge of such a system unless it is clear that the order is on its face wrong. For example when a private individual through an automated system places an order for 100 cakes it is usually apparent that there is a mistake in the order.[38] In such a situation it must be clear to the seller that this order is likely wrong and thus the seller must act in good faith and request confirmation from the buyer.[39]

---

35 E-Commerce Directive, Art 3 (3)(4)(i).

36 E-Commerce Directive, Art 9.

37 E-Commerce Directive, Art 10.

38 Rolf H Weber and Yvonne Jöhri, 'Vertragsschluss im Internet' in Rolf H Weber, Reto M Hilty and Rolf auf der Maur (eds), *Geschäftsplattform Internet* (Schulthess 2000) 43 51.

39 Alexander F Koch, *Internet Recht* (Oldenbourg 2005) 119.

b) Assessment of Different Forms of Digital Contracts

aa) Early Digital Contracts

Digital contracts as regularly used today are particularly valuable in situations in which many parties have to repeatedly sign similar contracts. Through an automated system these contracts can be dispatched to all parties involved in a project and receive their approval of the contract by allowing for digital signatures. All data relating to the contract and its approval are stored centrally and are available to be viewed by all the parties over the internet by logging into a secure platform. These platforms which encompass a workflow and signature repository are usually called Transaction Platforms (TP).

In addition to tracking the approval process of a contract TP allow parties to alter or propose changes to a contract which can be approved 'on the go' by the parties thus enabling a fast contract adjustment. This is particularly useful in an environment which requires constant adoption to changing circumstances. For example a construction project may need to adjust to the changes required by the builder or owner of the property. After a meeting in which the parties agree on the changes they can easily go online, log on to the database, adapt the contract accordingly (including costs and other factors) and have it approved by all parties through an electronic identity verification system. Such contracts can also be combined with progress reports which then trigger payments according to the degree of completion. These systems are semi-automated as they still require human input in order to cause any effects.

Currently many new technologies are presented which are all based on the underlying ledger and block chain technology of Bitcoins or other cryptocurrencies. Such a public or private ledger ensures the security of the transaction and can e.g. be used for a bond distribution. However, generally the other party is not known which is why a ledger is used in order to increase the safety of the transaction. The block chain leads to transaction transparency but not necessarily to identity transparency. Under current US law, however, the issuer of the bond must know who the beneficiary of the interest is as it may otherwise pay out the money to a company on a restricted list (e.g. terrorist organization).

bb) Automated Contract Drafting

A new form of automation in digital contracts has evolved parallel to the technological developments. Businesses as well as law firms deal on a regular basis with standard contracts, for example a license agreement or a sales contract. Drafting these contracts is usually very time consuming. Thus, new systems have been designed which allow customers to create these contracts or documents through automated software.

For example the London Stock Exchange (LSE) programmed its software to produce certain contract types automatically allowing only for a certain degree of alteration. This approach enabled the LSE employees to draft these contracts much faster and to be sure that they are in compliance with corporate policy as the software will not allow for non-compliant contracts.[40] This design significantly reduces time spent on drafting and also reduces legal costs as lawyers are only required if changes to the template are necessary or a new contract must be included in the system.

These automated contract tools are bound to revolutionize the way in which many businesses and law firms operate. What used to require hours of diligent contract review can today be done by computer software in minutes. However, with such technology always comes the risk of mistakes in instances when for example the software overlooks information which is highly relevant. In these cases clear rules are necessary to apportion the liability as on the one hand the software developer could have made a mistake in the programming or on the other hand the law firm did not adequately check the work product.

cc) Automated Contracts in the IoT

In the context of the IoT automated contracts allow a simple agreement to be entered into by a computer system based on data it receives from an IoT device. For example the sensor in an oil tank may signal that the heating oil is running low. Previously the customer would be alerted by some form of message via SMS or email of this fact and then could manually place an order with one of the available suppliers. However, with automated systems the order can be automatically placed when a certain

40 See also <http://www.business-integrity.com/customers/radiant-law/> accessed 30 November 2015.

level of oil is reached. The system can also determine which oil company is the cheapest and automatically place its order with this company. Thus, when something in the process goes wrong the question is who has formed this contract and who will be liable under it.

A computer cannot on its own enter into a contract, at first instance this order seems invalid. However, if the customer installs a system communicating to a group of potential sellers that they will be receiving an order from the system via a certain communication method the customer will be bound by any such communication as the seller must assume that it reflects the customer's intention. Acting in good faith on the prior intent to be bound by such an order the owner of the system will be estopped from bringing the argument that the order was placed automatically unless it is so unreasonable that it would fall outside the scope of his prior representation.

However, the legal reasoning behind the question whether a person can be bound by an order which was initiated by a computer varies very heavily between countries and thus requires a close examination of the applicable law.[41] As there has been no case law on the subject matter the conclusion and legal effect of such contracts remain mere speculation. Nevertheless, legislators must be aware of the growing forms of automated decision-making and find solutions to bridge the gap between traditional legal concepts and today's technology.

In the industrial context IoT data has gained increased importance and forms an integral part of a supply and production chain. Devices signal when stock is running low and automatically alert the seller to reship another batch. In this context the orders are subject to an overall contractual agreement which in most instances allows the receiving party to ship the goods back to the seller free of charge if an order has been wrongly placed. Thus, these risks and costs in the commercial context are placed on the seller as part of its business operation. As these transactions involve highly sophisticated parties which are in an ongoing business relationship they usually agree on extensive contractual provisions dealing with these sorts of risks as well as the measures to be taken in situations when an error has occurred. Additionally, their IoT devices and communication infrastructure are audited by external experts who ensure secure and reliable communications.

41 Melinda F Müller, 'Roboter und Recht' 2014 AJP 595.

In contrast, private individuals mostly deal with cheap IoT devices which are much more likely to be hacked and may communicate corrupted data. Thus, the use of such automated contracts for private individuals does not seem to be an ideal solution in light of the sophistication required to ensure their security and proper operation.

dd) Smart Contracts

The growth of digital cryptocurrencies such as Bitcoin have enabled a new era in digital contracting. Previously, an electronic sale of goods always carried two major risks, namely firstly the risk of non-delivery and secondly the risk that the payment did not go through based on a fraudulent transaction. Today, the whole contract formation and its enforcement can become part of a smart contract. This contract once agreed upon by two parties will track a package through GPS and after it has arrived at the predetermined location release the funds in form of Bitcoins to the new owner by supplying the necessary digital key. In doing so it is ensured that the parties to a transaction are in possession of the money which must be supplied in form of Bitcoins beforehand and that the seller is actually shipping a package to the customer. Furthermore, through the tracking and shipping the identity of both parties can be verified.

These smart contracts can create the trust necessary for business transactions to occur as they enable a secure transaction in which the party paying for a good or service place the money in 'escrow' (the smart contract) and the seller can be sure that he will receive the funds. In the context of consumer contracts such smart contracts would enable the inclusion of cooling-off periods in which the customer can return the goods and receive a refund. During this time the Bitcoins would not be released to the seller thus are safe from a potential insolvency or third party claims.

4. Special Contractual Duties

Generally the parties are free to choose what duties they impose on each other through an appropriate wording in their digital contract. However, when certain types of contracts are involved, specific laws apply. These rules are governed by the jurisdiction and the forum selected in the contract. If no law is chosen, the *lex fori* will apply. Nevertheless, if a consumer is party to the contract a choice of law is prohibited.[42]

The mere form of the contract being electronic does not place special contractual duties on any party to the transaction. It only potentially creates different risks which each party should guard against. A written contract for example will generally be stored in a secure place in order to preserve it whereas a digital contract should be stored on various redundant hard drives or media devices which enable retrievals. Furthermore, the contract is signed twice by both parties whereas each party receives the same document. This prevents one party from altering the contract after it has been signed as the other party will still be able to show the hardcopy. In the digital contract context such repudiation after the contract has been signed with both electronic signatures must be prevented. Appropriate security measures and redundant storage of the digital contract in a so called ledger will prevent any alteration after the fact. In this case a third party timestamp is essential for proving that the contract has been executed in a particular fashion when there are two competing versions.

As mentioned, protocols and asymmetric encryption should be added as part of the specifications of such a digital contract. This will ensure the secure communication between the parties. This approach would be in line with the EU Regulation 910/2014 e-IDAS[43] which encourages the use of certification systems.

Specific to smart contract are certain risks and organizational considerations. These are based in the way they operate. Firstly a contract is formed as a computer code. This code is then shared on the public registry in order to record the transaction. As the ledger automatically is updated and distributed through a vast system, third parties gain access to the content of the contract. Most vendors will therefore be reluctant to use such a technology because they do not want their terms to become public.

Through having a contract adduced in code, further risks can be created such as a potential difference between the English contract language and the code. This tension will strongly depend on whether the contract will be produced directly through code modules or whether there will be an actual

42 Arts 15–17 of the Lugano Convention of 2007.

43 EU e-IDAS: Regulation (EU) No 910/2014 of the European Parliament and of the Council of 23 July 2014 on electronic identification and trust services for electronic transactions in the internal market and repealing Directive 1999/93/EC [2014] OJ L 257/73.

digital contract in English beforehand. Moreover, coding bugs are common, thus creating further risks for the contract enforcement process as in a dispute the party alleging a bug must prove it.

Potentially the research of the Massachusetts Institute of Technology (MIT) in terms of encrypted processing may offer a solution to this issue in the future.[44] Additionally, new decentralized settlement approaches are being improved to keep certain information of a transaction secret.[45] In any case the transfer of assets to the ledger will have an effect on the liquidity as well as create novel questions in an insolvency situation.

A further special issue of automated digital contracts concerns the duty of the customer to adopt security measures. The customer is often the 'weaker' contract party, namely from a knowledge-based or financial perspective. Nevertheless, suppliers in the IoT have an interest that customers comply with the desirable or at least the necessary security measures. However, these measures are limited to standard security, antivirus software and to keeping the computer up to date.

In practice, customers would often like additional safeguards and assurances from their contracting parties. However, most parties are not willing to take on additional risks or are from a technical viewpoint ill-equipped to deal with the customer demand of added security. In the consumer context the businesses are more inclined to invest into added security as they generally bear most, if not all, of the transaction risks. Furthermore, the services sold online are generally not of high value. Thus a problem with the contract would only result in a minor loss for the business. Also data protection or other privacy concerns are not as dominant in the minds of the US service providers as they are mostly unfamiliar with the strong EU framework on data protection and privacy. The fines for a breach are very low in cases in which there was no gross negligence. All these factors do not currently encourage US based service providers which are the main parties using electronic contracts to add additional safety measures. In contrast, in the commercial settings involving large sums the contracting entities will mostly acquire external expertise to ensure that their IT operations are secure.

---

44 Guy Zyskind, Oz Nathan and Alex Pentland, 'Enigma: Decentralized Computation Platform with Guaranteed Privacy', White paper available at <http://enigma.media.mit.edu/enigma_full.pdf> accessed 30 November 2015.

45 See for example the private pools of Hyperledger, available at <http://hyperledger.com/> accessed 30 November 2015.

III. Allocation of Risk and Liability

1. Risks in Contract Formation and Allocation of Liability

Digital contracts only carry marginally more risk than a standard contract as long as the parties take proper precautions and have the appropriate IT infrastructure. The EU as well as the US law allow for a digital contract formation, thus the risks are simply based in the technology itself. Once the identity of a party has been established by a trusted certificate provider, the offer, counteroffer and acceptance only need to be communicated securely. When such a transaction involves sophisticated commercial parties they will have their own IT experts in order to ensure that the systems of the seller and buyer are fully compatible.

In instances in which there is a technical problem potentially no meeting of the minds has taken place because of opposing presumptions of the parties and thus no contract was formed. These cases pose challenges for all parties involved as the question then becomes who is at fault and what caused the issue and whether a party should have noticed that the communication did not reflect the intention of the other party. Furthermore, a fraudulent electronic contract can be induced more easily by way of sophisticated alterations to its programming than this would be possible in a written contract. By collecting information on a person's identity which is widely available online identity fraud has become a much more common occurrence. Generally online retailers only seek basic information as to a person's identity and will deliver goods on invoice expecting to get paid at a later date. Thus, in these instances the retailer will likely bear the burden of such a loss.

However, when a private user enters into a digital contract some protections apply which generally place the costs of any loss originating from the electronic contract formation on the business. For example because of a language coding problem the browser of the consumer may not display the entire contract. As a consequence, the customer is entering into a contract which he never intended to sign. In this respect, the common law and the civil law approach differ. Under common law no meeting of the minds has occurred thus the contract has not been formed and both parties have to return any benefit received under the contract.[46] However, under

46 Chris Turner, *Contract Law* (Routledge 2014) 143.

EU law if the mistake is based in the buyer's system, he or she will generally bear the cost of such a mistake. In relation to private buyers consumer protection law can remedy this position thus the difference only remains in regard to commercial contracts.

Once the issues as to contract formation, identity and other related aspects have been resolved the liability of the parties will be governed by the contract and general contract law. Thus, the additional liability of a party to the contract lies in the formation risks as well as the disclosure of information based on the electronic nature of the contract. These risks are insofar higher as electronic data is easily distributed or altered whereas the risk in a written contract is lower because of the need for physical access.

2. *Liability of Intermediaries in Digital Contract Formation*

The risks surrounding automated digital contracts are based on the contract type itself as well as on a potential tortious liability for a disclosure of personal information or other sensitive data. Generally, the risk of a transaction should be guarded against by the party creating the risk. Thus, when one party relies on its own IoT data that party should be liable for any costs or loss that occurs because of this data. However, often IoT data is supplied by a third party who is not party to the transaction under the digital contract. In such a case, the risk is generally allocated to the party ordering goods through the automated digital contract.

The E-Commerce Directive contains in Article 14 a provision limiting the liability of hosting providers which do not have knowledge of the illegality of the information stored on their systems or illegal conduct of their customers. However, this exemption does not cover the situation where a party involved in an electronic transaction stores personal data contrary to the Data Protection Directive (or the soon to be the General Data Protection Regulation). Thus, mere conduits, caching providers or hosting providers do not have a general obligation to monitor what information is communicated through their systems. In general, these provisions were a sensible solution in the 2000s as they insulated certain ancillary parties to the e-commerce transaction from liability for transactions to which they were no party and only provided the communication channel. However, in today's world in which not only simple electronic contracts are part of the commercial environment but new technologies such as smart contracts are evolving this exclusion must be re-examined in light of the functions of all parties involved.

New data protection laws such as the EU General Data Protection Regulation would classify the intermediary as a processor of personal data thus imposing a burden to process the data securely and in accordance with best practices. Thus, all parties involved in the digital contract process as well as any intermediaries facilitating the contract and providing the infrastructure are subject to the EU data protection laws. Any breach of these laws can result in fines which generally are imposed on the party in breach. Internally the parties can seek indemnification against such claims especially when the contract software is in a beta stage.

Today's growing number of automated processes and contract formations as well as their hugely varying level of sophistication involved in these computerized systems place some pressure on the current legal systems. Most definitions enshrined in contract and torts law are ill equipped to deal with automated systems carrying out automated contract formations for their owners. These surrounding issues concern the potential of a 'thing' entering into a contract on behalf of its owner as well as the liability that attaches to actions taken by such systems. Due to these issues the provider of a service will place the liability for actions taken by an automated system into the hands of the owner of that system through its contracts by requiring the customer to agree to the risk. Thus, in such a situation the provider must only check whether the communication was sent from the correct source and can then rely on its content.

3. Liability for Digital Contract Content

In addition to the law surrounding personal data the information transmitted through digital contracts may be sensitive and contain information which is a trade secret of one of the parties. If these contracts are automated and the contracts are formed without human interaction, no such information should be included or additional technical and organizational safeguards must be implemented in order to reduce the risk of a data breach.

As the disclosure of contract content can either be voluntary or involuntary through e.g. a hacker attack the parties should agree on how such situations are to be resolved. If the information is divulged by an employee of one of the parties the contract should include a liquidated damages clause whereas if an outside attack occurs it is more important that notice is given to all parties immediately. In such a situation forensic IT experts must be called immediately to assess the extent to which the confidentiality of the contract has been breached. Parties regularly entering into digital contracts in a commercial setting should implement secure systems for communicating their contracts in order to reduce outside hacking risks.

When costumer data is included in digital contracts the EU data protection laws will apply. However, the potential impact of disclosure is only high when the digital contracts are stored centrally and a third party gains access to this storage. A singular data breach, although burdensome and a violation of the data protection laws, does not carry significant risks for the business.

New methods of transferring information through an encrypted system are currently being developed and refined. These would allow the storing of information in the encrypted digital contract itself which would only be accessible by the party once the data is decrypted with the correct key.[47]

Placing most of the liability on the consumer through terms and conditions will likely be subject to a high level of scrutiny and limitations. Thus, only in the commercial setting contracting parties are free to agree which party should bear what type of risk in a fully automated digital contract.

IV. Outlook

In view of the changing technological environment, legislators must become aware of the growing forms of automated decision-making and find solutions to bridge the gap between traditional legal concepts and modern technology. Nevertheless, it should not be overlooked that digital contracts only carry marginally more risks than 'traditional' contracts as long as the parties take adequate precautions and have the appropriate IT infrastructure; in other words, the critical issues lie more in the understanding and application of technology than in the inappropriateness of the

47 Rolf H Weber and Simone Baumann, 'FinTech – Schweizer Finanzmarktregulierung im Lichte disruptiver Technologien' Jusletter 21 September 2015, N 29.

legal framework. Nevertheless, the following recommendations in view of the Digital Single Market Strategy can be given:

- Improved transparency and disclosure in respect of technological features in the contract formation would be desirable.
- The definition of 'contract' needs an adaptation insofar as it should also include agreements entered into by a 'thing'.
- The limitations of responsibility and liability as foreseen in Arts 12–14 of the E-Commerce Directive should be re-examined in the light of the new technologies.
- The incoherence between the E-Commerce Directive and the Data Protection Regulation related to the treatment of intermediaries should be eliminated.
- Legalistic differentiations between 'sales' and 'services' in e-commerce markets need to be abolished.
- Payment schemes, mainly if based on the block chain technology, merit much more attention.

Apart from these specific recommendations other issues in the context of the IoT are even of higher importance. The legislator needs to address data security and privacy[48] in order to improve trust and confidence in the use of the new technologies. Already in 2014 Jean-Claude Juncker highlighted that the EU's Single Digital Market Strategy would lead to a growth of 250 billion Euros by streamlining and facilitating online services and sales through the appropriate legal framework. In May 2015 the EU Commission has published a Communication to the EU Parliament and the Council outlining the goals of such a Digital Single Market Strategy including a timetable for their implementation.[49] The first steps towards this goal have been taken with the agreement on the EU data protection reform in December 2015.[50]

---

48 See Rolf H Weber, 'The digital future A challenge for privacy?' (2015) 31 Computer Law & Security Review 234, 234–242; Rolf H Weber, Dominic N Staiger, 'Bridging the gap between individual privacy and public security' (2014) 2 [2] Groningen Journal of International Law 14, 14–32.

49 European Commission, A Digital Single Market Strategy for Europe, COM(2015) 192 final, Brussels, 6.5.2015.

50 European Commission, Agreement on Commission's EU data protection reform will boost Digital Single Market, Brussels, 15 December 2015.

Consumer Contracts and the Internet of Things

Christiane Wendehorst[*]

I. Introduction

The Internet of Things (IoT) is a current buzzword. It describes the network of physical devices of any kind (cars, TV sets, watches, garments, food packaging, etc.), which are embedded with electronics, software, sensors, and network connectivity to enable them (i) to collect and exchange data (ii) to be uniquely identifiable and addressable and/or (iii) to be sensed and controlled remotely across existing network infrastructure.[1] In the narrowest sense, IoT covers only devices with their own IP address. In a wider and more meaningful sense, however, IoT includes devices that exchange data via other protocols (such as Bluetooth) and connect to the Internet by way of a bridge. Although ambient intelligence and autonomous control are often associated with IoT, they are not essential features of every device that is part of the IoT.

The market value of IoT in the EU could potentially exceed one trillion euros in 2020,[2] and in March 2015 an Alliance for Internet of Things Innovation (AIOTI) was initiated.[3] Intuition suggests that the emergence of IoT must have a profound impact also on the law of contract. However, hardly anyone has so far spelt out the exact implications and what is required in order to make contract law fit for the 21st century in general and IoT in particular. In this chapter, it will be argued that, despite the fact

---

* Christiane Wendehorst is Professor of Civil Law at the University of Vienna.

1 For more details see, e.g., Rolf Weber and Romana Weber, *Internet of Things. Legal perspectives* (Springer 2010) 1 et seq.

2 Commission, *Definition of a Research and Innovation Policy Leveraging Cloud Computing and IoT Combination* (Publications of the European Union 2014) 9 et seq available at <https://ec.europa.eu/digital-agenda/en/news/definition-research-and-innovation-policy-leveraging-cloud-computing-and-iot-combination> accessed 14 December 2015.

3 <https://ec.europa.eu/digital-agenda/en/alliance-internet-things-innovation-aioti> accessed 14 December 2015.

that a technologically neutral attitude towards contract law is preferable,[4] the emergence of smart things and IoT calls for some new rules and new concepts.

II. Challenges Posed by Smart Devices and IoT

On 9 December 2015, the European Commission tabled two legislative Proposals, one on contracts for the supply of digital content[5] (hereinafter 'Digital Content Proposal') and the other on contracts for the online and other distance sales of goods[6] (hereinafter 'Distance Proposal'). Despite the fact that smart things, such as smartphones or connected cars, combine the features of tangible goods and of digital content, both Proposals treat smart things like ordinary tangible goods.[7] This implies that the supply of smart things is subject to a scheme of contractual liability that is not very different from the established scheme used for the sale of the broadest variety of consumer goods, ranging from a bottle of whisky in the supermarket to a trendy watch, and from a TV set to a family car. But why should new rules suddenly be needed just because an embedded device in the watch communicates with the car, conveying my body temperature to the car's heating system in order to ensure an optimized climatic experience? Or because a printed sensor tag with Near Field Communication

4 The three principles of non-discrimination, technological neutrality, and functional equivalence have been the pillars for any legislative action in the area for decades, see e.g. the UNCITRAL Model Law on Electronic Commerce 1996 available at <http://www.uncitral.org/uncitral/en/uncitral_texts/electronic_commerce/1996 Model.html)> accessed 14 December 2015.

5 Commission, 'Proposal for a Directive of the European Parliament and of the Council on certain aspects concerning contracts for the supply of digital content' COM(2015) 634 final ('Digital Content Proposal').

6 Commission, 'Proposal for a Directive of the European Parliament and of the Council on certain aspects concerning contracts for the online and other distance sales of goods' COM(2015) 635 final ('Distance Proposal').

7 See Digital Content Proposal, recital 11 and Distance Proposal, recital 13: '*However, this Directive should apply to digital content integrated in goods such as household appliances or toys where the digital content is embedded in such a way that its functions are subordinate to the main functionalities of the goods and it operates as an integral part of the goods.*'

(NFC) on the whisky bottle[8] sends cocktail recipes and promotional offers to my smartphone? Or because my car realises I have twice yawned, it reminds me to take a rest, automatically reduces the speed, and transfers the information, amongst others, to my car insurance company?

1. Functionality, interoperability, suitability

The more sophisticated and complex consumer goods are, the more difficult it is to draft product information in a way consumers will understand. In the case of smart devices, the question arises of how much information the trader has to provide under the rules of the Consumer Rights Directive[9] (CRD); in particular, whether smart devices are subject to additional information requirements on the functionality and interoperability of digital content under CRD Articles 5(1)(g) and (h), 6(1)(r) and (s). This information includes, where applicable, the functionality, including applicable technical protection measures, of digital content and any relevant interoperability of digital content with hardware and software that the trader is aware of or can reasonably be expected to have been aware of.

Among the many aspects listed in the DG Justice Guidance Document on the CRD of June 2014[10], the following might be of particular importance not only with respect to isolated digital content but also with respect to smart devices: (i) language of the content, and, if different, language of any instructions included with the content; (ii) commitment or absence of commitment by the trader or a third party to maintain or update the product; (iii) any conditions for using the product to the described extent not directly linked to interoperability, such as tracking and/or personalization, the requirement of an internet connection and its technical requirements (e.g. minimum download and upload speed) in order to use the products, need for other users to have specific software installed (e.g., for

---

8 <http://www.diageo.com/en-row/ourbrands/infocus/Pages/diageo-and-thinfilm-unveil-the-connected-smart-bottle.aspx> accessed 15 December 2015.

9 Directive 2011/83/EU of the European Parliament and of the Council of 25 October 2011 on consumer rights, amending Council Directive 93/13/EEC and Directive 1999/44/EC of the European Parliament and of the Council and repealing Council Directive 85/577/EEC and Directive 97/7/EC of the European Parliament and of the Council [2011] OJ L304/64 ('CRD').

10 See at <http://ec.europa.eu/justice/consumer-marketing/files/crd_guidance_en.pdf> accessed 15 December 2015, 67, 68.

communication software); (iv) any limitations to the use of the product (e.g. restrictions based on the location of the consumer's device; any functionalities that are conditional on additional purchases, such as paid content, club memberships, additional hard- or software); (v) devices that the content can be used with, such as the hardware, the necessary operating system and additional software (including the version number).

The Recitals and Commission guidance are not very clear as to the fact whether these additional information duties apply to smart devices with embedded digital content. On the one hand, the European legislator seems to consider tangible goods and digital content as two mutually exclusive types of merchandise, as is confirmed by the two Proposals submitted on 9 December 2015. On the other hand, the information duties concerning digital content must undoubtedly apply also to digital content supplied on a tangible medium, such as a CD or USB stick, and a smart device with embedded digital content is nothing but a tangible medium. Of course, the same details could still be subsumed under 'the main characteristics of the goods or services, to the extent appropriate [...] to the goods or services', but this is much less clear, in particular as the main characteristics of, for example, a car will rather cover such aspects as dimensions, space, maximum speed, fuel consumption, and the like.

Whether the trader needs to provide the information relating to digital content at all is just one question that arises in the context. Another question is whether that information is helpful to consumers, in particular consumers with a limited degree of digital literacy. This issue is all the more problematic when consumers no longer have a choice but to buy smart devices. Already today anyone who wants a TV set above a certain minimum screen size is forced to buy a smartTV, whether or not that person is in a position to handle the device. Due to full harmonisation under the CRD,[11] no additional pre-contractual information duties, such as concerning the suitability of the device for the individual consumer, may be imposed by Member States, at least not for distance or off-premises contracts.[12]

11 See CRD, Art 4.

12 But see CRD, Art 5(4) for on-premises contracts.

2. *Data as counter-performance*

A characteristic feature of many smart devices is the continuous processing of data generated through the consumer's use of the device. Smartphones or modern cars generate almost complete movement profiles of their owners, and they record any telephone or browser history, driver behaviour and even all voices in a car as if it were the cockpit of a plane. Even where the original data are pseudonymised, the density of data coverage means that almost anything can be traced back to the data subject. The outcome is the creation of a profile of every citizen. The profile may be more complete than anything the citizen might remember about herself, but it may also be falsely attributed to a particular citizen. Furthermore, algorithms may use this profile to draw some unusual conclusions, such as a high susceptibility for depression, which then could have potentially detrimental effects if such data is leaked to the wrong person. More sophisticated devices, such as smart watches or fitness equipment, give a full record of many health data; for other smart devices there is a huge untapped potential.

The CRD provides that the consumer is to be informed of the total price of the goods,[13] with price being defined as a sum of money to be paid to the trader.[14] In Article 3(1) of the Digital Content Proposal the European Commission has rightly extended the scope to digital content for which 'in exchange, a price is to be paid or the consumer actively provides counter-performance other than money in the form of personal data or any other data'. However, no conclusions have been drawn so far concerning pre-contractual information duties, and the Distance Proposal does not even mention data as counter-performance.

Both are surprising – if data is a form of counter-performance, why should there be no corresponding pre-contractual information duty, and why should the same not be mentioned in the context of smart tangible goods? Admittedly, smart devices are usually delivered only in exchange for an – often significant – sum of money. However, money is not the only

---

13 CRD, Arts 5(1)(c) and 6(1)(e).

14 This is not explicitly stated in the CRD. However, it is clear from the context that the same definition applies as was to be found in the Distance Proposal, Art 2(i) of: 'price' means money that is due in exchange for goods sold, digital content supplied or a related service provided. See also Digital Content Proposal, Arts 2(6) and 3(1).

counter-performance as smart devices are usually delivered in exchange for a mixed counter-performance: a sum of money plus personal data or user-generated content.

3. The role of product monitoring and maintenance

The new Distance Proposal does not mention maintenance or after-sale services as a criterion to establish conformity of goods with the contract. This is all the more surprising as an increasing number of tangible devices, in particular those featuring embedded software and other digital content or sensors, require intensive product monitoring and after-sale maintenance in the form of patches or updates. This may not be the case with simple content, such as a music or video file, but certainly with any core software components. Stricter requirements concerning product monitoring and maintenance are particularly necessary where the data stored on the device is especially critical, where the device is closely connected with other devices and where more harm can be caused by a malfunction of the device. New malware taking benefit of inevitable security gaps makes continuous updating a must. News items on hackers gaining control of a jeep and stopping it at full speed on the motorway[15] have concerned drivers all over the world and led to a major recall of cars by the manufacturer, and a security flaw in the software of Samsung smart fridges resulted in the leakage of access data for their owners' gmail accounts.[16] If the owner of a smart home can use his mobile phone to open the front door and turn on the lights while lying on a beach 2000 miles away, it is not far-fetched to suggest that others could also open that owner's front door. As the case may be, smart devices may become worthless or even extremely dangerous without patches to fix bugs in the original embedded software and/or to adapt the software to a changing digital environment.

Bugs that would already have been considered to be a lack of conformity at the time the goods were delivered to the consumer are certainly catered for, both by the existing law and by the new Distance Proposal. However, there is no such thing as bug-free software, and security gaps

---

15 <https://www.youtube.com/watch?v=MK0SrxBC1xs> accessed 15 December 2015.

16 <http://www.consumerreports.org/cro/topfreezerrefrigerators/smart-refrigerators-privacy> accessed 15 December 2015.

that were unforeseeable at the time of delivery may not be considered to amount to a lack of conformity with the contract. Even if the burden of proof is on the seller, and even if this is now for a period of two years[17] and if – as the Court of Justice has ruled recently in *Faber*[18] – the consumer does not have to demonstrate what has caused the apparent lack of conformity, it will often be possible for the seller to show that the particular security gap could not have been foreseen at the point of delivery. Similarly, Article 7(e) Product Liability Directive (PLD)[19] declares the producer to be exempt from liability where 'the state of scientific and technical knowledge at the time when he put the product into circulation was not such as to enable the existence of the defect to be discovered'. Accordingly, the consumer may not have any remedies (depending on the applicable national law of contract and tort/delict) where a purchased smart device could be considered as sufficiently secure at the point it was put into circulation or delivered although it was foreseeable that it might become insecure at a later point in time. National tort/delict law may impose an obligation on producers to monitor products and issue warnings and/or product recalls if necessary, but Member States are not required to do so under the PLD, nor may they impose such an obligation under product liability law due to the effect of full harmonisation.[20]

4. *Dispersion of responsibility and outsourcing of functions*

According to Article 8(3) Distance Proposal, any lack of conformity with the contract which becomes apparent within two years from delivery is presumed to have existed at the time of delivery unless this is incompatible with the nature of the goods or with the nature of the lack of confor-

17 Distance Proposal, Art 8(3).

18 Case C–497/13 *Froukje Faber v Autobedrijf Hazet Ochten BV* [2015] ECR I–nyr.

19 Directive 1999/34/EC of the European Parliament and of the council of 10 May 1999 amending Council Directive 85/374/EEC on the approximation of the laws, regulations and administrative provisions of the Member States concerning liability for defective products [1999] OJ L141/20.

20 See Cases C–52/00 *Commission v French Republic* [2002] ECR I–3827; C–154/00 *Commission v Hellenic Republic* [1989] ECR I–2965; C–183/00 *María Victoria González Sánchez v Medicina Asturiana SA* [2002] ECR I–3901; C–402/03 *Skov Æg v Bilka Lavprisvarehus A/S and Bilka Lavprisvarehus A/S v Jette Mikkelsen and Michael Due Nielsen* [2006] ECR I–199.

mity. This is a very important rule for the consumer as it largely places the burden of proof on the seller. However, even according to the decision in *Faber*, the consumer would still have the burden of proving that a particular good is, for whatever reason, not or no longer in conformity with the contract. For the majority of goods this is not very difficult, and in the case underlying the *Faber* judgment it was sufficient for the consumer to show that the car had caught fire and was therefore obviously no longer in a condition that could be considered as in conformity with the contract. However, in the case of multiple interoperating devices, it may be extremely difficult to prove which of the devices is not in conformity with the contract. A simple example can illustrate this point well: the smart home garden fails to be watered automatically and damage results. The complexity arises from the multitude of possible actors: the control panel was bought from seller X and produced by A, the water fountain was bought from seller Y and produced by B, service provider Z installed the control panel and fountain, and the control panel receives meteorological data from the Internet weather service C. In such an example, Article 8(3) Distance Proposal will not be of great help to the consumer due to the difficulties in demonstrating that the non-conformity relates to either the control panel or the water fountain: it could be either, or there could be a problem of interoperability between both for which A, B, or Z may or may not be responsible, or it could in fact be neither but rather a problem resulting from internet service provider C.

The more functions are outsourced from a device to other devices, to particular Internet service providers, or to generally available Internet sources, the more difficult it becomes to localise a problem and hold a particular seller or producer liable if something goes wrong.

5. *Intellectual property law and EULAs*

A characteristic difference between traditional sales contracts and contracts for the supply of smart products is the role of intellectual property law. The main reason why IP law is not a concern when we buy a designer chair lies in the exhaustion principle (first sale doctrine): the resale of a chair sold with the consent of the rightholder is permitted, and the rightholder may not prohibit further circulation of the chair or ask for a royalty. Needless to say, however, the design of the chair may still be protected under IP law, and it would usually not be permissible to simply copy the chair using a 3D scanner and printer and to sell the copies. Another reason why IP law is not a tremendous cause for concern, in particular why there is no practice of asking end users to sign a licence or similar agreement when they buy a designer chair, or in fact a printed book, is that any limitations on the use of the chair or the book that go beyond the limitations already stipulated by law would be of little economic value to the rightholder, unattractive to buyers, extremely difficult to enforce, and prone to be held unconscionable by courts.

Digital content, however, complicates the situation considerably as it also has two elements: the binary code as such, which is usually protected (at least by copyright law), and the concrete copy. The CJEU has held in the famous *UsedSoft* judgment[21] that, at least as far as software is concerned, a licence allowing the use of a copy of digital content for an indefinite period makes the user's legal position comparable to ownership in a tangible asset, even where the software is not transferred on a tangible medium but downloaded from the rightholder's server, and even as far as the right to receive updates and patches under a maintenance contract is concerned. However, the *UsedSoft* judgment itself is highly disputed and may not reflect a final position on the matter.[22] Even more so it is highly disputed whether and to what extent similar principles should apply to other digital content such as music, films, e-books etc.[23]

---

21 Case C–128/11 *UsedSoft GmbH v Oracle International Corp* [2012] ECR I–nyr.

22 Thomas Vinje, Vanessa Marsland and Anette Gärtner, 'Software Licensing After Oracle v. UsedSoft' (2013) 13 [4] Computer Law Review International 97, 99 et seq; Maša S Galič, 'The Legality of Resale of Digital Content after UsedSoft in Subsequent German and CJEU Case Law' [2015] European Intellectual Property Review 414, 427; Alexander Göbel, 'The principle of exhaustion and the resale of downloaded software – the UsedSoft % Oracle case' (2012) 9 European Law Reporter 226, 228 et seq; Péter Mezei, 'Digital First Sale Doctrine Ante Portas' (2015) 6 Journal of Intellectual Property, Information Technology and E-Commerce Law 23, 40 et seq; Christopher Stothers, 'When is Copyright Exhausted by a Software Licence? UsedSoft v. Oracle' (2012) 11 European Intellectual Property Review 788, 790.

23 See Maša S Galič, 'The Legality of Resale of Digital Content after UsedSoft in Subsequent German and CJEU Case Law' [2015] European Intellectual Property Review 414, 418 et seq, 421 et seq; Péter Mezei, 'Digital First Sale Doctrine Ante Portas' (2015) 6 Journal of Intellectual Property, Information Technology and E-Commerce Law 23, 38 et seq. This issue will presumably be addressed in Case C–174/15 *Vereniging Openbare Bibliotheken* [2015] ECR I–nyr.

In any case, digital content usually comes with an end user licence agreement (EULA) which is not just the equivalent to ownership in a tangible asset as suggested by the CJEU in *UsedSoft* but creates a separate contractual relationship between the consumer and the rightholder. This contractual relationship is separate from the (sales or other) contract the user will have concluded with a retailer, and the user is normally forced to assent to the EULA if he wants to use the digital content. EULAs normally do not ask for an extra royalty in addition to the price but impose a variety of restrictions on the use of the content, disclaimers of warranty and exclusion of liability and often foresee far reaching rights for the licensor, e.g. the right to install spyware on the user's device, to collect all sorts of data, and even to delete disapproved content from the user's device. Some of these terms are grossly unfair under national law implementing the Unfair Contract Terms Directive,[24] and arguably most buyers would be entitled to use the content without assenting to the EULA, but in practice they are left without a choice. In addition, with smart devices, there is a widespread practice to push end users into EULAs, in particular where the smart device features a display and some buttons (e.g. smartphone, smartTV, car), thus allowing for a clickwrap agreement in the course of the initial setup run.

6. *Post-sale clickwrap agreements*

The practice of pushing end users into separate agreements with the manufacturer or other third parties is not restricted either to EULAs or to copyrighted content. If they could most manufacturers would probably ask end users to enter into such agreements, using wording such as: 'Before you use your product for the first time make sure you fill in and sign this form and register with us […]' – which does arise with guarantee agreements – or to allow items to be tracked in linking the serial number with the identity of the new owner. However, agreements of this kind are purely optional for the end user. With traditional products, there is little manufacturers could put into an end user agreement and which would stand a reasonable chance of being enforceable against the end user, both for prac-

24 Council Directive 93/13/EEC of 5 April 1993 on unfair terms in consumer contracts [1993] OJ L95/29 ('Unfair Contract Terms Directive').

tical and for legal reasons; besides, response rates would be low, and administration costs plus the risk of scaring off customers would more than outweigh any benefits.

With the emergence of smart devices, however, this has changed fundamentally: almost anything can be enforced against the end user in practical terms, all user data being available to, and functionality of the device being fully dependent on and controllable by the manufacturer or other third parties. Where the device has a display and a button the end user can activate in order to signal assent, there is nothing to stop manufacturers from pushing end users into all kinds of additional post-sale agreements with the manufacturer itself and/or with a variety of third parties, that either belong to the same corporate group or that pay the manufacturer for the acquisition of new customers.

Most of these post-sale agreements concern digitally provided services of some kind, such as cloud services or email hosting, or they may be framework agreements with digital marketplaces (e.g. app stores). Usually, everything is combined with separate or integrated agreements concerning the collection, processing and exploitation of user data. Some of the agreements may be clearly optional, e.g. the buyer of a smartphone will find a broad range of pre-installed apps which, upon their initial activation, ask the buyer to agree separately to terms and conditions of the relevant service. While this may be a point of concern for the competition lawyer, or for the lawyer in charge of drafting contracts between the businesses involved, it is usually not problematic with regard to end user contracts. However, some post-sale agreements are not optional, but rather the end user cannot reasonably use the smart device without concluding the additional agreement. Frequently, agreements lie somewhat in between optional and coercive, i.e. while it is technically possible to use the smart device without concluding the additional agreement the average end user is placed under the impression that it is not.

7. Dependency on digital infrastructure services

Evidently, the most serious problems are posed by additional digital services the customer has to subscribe to in order to be able to use the smart device, or that are required for logging into the device, or in any other way for maintaining its functionalities.

a) Discontinuation or modification of features

Traditional products may depend on particular services. Any TV set is of little use unless the buyer subscribes to some kind of TV broadcasting service. However, there are different broadcasting services from which the buyer can choose – usually they are not in any way linked with the manufacturer of the TV set, and if one of them disappears from the market another will crop up. Equally, traditional products may be dependent on the availability of spare parts. This may pose a serious problem to buyers, but at least where the manufacturer was a large company and disappears from the market or stops producing spare parts usually another producer will step in – there are economic incentives for doing so as spare parts are sold for money, they are often not protected by patent or design rights, and furthermore refusing a license may amount to abuse of a dominant market position. In the motor vehicle sector, some of the problems have been solved by way of block exemption regulations,[25] and many Member States have enacted special legislation concerning spare parts, ranging from information duties to an obligation to provide for spare parts for the entire expected lifespan of a product.[26] However, where some 'invisible' digital service (for which the end user has already paid in advance because it was included in the purchase price) suddenly disappears from the market, nobody will usually step in. This consequence results from the full copyright protection of most of these services,[27] and the lesser willingness of

25 E.g. Commission Regulation 330/2010 of 20 April 2010 on the application of Article 101(3) of the Treaty on the Functioning of the European Union to categories of vertical agreements and concerted practices [2010] OJ L102/1; Commission Regulation 461/2010 of 27 May 2010 on the application of Article 101(3) of the Treaty on the Functioning of the European Union to categories of vertical agreements and concerted practices in the motor vehicle sector [2010] OJ L129/52.

26 See e.g. <http://europakonsument.at/sites/europakonsument.com/files/Commercial_Warranty_EN_2015.pdf> accessed 15 December 2015, 32–33, for an overview of the current situation.

27 See Directive 2001/29/EC of the European Parliament and of the Council of 22 May 2001 on the harmonisation of certain aspects of copyright and related rights in the information society [2001] OJ L167/10, recital 29: '*[...] The question of exhaustion does not arise in the case of services and on-line services in particular. This also applies with regard to a material copy of a work or other subject-matter made by a user of such a service with the consent of the rightholder. [...] every on-*

end users to pay additional money for the continuation of a service than for spare parts.

It is not only that a service may be discontinued, possibly even with a view to sanctioning certain consumer behaviour or to enforcing a claim for payment, but also that the service provider may alter technical features, causing dissatisfaction on the part of the customer and forcing the customer to subscribe to an enhanced version against additional payment. Article 15 Digital Content Proposal explicitly grants the service provider a right to do so if it was stipulated in the (standard term) contract.

b) Personalisation of assets

A related problem is the technical possibility to personalise the smart device in a way that cannot easily be reversed by the user, such as by irreversibly entering a user name and password during the initial setup. Of course, traditional products can also be personalised, such as by engraving a name, or they may not be suitable for being passed on, such as made-to-measure clothes. However, this is either inherent in the goods by their very nature, or stems from the free decision of the owner. Smart devices, however, are sometimes personalised in a way that is controlled solely by the manufacturer or third party providers.

Needless to say, this may cause problems when the buyer wishes to resell the asset as the new owner will want to have the same degree of personalisation and control as the previous owner. Likewise, the previous owner will have an interest that all personal data are deleted or at least made inaccessible for the new owner.

c) Remote control

Digital infrastructure services, together with the processing of user data, also allow for remote control, both of the smart device itself and of its owner's user behaviour. Many modern smartTV sets with an inbuilt DVD player, for instance, would not only remain connected with the manufacturer and a variety of service providers but would also recognise copyright

line service is in fact an act which should be subject to authorisation where the copyright or related right so provides'.

infringements, such as the display of illegal copies of DVDs or the consumption of full movies wrongfully uploaded by third parties on file hosting sites. In the event a copyright infringement is identified, the device would then send a warning to the user urging him to stop immediately in order to avoid legal sanctions, or it would simply refuse to function. Modern cars would recognise when the driver yawns, or when his hand faintly trembles, and remind the driver to stop and take a rest; more advanced models would deny service where the driver intends to go significantly beyond the speed limit. Ultimately, it is not so much the user controlling the device, but rather the device, and the providers feeding the device with data, who are controlling the user.

III. Waving Goodbye to Sales?

This brief overview has served to demonstrate that the emergence of IoT is a serious challenge for traditional rules of contract and contractual liability. Some of the problems encountered are merely gradual in nature. There are, however, some more fundamental issues as smart devices and IoT call into question the very notion of sale and ownership. This notion rests on the assumption that, at a particular point, physical control of a thing plus – at least in civilian terminology – the 'absolute' right to proceed with the thing as one deems appropriate, within the limits imposed by the law and other people's freedoms, passes from the previous owner to the buyer. With many smart devices this is the case only in very formal and superficial terms: the substance of the smart TV set or connected car may be owned by the buyer but many or even all of the functions depend on the ongoing provision of a particular data infrastructure (usually cloud based) by a particular provider. The future lies in 'device as a service', i.e. the value of what is physically controlled or owned by the buyer is negligible compared with the value of the whole device, which comes as a package of good and service. In addition, remote control gives third parties almost as much physical control over the thing as the owner. Moreover, the thing is not only used by and for the benefit of its owner, but rather it collects and transmits data to one or several third parties and is about as much 'run by' this party as by the owner.

1. What makes a contract a sale?

To some extent contract typology is a very civilian concern, but also common law jurisdictions need to classify contracts in one or the other context, such as in deciding whether to apply the Sale of Goods Act 1979 or Chapter 2 of the Consumer Rights Act 2015. In any case, the idea that there is a rather clear notion of sale, which implies the transfer of ownership in goods, has been a recurring theme in EU legal instruments such as the Consumer Sales Directive,[28] the CRD or the Proposal for a Common European Sales Law (CESL)[29].

The first reason why one could be inclined to doubt that the sale of a smart device is really a sale is that smart devices are usually goods with embedded digital content. Despite the ruling in *UsedSoft*[30] it is still not clear to what extent a copy of licensed content can be owned in the same way as a tangible good. But if the obligation on the part of the seller to transfer ownership to the buyer is the characteristic feature that makes a sale a sale, how can one be sure there is something like ownership in smart devices? A rather simplistic answer would be as follows: the digital content is, from a technical point of view, nothing but a certain condition of the tangible asset on which it is stored or in which it is embedded. If ownership in the tangible asset is transferred, it is ownership in the tangible asset in its current condition. Of course, some of the digital content may be protected under copyright, patent, or other kind of intellectual property legislation, and third parties may have certain rights if the copy embedded in the smart device was an illegal copy. But these rights would be comparable to a pledge or other right that is enforceable vis-à-vis the owner. This line of reasoning may be called the 'third party rights' theory. Another line of reasoning would be: if the digital content stored on or embedded in the tangible asset is protected under copyright or other intellectual property legislation, the powers that come with the intellectual property right may be exhausted under the first sale doctrine. Where copyright in software is concerned, the power to control distribution of a copy

28 Directive 1999/44/EC of the European Parliament and of the Council of 25 May 1999 on certain aspects of the sale of consumer goods and associated guarantees [1999] OJ L171/12.

29 Commission, 'Proposal for a Regulation on a Common European Sales Law (CESL)' COM(2011) 635 final.

30 Case C- 128/11 *UsedSoft GmbH v Oracle International Corp* [2012] ECR I–nyr.

of the software would be exhausted with the first sale in the EU by the rightholder or with his consent, with the exception of the power to control further rental of the program or a copy thereof, as under Article 4(2) Software Directive.[31] Similarly, the power to control the distribution of other digital content may be exhausted under Article 4(2) InfoSoc Directive.[32] Where a tangible asset is sold with embedded digital content, e.g. a smart fridge, there are usually no opportunities for the average buyer to pursue any kind of activity reserved to the rightholder, at least not if we assume that rental of the fridge would not amount to rental of the digital content.[33] This approach can be called the 'exhaustion theory'.

2. *Between ownership and access*

This being so, is there any reason to call into question the notion of sale and ownership with relation to smart devices? No and yes. The problem is not so much that of ownership in a formal sense, but rather ownership in a more substantive and meaningful sense, of being both entitled and enabled to fully control the use of the asset in accordance with its nature. Of course, no owner ever has full control. The owner of flowers, for instance, cannot prevent their decay, and the owner of a machine cannot prevent that the machine will at some point need repairing. But things are different where the lifespan and fate of a device after delivery are subject to continuous and uninterrupted control by one or several third parties and/or other interacting machines. In this case the buyer acquires something in between ownership and access.

---

31 Directive 2009/24/EC of the European Parliament and of the Council of 23 April 2009 on the legal protection of computer programs [2009] OJ L111/16.

32 Directive 2001/29/EC of the European Parliament and of the Council of 22 May 2001 on the harmonisation of certain aspects of copyright and related rights in the information society [2001] OJ L167/10.

33 Cf also Art 11 of the Agreement on Trade-Related Aspects of Intellectual Property Rights (TRIPS) [1994] OJ L336/1: '*...In respect of computer programs, this obligation does not apply to rentals where the program itself is not the essential object of the rental.*'; Art 7(2) WIPO Copyright Treaty (WCT) [2000] OJ L89/6: '*Paragraph (1) does not apply (i) in the case of computer programs, where the program itself is not the essential object of the rental...*'; Thomas Söbbing, 'Embedded Software' (2013) 7 Der IT-Rechts-Berater (ITRB) 162 [164].

Does it matter? For legislation on non-embedded digital content, such the Digital Content Proposal or Chapter 3 of the UK Consumer Rights Act 2015, it does not: What counts is what the contract says, no matter whether this can be called ownership, access, or something in between, under whatever sort of doctrinal classification. The huge advantage of this approach is that it is flexible and relatively future-proof. Its drawback is that it relies heavily on the description of the product provided by the supplier, and there is little room for submitting the definition of the mutual obligations of the parties to a fairness control.[34] In any case, according to the two Proposals of 9 December 2015, this approach does not apply to the supply of smart tangible devices.[35] If, for tangible devices, the division into sales and services remains, the question arises whether a third track must be introduced between the two or whether the supply of smart devices is simply a sale combined with related services, which was the concept reflected, inter alia, in the CESL, at least for two-party relationships.[36] Arguably, the latter is the much simpler and clearer approach even if, in the case of smart devices, there is usually a three-party- or even multi-party-relationship. At least where there is a possibility to conclude clickwrap agreements the seller is (under the applicable national contract law) usually not a party to the related agreements. Rather, the agreements are concluded directly between the end user and the rightholder, manufacturer or other third party. However, where the seller has not made this sufficiently clear before the contract was concluded it may well be the case that national contract law holds him as the person who has promised to deliver the whole package of sale and service. In such case, the manufacturer or other third party would be considered as the seller's subcontractor to whom the seller has delegated the fulfilment of particular obligations under the contract. The applicable national contract law may also consider both the seller and the manufacturer or other third party as being liable for fulfilling the obligations under the service and other agreements.

34 Unfair Contract Terms Directive, Art 4(2): '*Assessment of the unfair nature of the terms shall relate neither to the definition of the main subject matter of the contract nor to the adequacy of the price and remuneration, on the one hand, as against the services or goods supplies in exchange, on the other, [...]*'.

35 Digital Content Proposal, recital 11 and Distance Proposal, recital 13.

36 See Commission, 'Proposal for a Regulation on a Common European Sales Law (CESL)' COM(2011) 635 final, Art 2(m) (CESL).

3. *Sale of goods and provision of digital services under the Proposals of 9 December 2015*

Ultimately, it is therefore still possible to work on the basis of the traditional dichotomy of sales and services, defining the supply of smart devices as a combination of both. With regard to the two Proposals of 9 December 2015 this means that the sale of the tangible device is covered by the Distance Proposal whereas the provision of the service, or various services, definitely is not.[37] Whether or not the latter is covered by the Digital Content Proposal is not entirely clear. On the one hand there is no indication in the text of the Digital Content Proposal that the provision of digital infrastructure which is required for the use of a tangible device should be excluded. On the other hand it seems that the Commission wanted to see the supply of smart devices and everything that comes with it to be covered solely by the Distance Proposal plus, where relevant, applicable national contract law, given that the supply of digital content embedded in a tangible device is explicitly excluded from the scope of the Digital Content Proposal.[38] In any case, even if the rules of the Digital Content Proposal applied they would not appropriately address a situation where the supply of digital content forms an integral part of another contract under which a tangible device was delivered in return for a one-time payment: any rights under the Digital Content Proposal would be restricted to the digital content itself, and if the consumer intended to exercise remedies with regard to the device it would have to be under national rules concerning linked contracts, such as *clausula rebus sic stantibus*, if such rules remain at all applicable despite full harmonisation.

IV. Challenges Accepted: Which Contract Rules for the Brave New World?

Ever since automated vehicles made it from the labs to the roads (and Google and other companies are announcing the imminent of entirely self-driving cars) a good deal of legal literature has been published on the

37 Distance Proposal, Art 1(2).

38 Digital Content Proposal, recital 11 and Distance Proposal, recital 13.

possible implications for tort and insurance law,[39] as well as for privacy, security and anti-discrimination law.[40] In contrast, the contractual side of the phenomenon has hardly ever been addressed. Needless to say, a thorough analysis of the situation and the development of a draft would require much more time and research than was possible in the scope of this chapter. What will be presented here is therefore merely a rough sketch that is very much work in progress.

1. *Pre-contractual information and related duties*

A first start could be made with pre-contractual information duties under the CRD. As has been pointed out in more detail above, it is currently unclear whether the specific information duties relating to digital content equally apply to smart devices with embedded digital content. In comparing the terminology and concepts of the various instruments and draft instruments one could probably draw the conclusion that, at least from the point of view of those who originally drafted the provisions, the duties relating to digital content do not apply to smart devices. However, they definitely should apply when considering the purpose of the rules.

An information duty concerning counter-performance other than money is currently absent, or at least it does not play a very prominent role but is, if at all existent, hidden within the information duty concerning 'main characteristics' or 'functionality'. The European legislator seems to have been under the impression that the giving of data as counter-performance is a phenomenon restricted to digital content. However, the phenomenon is much broader, and for many smart devices the consumer simply pays twice: once with money, and another time with his data or user-generated content. Needless to say, the fact that the consumer is also charged a considerable sum of money, in addition to using his data, makes him still

39 For the latest developments in the EU see the contribution by Hans Schulte-Nölke in Egon Lorenz (ed), *Karlsruher Forum 2015: Europäisierung des Haftungsrechts und des Versicherungsvertragsrechts* (forthcoming, 2016); for the U.S.A. see Dorothy J Glancy, Robert W Peterson and Kyle F Graham, *A Look at the Legal Environment for Driverless Vehicles* (pre-publication October 2015), available at <http://onlinepubs.trb.org/onlinepubs/nchrp/nchrp_lrd_069.pdf> accessed 15 December 2015, each with further references.

40 For recent research see, e.g., Scott Peppet, 'Regulating the Internet of Things' (2014) 85 Texas Law Review 93, with further references.

more vulnerable and in need of protection. For this reason, a corresponding information duty needs to be imposed on the trader. Breach of this duty would have the effect that user data may not be processed.[41]

Finally, there should be some clarification that neither Article 5 nor, more importantly, Article 6 CRD prevent Member States from imposing on traders a duty to provide to consumers appropriate advice concerning the suitability of, inter alia, smart devices, and to take reasonable steps to ascertain the consumer's digital and other environment. Taken together, this could mean a rule along the lines of the following:

Pre-contractual information duties

1. The information the supplier has to provide, in a clear and comprehensible manner, to the consumer under Articles 5(1)(c) and 6(1)(e) of Directive 2001/83/EU before the consumer is bound by a contract, or any corresponding offer, shall be deemed to include any counter-performance other than money which the consumer has to provide in exchange for goods, digital content or services and any data the supplier intends to collect in relation to the goods, digital content or services.
2. The information duties under Articles 5(1)(g) and (h) and 6(1)(r) and (s) of Directive 2001/83/EU shall apply equally to goods in which digital content is embedded, or on which digital content is stored, or which can otherwise connect digitally with the internet or with other tangible assets.
3. Articles 5 and 6 of Directive 2011/83/EU shall be without prejudice to, inter alia, any duty of the supplier under the applicable national law
   (i) to provide to the consumer competent, unprejudiced and otherwise appropriate advice concerning the suitability of the goods, digital content or services for the needs and abilities of the individual consumer; and
   (ii) to take reasonable steps to ascertain the consumer's digital and other environment with a view to identifying potential issues of interoperability and compatibility, where applicable.

2. Agreement on contract terms

Pre-contractual information concerning post-sale agreements which the consumer has to conclude after the acquisition of the smart device in order to be able to use the device in accordance with the contract must be considered part of the 'main characteristics' of the device under Articles 5(1)(h) and 6(1)(s) CRD. However, mere pre-contractual information

41 See CRD Art 6(6) for distance and off-premises contracts. A similar provision is missing for on-premises contracts, but arguably follows from general principles underlying the CRD.

duties on the part of the trader would not be sufficient. Instead, there must be direct consequences also for the validity of contract terms, in particular terms not individually negotiated.

In the first place it should be made clear that terms of a post-sale contract cannot be invoked against the consumer unless they have been sufficiently brought to the consumer's attention already when the sales contract was concluded. The post-sale contract as a whole, or individual terms thereof, cannot be invoked against the consumer where it was of such a surprising nature that the consumer could not have expected the contract or the relevant terms. Rules on how contract terms, in particular not individually negotiated contract terms, are agreed upon do not exist at European level – the Unfair Contract Terms Directive is only about unfairness control. Therefore, the consequences must be spelt out at the level of national law. However, if such rules existed at European level they could be phrased along the lines of the following:

Agreement on not individually negotiated terms

1. The supplier must make available to the consumer the terms on the basis of which the supplier is prepared to conclude the contract and take reasonable steps to draw the consumer's attention to contract terms that are not individually negotiated. Such terms are not sufficiently brought to the consumer's attention unless they are
   (i) presented in a way which is suitable to attract the attention of the consumer to their existence; and
   (ii) given or made available to the consumer by a trader in a manner which provides the consumer with an opportunity to comprehend them before the contract is concluded.[42]
2. Where the consumer cannot reasonably be expected to refrain from concluding a contract because it is necessary for achieving the purpose of an existing contract, and the two contracts form a commercial unit the requirements under paragraph (1) must be met already when the first contract is concluded. A commercial unit shall be deemed to exist, in particular, where the supplier himself is party to the first contract or, if the first contract is with another party, where the supplier uses the services of that other party in connection with the conclusion or preparation of the contract.[43]
3. Where the supplier has not complied with the duties under this Article the supplier may not invoke contract terms supplied by him against the customer.

42 Adapted version of the European Parliament's legislative resolution of 26 February 2014 on the CESL, P7_TA(2014)0159, see Amendments 148, 149.

43 Adapted from Directive 2008/48/EC of the European Parliament and of the Council of 23 April 2008 on credit agreements for consumers and repealing Council Directive 87/102/EEC [2008] 133/66, Art 3(n)(ii).

Surprising terms

1. The supplier may not invoke contract terms that are not individually negotiated against the customer where they are of such a surprising nature that the customer could not have expected the proposed term.[44]
2. The same applies where, in a situation defined under Article [Agreement](2), the customer could not have expected the proposed terms, or the contract as a whole, in the context of the first contract.

Needless to say, the same must apply in the context of unfairness control. However, there also needs to be a specific black list of unfair terms for digital content, including EULAs, and also for smart products. It is unfortunately not possible in this article to present a draft black list as further research would be required.

Unfair contract terms

1. A contract term that is not individually negotiated shall be regarded as unfair if, contrary to good faith, it causes a significant imbalance in the parties' rights and obligations arising under the contract, to the detriment of the customer.
2. When assessing the unfairness of a contract term regard is to be had to: …
3. In a situation defined under Article [Agreement](2) the unfairness of a contract term, or the contract as a whole, shall be assessed also in the light of the first contract.

Contract terms which are always unfair

1. Terms in a consumer contract shall always be regarded as unfair if they have the object or effect of:
   (a) excluding or limiting in any way the consumer's right as a data subject to withdraw, at any time, his or her consent to the processing of personal data;
   (b) excluding or limiting in any way the consumer's right to re-sell, rent out or otherwise utilize a product in which the consumer has lawfully acquired ownership or another right to use the product for an indefinite period of time;
   (c) …

A particularly important example of a post-sale contract is a data processing agreement, often not even called an 'agreement' but rather a 'privacy policy' or the like which the consumer is pushed to accept. The nature and validity requirements for such agreements are, so far, not altogether clear. There is therefore a danger that certain consumers, such as minors, can enter into data processing agreements even though they would not be able to enter into other contracts under the applicable national law.

44 Adapted version of the European Parliament's legislative resolution of 26 February 2014 on the CESL, P7_TA(2014)0159, see Amendment 156.

There is also a danger that the processing of data is justified by way of reference to a rule that would be Article 6(1)(b) in the latest draft of the General Data Protection Regulation (GDPR):[45] the processing of personal data is justified where it is necessary for the performance of a contract to which the data subject is party, even in cases where the formal requirements for obtaining a data subject's consent under Articles 6(1)(a) or 9(1)(a) GDPR have not been met. This calls for some additional clarifications along the lines of the following:

Data processing contracts

1. Where, in the context of the conclusion of a contract, the consumer is asked to consent to the processing of personal data that will be generated directly or indirectly through the conclusion of the contract, including by the use by the consumer of a product supplied under the contract, this shall be considered a contract with the party asking for the consent and shall be subject to the provisions on contract terms, in particular not individually negotiated contract terms, and to the validity requirements such as capacity that would be applicable to contracts in general under national law.
2. The consumer's agreement to the data processing contract must also fulfil the requirements under Article 6(1)(a) or, where applicable, Article 9(1)(a) of the General Data Protection Regulation, and the trader must inform the consumer, before the consumer is bound by the contract or any corresponding offer, about the consumer's right to withdraw his consent to the processing of personal data and the effects a withdrawal of consent would have on the further performance of the contract.

3. *Conformity of goods with the contract*

The definitions of conformity with the contract for digital content on the one hand and for goods on the other hand differ to a significant extent between the two Proposals. Regrettably, the European Commission has opted primarily for a subjective test in the Digital Content Proposal, which means that what counts foremost are the supplier's standard terms. However, this is not the concern of this chapter, which is about smart devices and the Distance Proposal. The latter takes a much better approach concerning the relationship between subjective and objective test. However, it fails to take account of the specific characteristics of smart goods, which is why it is suggested to add some provisions.

45 Council compromise text of 11 June 2015, <http://data.consilium.europa.eu/doc/document/ST-9565-2015-INIT/en/pdf> accessed 15 December 2015.

a) Quality aspects

The relevant test for conformity of goods with the contract in terms of quality is to be found in Articles 4 to 6 Distance Proposal. It corresponds, by and large, with earlier rules that had been drafted, in particular, in the context of the CESL Proposal.[46] The test seems to work well for traditional goods. Smart goods, however, combine the elements of tangible goods and digital content and thus would call for a combination of the relevant tests. The Distance Proposal as it currently stands tends to put too much stress on normal qualities and fitness for use and to omit other aspects, which could potentially mean that a smart fridge that keeps the food fresh and cool is in conformity with the contract even where, due to a security flaw, it discloses the access data of its owners' gmail accounts[47] or ceases to interoperate with the control panel of a smart home scheme. At least for the sake of clarity it would be preferable to mention interoperability and other performance features such as accessibility, continuity and security, explicitly also in the Proposal on sale of goods.

More importantly, the related service of product monitoring and maintenance should be included as an additional criterion for establishing conformity with the contract. This could, at first sight, be considered to be an alien element in sales law. However, it should be obvious that goods are normally not in conformity with the contract where they cannot be used by the consumer for want of a particular digital infrastructure or where they might, unless updated as necessary, cause personal injury to the buyer or at least put at risk his other belongings and personal data. In a situation where continuous product monitoring is required for not more than 1% of consumer products it may seem disproportionate to modify general sales law which, after all, is good for 99.999% of cases. Contrastingly, in a situation where suddenly 50% of things sold may potentially pose serious security and/or privacy risks if not monitored and maintained on a regular basis, a legislator is simply failing to do its job if the law is not changed to reflect this new reality. The most difficult problem in this context is the relevant time for establishing conformity and any applicable time limits. In order not to put too much burden on sellers the time limit suggested by Article 14 Distance Proposal should still apply.

---

46 CESL, Annex I.

47 <http://www.consumerreports.org/cro/topfreezerrefrigerators/smart-refrigerators-privacy> accessed 15 December 2015.

It is further suggested to have a rule on 'privacy by design', i.e. a design of goods that takes account of privacy concerns and does not allow for more user data being collected and processed than are strictly necessary for the functionality of the goods in accordance with the contract. The same holds true for 'privacy by default', i.e. the programming of embedded software in a way that takes non-disclosure of personal data as the default setting where there are relevant options among which the user can choose. Privacy by design and privacy by default might be subsumed under 'quality' or 'performance features'. However, this aspect seems to be so important that it deserves to be mentioned separately as an additional criterion for assessing conformity with the contract. Besides, it differs from the other conformity criteria listed in Article 5 insofar as the standard should go beyond what is 'normal' given that, regrettably, this requirement is usually ignored in practice.

The slightly revised Articles 4 and 5 Distance Proposal could read as follows (revisions underlined):

Article 4
Conformity with the contract

1. The seller shall ensure that, in order to conform with the contract, the goods shall, where relevant:
   (a) be of the quantity, quality and description required by the contract, which includes that where the seller shows a sample or a model to the consumer, the goods shall possess the quality of and correspond to the description of this sample or model;
   (b) be fit for any particular purpose for which the consumer requires them and which the consumer made known to the seller at the time of the conclusion of the contract and which the seller has accepted; and
   (c) possess the qualities, functionality, interoperability and other performance features such as accessibility, continuity and security indicated in any pre-contractual statement which forms an integral part of the contract.
2. In order to conform with the contract, the goods must also meet the requirements of Articles 5, 6 and 7.
3. Any agreement excluding, derogating from or varying the effects of Articles 5, 6 and 7(2) to the detriment of the consumer is valid only if, at the time of the conclusion of the contract, the consumer knew of the specific condition of the goods and the consumer has expressly accepted this specific condition when concluding the contract.

Article 5
Requirements for conformity of the goods

The goods shall, where relevant:
(a) possess qualities, functionality, interoperability and other performance features such as accessibility, continuity and security which are normal in

goods of the same type and which the consumer may expect given the nature of the goods and taking into account any public statement made by or on behalf of the seller or other persons in earlier links of the chain of transactions, including the producer, unless the seller shows that:
  - (i) the seller was not, and could not reasonably have been, aware of the statement in question;
  - (ii) by the time of conclusion of the contract the statement had been corrected; or
  - (iii) the decision to buy the goods could not have been influenced by the statement.
- (b) be fit for all the purposes for which goods of the same description would ordinarily be used;
- (c) be delivered along with such accessories including packaging, installation instructions or other instructions as the consumer may expect to receive;
- (d) be maintained, including by providing a necessary digital infrastructure and updating embedded digital content, as the consumer may expect given the nature of the goods, the counter-performance provided by the consumer, potential security risks and taking into account any public statement within the meaning of point (a); and
- (e) be designed so as not to process more personal data generated by the use of the goods than are strictly necessary, and programmed so as to have non-disclosure of personal data as the default setting where the consumer can choose among several options.

Article 8
Relevant time for establishing conformity with the contract

...

4. Where conformity of the goods with the contract implies that they are maintained, including by providing a necessary digital infrastructure and updating embedded digital content, the seller shall be liable for any lack of conformity with the contract which results from a failure to maintain and which exists at the time when maintenance would have been due. For the purpose of Article 14 the relevant time for establishing conformity shall be the time indicated in paragraphs 1 and 2.

b) Legal aspects

Article 7 of the Distance Proposal concerns the legal aspects of conformity. Titled 'Third party rights' it is a true reflection of what has been called 'third party rights theory'. In principle, this works for goods, but it would be preferable to state explicitly that the seller is under an obligation to transfer full ownership to the buyer, at the latest when the price for the goods has been fully paid, and also to state explicitly that the consumer must be not only in a position to use the goods in accordance with the contract, but also to re-sell them.

This is crucial for smart devices as the manufacturer, or whoever else remotely controls the goods, has the technical means to prevent re-sale of the goods. Therefore the consumer must have the right to re-sell the goods, and whoever controls the goods must provide easy and reasonable means to de-personalise goods, such as by deleting user names and passwords of the previous owner and blocking access to his personal data, and to re-personalise the goods and grant the new owner the same degree of control as the previous owner had. This is one of the reasons why, for smart goods, a much more elaborate rule on the legal aspects of conformity would be required.

Another reason is that there is a range of possibilities as to how the manufacturer or any other party remotely controlling the use of the goods, in particular by providing continuing access to a particular digital infrastructure, can force the consumer to conclude further contracts, or simply discontinue a service, or alter its performance features to the detriment of the consumer as is explicitly stipulated as a right of any supplier of digital content in Article 15 of Digital Content Proposal. If the manufacturer or any third party remotely controlling the goods reserves this right it has the same effect as a right in rem, or intellectual property right, of a third party.

Finally, it should be noted that, even if updates of embedded digital content are usually to the consumer's benefit and will even be required in many cases, updates may have the same effect as discontinuation of the service or alteration of features to the detriment of the consumer. This is the case because, even if the overall purpose of an update is to enhance performance features, the concrete effect for the individual consumer may be that the consumer is no longer in a position to use the goods due to some problem of compatibility and interoperability. The consumer must therefore have a right to maintain a previous version of digital content;[48] otherwise an update, though being very desirable as such, might have

48 Obviously, this would have to be largely at the consumer's own risk in terms of any security gaps the update was intended to close, and the consumer would need to have a right against the supplier to be informed about those security gaps. The consumer would then have to decide whether she is prepared to accept the risk or prefers to rely on decompilation (reverse engineering) to solve the interoperability issue, cf Art 6 Software Directive.

similar expropriating effects as some undesirable activities on the part of the supplier.

Taken together, these suggestions would mean significant modifications of the existing Article 7 Distance Proposal (revisions underlined):

Article 7
Conformity with the contract in legal terms

1. The consumer must, at the latest when the price has been fully paid, acquire ownership in the goods, and the goods must be free from any right of a third party, including based on intellectual property, so that the goods can be used, exploited and re-sold in accordance with the contract.
2. Goods do not conform with the contract if the consumer cannot use, exploit or re-sell the goods in accordance with the contract unless he concludes another agreement with the seller or with a third party designated by the seller which involves further duties or obligations on the part of the consumer or the conclusion of which can be refused by the seller or third party.
3. Goods do not conform with the contract if their use, exploitation or re-sale in accordance with the contract depends on the continuing supply of digital content, including continuing access to a digital infrastructure, and the supplier of that digital content
   (a) reserves the right to alter performance features of the digital content which are relevant for the use or re-sale of the goods to the detriment of the consumer;
   (b) reserves the right to discontinue the provision of updates where such provision is required under the contract; or
   (c) fails to grant the consumer the right and reasonable means, during the normal lifespan of the goods, to maintain a previous version of the digital content where the digital content has been updated and the update may cause problems of interoperability or compatibility with the consumer's digital environment.
4. Re-sale within the meaning of this Article includes reasonable technical means to de-personalise the goods, such as by deleting user names and passwords and blocking access to personal data of the previous owner, and to re-personalise the goods by granting the new owner the same degree of control as the previous owner had.

4. Liability of the producer and the supplier of digital content

Any extended notion of non-conformity in Article 7 Distance Proposal can lead to liability of the seller only where a problem was already existent at the relevant time for establishing conformity, as defined in Article 8 Distance Proposal. This means that the goods are not in conformity with the contract in legal terms where the manufacturer or some other trader reserves the right, e.g. in a relevant service contract with the consumer or with the seller, to refuse to conclude a contract that is necessary for the goods to be used or re-sold, or to alter performance features, or to discontinue the service altogether, or to simply replace digital content by updated digital content without giving the consumer a right to maintain a previous version. However, even where the manufacturer or other trader does not explicitly reserve such a right, there is a danger of *de facto* expropriation of the consumer at a later point in time if the manufacturer or other trader simply fails to comply with what they promised.

To some extent, this issue is addressed by the suggested inclusion of maintenance in Article 5 Distance Proposal. However, it would arguably not be appropriate to hold the seller liable for a longer period than that indicated in Article 14 Distance Proposal, in particular as the seller is often not in any position to control the manufacturer or other relevant third party providers. This is why the consumer should also have remedies against both the supplier who is in breach of duties and the producer within the meaning of Article 3 PLD.[49] As far as remedies for non-conformity are concerned, they should be limited to the normal lifespan of the product, calculated from the time indicated in Article 8 Distance Proposal. However, when it comes to death, personal injury or destruction of, or damage to, any item of property other than the goods themselves the supplier and/or the producer should be liable under the same conditions as the producer of defective movables under the PLD.

This could be phrased as follows:

Liability of the producer and supplier of digital content

1. Where the normal use or re-sale of goods depends on the continuing supply of digital content, including continuing access to a digital infrastructure, by a particular supplier and the supplier of that digital content, at any time during the normal lifespan of the goods,
   (a) alters performance features of the digital content which are relevant for the use or re-sale of the goods to the detriment of the consumer;
   (b) discontinues the provision of updates where such provision is required for security reasons; or
   (c) fails to provide to the consumer reasonable means to maintain a previous version of the digital content where the digital content has been updated and

49 Directive 1999/34/EC of the European Parliament and of the council of 10 May 1999 amending Council Directive 85/374/EEC on the approximation of the laws, regulations and administrative provisions of the Member States concerning liability for defective products [1999] OJ L141/20.

> the update may cause problems of interoperability or compatibility with the consumer's digital environment;
>
> and where this results in the goods no longer being in conformity with the contract, the supplier and the producer of the goods within the meaning of Article 3 of Directive 85/374/EEC shall be jointly and severally liable to the consumer to the same extent as the seller would have been liable if the lack of conformity had existed at the point in time referred to in Article 8.
>
> 2. The same applies where the supplier fails to
>   (a) conclude, where applicable, a new contract under the same conditions with any third party to whom the consumer has re-sold the goods or that are otherwise designated by the consumer;
>   (b) provide reasonable technical means to de-personalise the goods, such as by deleting user names and passwords and blocking access to personal data of the previous owner, and to re-personalise the goods by granting the new owner the same degree of control as the previous owner had.
> 3. Where death, personal injury or destruction of, or damage to, any item of property other than the goods themselves is caused by a defect in the goods which has its origin in the supply of the goods with defective digital content, the supplier of that defective digital content shall be liable under the same conditions as the producer of defective movables under Directive 85/374/EEC. Where the supply of the digital content by that particular supplier occurred with the assent of the producer of the goods within the meaning of Article 3 of Directive 85/374/EEC that producer and the supplier shall be jointly and severally liable to the same extent as if the defect had existed at the time the goods were brought into circulation.

4. Abuse of remote control

Under many legal systems, a contracting party, or in fact also a non-contracting party, may have a right to withhold performance until the other party to the relationship has fulfilled its own obligations vis-à-vis the first party. While this is – generally speaking – justified, the possibility of putting pressure on the consumer by simply using remote control to prevent the normal use of goods the consumer has acquired would be an undesirable abuse of power. Where, for example, the consumer is in default with paying instalments for the device he has bought, or is in default with paying his e-mail host provider, no creditor should have the right simply to disable the functions of the device in order to put pressure on the consumer, or to instigate other traders to do so. This would, in essence, have the same effect as if the seller or other trader came to the consumer's premises at night and clandestinely removed the device, which is, for good reasons, prohibited under most legal systems. Of course, there should be a possibility for the seller to resort to such a move, but only where a court or competent authority has given a decision to that end under national law. This could mean an additional rule along the lines of:

> *Abuse of remote control*
>
> 1. The supplier of digital content that is necessary for the normal use or re-sale of goods, or any other trader who can in any way remotely control the use or re-sale of the goods by the consumer, such as by making the goods not accessible to the consumer or disabling the user account of the consumer or reducing the functionalities of the goods, may not exercise this power for the purpose of enforcing a claim against the consumer or any other purpose that would be incompatible with the consumer's ownership in the goods.
> 2. Paragraph (1) is without prejudice to any such action being permitted, or ordered, by the decision of a court or authority that must be recognised and enforced under the applicable EU and national law.
> 3. The trader who is in breach of the duties under this Article and the producer of the goods within the meaning of Article 3 of Directive 85/374/EEC shall be jointly and severally liable to the owner of the goods for any damage caused.

5. *Burden of proof*

As has been explained in more detail above, the consumer would, despite Article 8(3) Distance Proposal, still have the burden of proving that a particular good is, for whatever reason, not or no longer in conformity with the contract. In the case of interoperating devices, it may be difficult for the consumer to demonstrate which of several interoperating devices fails to be in conformity with the contract. This is why it is suggested to have some additional rules applicable to interoperating devices.

Holding a trader liable for defects in a product sold by another trader would normally not be justified. However, this may be different where the two contracts form a commercial unit within the meaning of Article 3(n) (ii) Consumer Credit Directive[50], i.e. in particular where one of the traders uses the services of the other trader in connection with the conclusion or preparation of the contract. This should apply not only where the other contract was a sales contract but equally where the other contract was a contract for, in particular, supply of digital content within the meaning of

50 Directive 2008/48/EC of the European Parliament and of the Council of 23 April 2008 on credit agreements for consumers and repealing Council Directive 87/102/EEC [2008] OJ L133/66.

the Digital Content Proposal. Needless to say, such a rule would need to be accompanied by an appropriate rule on a trader's right to redress.

It is also suggested to have a rule stating that, where goods are intended to interoperate with other goods or digital content and there is an issue of interoperability or compatibility, the seller shall have the burden of proof with respect to the conformity of the goods regarding the interoperability or compatibility in question. This rule would ensure that it is not for the consumer to prove that the lack of interoperability or compatibility amounts to non-conformity, the latter applying where, e.g., the seller has breached its duties under CRD Articles 5(1)(c) and 6(1)(e) and, in the absence of any pre-contractual information on interoperability issues, full interoperability has become a term of the contract, or where full interoperability would have been normal in goods of the relevant type and would have been what the consumer can reasonably expect.

Taken together, this could (tentatively) mean a provision along the lines of the following:

Goods intended to interoperate

1. Where goods are, by their nature, intended to interoperate with other goods, and the consumer cannot reasonably be expected to prove which out of several goods fails to conform with the contract under which the goods were bought, the consumer may exercise remedies for non-conformity with relation to both or all relevant goods if the respective contracts form a commercial unit. A commercial unit shall be deemed to exist, in particular, where the goods were bought from the same seller or, if they were bought from different sellers, where one of the sellers uses the services of the other seller in connection with the conclusion or preparation of the contract.
2. Paragraph (1) applies accordingly where goods are intended to interoperate with digital content supplied under a contract for the supply of digital content within the meaning of [Proposal COM(2015) 634 final].
3. Where goods are intended to interoperate with other goods or digital content and there is an issue of interoperability or compatibility the seller shall have the burden of proof with respect to the conformity of the goods in terms of the interoperability or compatibility in question.

6. *Effects of termination*

Last but not least, the effects of termination on a contract for the sale of smart devices may require some additional rules, which are, to a certain extent, copied from Article 13 Digital Content Proposal. However, it is suggested to have also a rule on reasonable reimbursement where data cannot be deleted because they have already been processed and the act of processing is irreversible (revisions are underlined):

Article 13
The consumer's right to terminate the contract

1. The consumer shall exercise the right to terminate the contract by notice to the seller given by any means.
2. Where the lack of conformity with the contract relates to only some of the goods delivered under the contract and there is a ground for termination of a contract pursuant to Article 9, the consumer may terminate the contract only in relation to those goods and any other goods, which the consumer acquired as an accessory to the non-conforming goods.
3. Where the consumer terminates a contract as a whole or in relation to some of the goods delivered under the contract in accordance with paragraph 2 the seller shall
   (a) return to the consumer the price paid without undue delay and in any event not later than 14 days from receipt of the notice and shall bear the cost of the reimbursement;
   (b) refrain from the use of any counter-performance other than money which the consumer has provided in exchange for the goods and any other data collected by the supplier in relation to the supply of the goods; or pay a reasonable amount for the use of such counter-performance, in particular where the data have already been processed and the act of processing is irreversible;
   (b) provide the consumer with technical means to retrieve all user generated content provided by the consumer and any other data produced or generated through the consumer's use of the goods. The consumer shall be entitled to retrieve the content free of charge, without significant inconvenience, in reasonable time and in a commonly used data format.
4. Where the consumer terminates a contract as a whole or in relation to some of the goods delivered under the contract in accordance with paragraph 2 the consumer shall
   (a) return, at the seller's expense, to the seller the goods without undue delay and in any event not later than 14 days from sending the notice of termination;
   (b) where the goods cannot be returned because of destruction or loss, pay to the seller the monetary value which the non-conforming goods would have had at the date when the return was to be made, if they had been kept by the consumer without destruction or loss until that date, unless the destruction or loss has been caused by a lack of conformity of the goods with the contract; and
   (c) pay for a decrease in the value of the goods only to the extent that the decrease in value exceeds depreciation through regular use. The payment for decrease in value shall not exceed the price paid for the goods.

V. Summary

Smart devices combine the features of goods and of digital content, and their supply combines the features of sales and of services. Any future regime for contracts concerning the sale of goods and supply of digital content will have to address this phenomenon in an appropriate way. The two Proposals for Directives published by the European Commission on 9 December 2015 have failed to take due account of the specific challenges posed by smart devices and the IoT. By submitting the supply of smart devices to a traditional sales law regime fundamental concerns of consumers are being ignored, such as interoperability, privacy, provision of patches or updates for embedded software, outsourcing of functions to third parties, or dependency on the continuous access to a particular digital infrastructure. In other words, the Distance Proposal fails to reflect the ongoing transition from the sales paradigm based on ownership to the service paradigm of continuous access and supply.

To some extent, the problem might be solved by submitting embedded digital content and technology as such to the provisions of the Digital Content Proposal, along the lines of what the English law provides in Article 16 UK Consumer Rights Act 2015. However, this would raise issues of coherence, and also the Digital Content Proposal fails to cater for many provisions that would be essential for effective consumer protection in the field. What is really called for is a more holistic approach, which not only focuses on the relationship between the buyer and the seller but equally on the relationship between the end user and the producer or the supplier of necessary digital infrastructure.

In this contribution, some draft provisions have been presented, which may serve as a source of inspiration and hopefully spark a debate, but which are still immature and very much work in progress. They concern, in particular, pre-contractual information duties, validity of standard contract terms, provision of patches and other updates, provision of necessary digital infrastructure, privacy by design and by default, post-sale clickwrap agreements, re-sale of goods, product liability for digital infrastructure services, abuse of remote control, burden of proof, and the effects of termination.

The draft provisions presented in this chapter have been formulated so as to fit into the Distance Proposal. At the end of the day, however, they should not remain restricted to distance sales, and what would be preferable is a consolidated approach covering rules for the supply of both goods and digital content in one coherent instrument.

Liability and Risk Management in Robotics

*Prof. Dr. Erica Palmerini / Dr. Andrea Bertolini, LL.M. (Yale)**

I. The potential impact of liability rules on the market for robotic products

A converging series of claims, opinions, and views expressed in the media,[1] in private interviews or public meetings,[2] and in independent reports[3] supports the belief that a clear and sound legal framework could

* Erica Palmerini is Associate Professor of Private Law at the Scuola Superiore Sant'Anna (SSSA), she holds a Ph.D. in Private Law from SSSA, and is responsible for §§ I, II, III. Andrea Bertolini is Assistant Professor of Private Law at SSSA, holds a Ph.D. in Private Law from SSSA and an LL.M. from Yale Law School. He is responsible for §§ II.1.a, III.1, III.2, IV and V.

1 'Special Report, Robots. Immigrants from the future' *The Economist* (London, 29 March 2014). This report stresses the fact that manufacturers' technical ability to produce robots that can help in the home might easily outrun their capacity to deal with the resulting liability issues, especially if the robots operate in the homes of elderly people with cognitive difficulties. See also Mark Piesing, 'Beyond Asimov: the struggle to develop a legal framework for robots' <http://www.wired.co.uk/news/archive/2013-02/18/robolaw> accessed 20 November 2015.

2 Among the claims made by experts at the International Transport Forum, which took place in Leipzig on May 28, 2015, were: 'neither the available and foreseeable vehicle and infrastructure technology, nor the legal framework can make a scenario where vehicles can drive anywhere autonomously all the time a reality over the next 15 to 20 years': Joy Fang, 'Legal liability issues "preventing mass-adoption of self-driving cars"' *Today* (29 May 2015) <www.todayonline.com/singapore/legal-liability-issues-preventing-mass-adoption-self-driving-cars> accessed 16 November 2015.

3 With regard to healthcare robotics, a study commissioned by the European Commission affirms that 'The most important political factor in the domain of robotics for healthcare are legislation and regulation, governmental support and the political agenda': Maurits Butter and others, 'Robotics for Healthcare. Final Report' (European Commission, 3 October 2008). With regard to autonomous vehicles, it has been stated that 'States and Local law Legislation, or lack thereof, will impact the speed and trajectory of adoption (...) A legal framework will be necessary to deal with the potentially complex liability issues that may come with self-driving cars (...) legal concerns (...) will need to be addressed for convergence solutions to gain mass-market adoption': KPMG and Center for Automotive

hasten the development of an advanced market of robotic products and services. On the other hand, legal uncertainties and/or legal gaps, together with technological roadblocks and socio-cultural constraints, are considered a potential barrier to the advent of robotics as a widespread phenomenon.[4]

The main concerns in terms of instituting a reliable legal environment focus on liability issues. Liability claims are feared especially by manufacturers, who are the most likely to be identified as being responsible for the accidents caused by robotic products, and thus would bear the costs associated therewith, both in monetary terms and reputation. On the one hand, potential ambiguities affect the task of determining the rules applicable to robotic products. On the other, the production and distribution chain for robotic applications involves multiple actors and the potential causes of failures would be spread across the entire process. Thus, in the case of

---

Research, 'Self-driving cars: The Next Revolution' 2012, 21 <http://www.kpmg.com/US/en/IssuesAndInsights/ArticlesPublications/Documents/self-driving-cars-next-revolution.pdf> accessed 20 November 2015. See also Nikolaus Lang and others, 'Revolution Versus Regulation. The Make-Or-Break Questions About Autonomous Vehicles' (The Boston Consulting Group 2015) <http://www.bcg.com.cn/export/sites/default/en/files/publications/reports_pdf/BCG-Revolution-Versus-Regulation-Sep-2015.pdf> accessed 20 November 2015. The regulatory and legal challenges advanced robotics will pose are also listed in James Manyika and others, 'Disruptive technologies. Advances that will transform life, business, and the global economy' (McKinsey Global Institute 2013) 21, 84 <www.mckinsey.com/insights/business-technology/disruptive_technologies> accessed 20 November 2015. See also UK Robotics and Autonomous Systems Special Interest Group, 'RAS 2020. Robotic and autonomous systems' (July 2014) <https://connect.innovateuk.org/documents/2903012/16074728/RAS%20UK%20Strategy?version=1.0> accessed 20 November 2015.

4 According to a survey on the attitudes of European citizens towards robots, the most significant worries included the concern that increasing automation and robotics will reduce job opportunities, and that robots could increase social isolation and reduce human contact, in particular in applications targeted at the disabled, elderly people and children: Special Eurobarometer 382 'Public Attitudes Towards Robots', conducted by TNS Opinion & Social at the request of Directorate-General for Information Society and Media (INSFO) and coordinated by Directorate-General for Communication (DG COMM), September 2012 <ec.europa.eu/public_opinion/archives/ebs/ebs_382_sum_en.pdf> accessed 19 November 2015. A further investigation confirmed these data: TNS Opinion & Social, Special Eurobarometer 427 'Autonomous Systems' Report, June 2015 <ec.europa.eu/public_opinion/archives/ebs/ebs_427_en-pdf> accessed 19 November 2015.

injuries to people or damage to properties, identifying the wrongdoer to whom responsibility should be ascribed could prove difficult.

In order to understand the specificity of the problems faced by producers of robotic devices we need to address those particular features that characterise them, ranging from their novelty and technological complexity to their – often – multipurpose nature, making it hard to identify the different uses they could be put at, and the various contexts in which they could be deployed. This directly impinges on the ability to assess the types and probability of risks associated with their use, ultimately impairing the very possibility of obtaining adequate insurance.

Overall, *ex ante* uncertainty with respect to the applicable regime and the – legal – risks the producer faces by distributing the application on the European market may cause a technology-chilling effect, delaying or preventing the emergence of otherwise desirable products and the establishment of a European industry for robotics.

II. The sources of uncertainty

Ex ante certainty with respect to the applicable legal framework represents a fundamental driver for technological development. Thence, we will now identify and discuss the sources of existing uncertainty, with the aim of uncovering those problems that are only apparent, and at the same time devise strategies to overcome real legal hindrances.

1. Defining a robot

The first difficulty resides in the very notion of robots and robotic products. The technological basis on which any legal reasoning impinges upon is slippery in itself, since robots can be very different in terms of shape (or embodiment), material that they are made from, abilities, type of control, level of interaction with humans, functions, etc. This variety of forms in which a robotic device can appear reflects the many contexts of use and the numerous tasks that can be executed by a robot or with the assistance of a robot. The multifaceted nature, as well as the types of performance, of robotic products confirm that assessing the risks involved in their use is problematic and that any general and unspecific evaluation is thus doomed to be unreliable.

a) The attempt at identifying an all-encompassing definition: a pointless exercise

Quite clearly, the notion of robot diffused today among the public at large is influenced by the literary depictions[5], rather than by the complex and articulated taxonomies offered by scholars, which include applications such as the steering aid mounted on tractors[6].

Indeed, the Merriam-Webster Online Dictionary defines the term 'robot' as such:

1a: a machine that looks like a human being and performs various complex acts (as walking or talking) of a human being; also: a similar but fictional machine whose lack of capacity for human emotions is often emphasised … 2: a device that automatically performs complicated often repetitive tasks; 3: a mechanism guided by automatic controls.

This definition is incomplete, since many applications do not walk or talk and can either be quite simple, such as a vacuum cleaner, or complex, like a surgical or industrial robot. Some are conceived to mimic human emotions or animal behaviours, for the purpose of keeping the elderly or children company.[7] Others are being developed to perform operations that entail a certain degree of creativity (softbots) or even provide a first assessment of the medical condition of a patient,[8] thus elaborating complicated data in a very different fashion from one time to another. Finally, as concerns the resemblance to human traits, studies show that, beyond a given point, users find that aspect awkward and unsettling, and so designers tend to preserve clear-cut signs of the mechanical and artificial

5 See Fiorella Battaglia and Nathalie Weidenfeld, 'Robots in film. Deepening philosophical arguments through storytelling' in Fiorella Battaglia and Nathalie Weidenfeld (eds), *Roboethics in Film* (Pisa University Press 2014) 7 et seq; Barbara Henry, 'Embodied imaginaries and robotic plots' in Fiorella Battaglia and Nathalie Weidenfeld (eds), *Roboethics in Film* (Pisa University Press 2014) 33 et seq.

6 See Michael Decker, 'Technology Assessment of Service Robotics. Preliminary Thoughts Guided by Case Studies' in Michael Decker and Mathias Gutman (eds), *Robo- and Informationethics Some Fundamentals* (Lit Verlag 2012) 64.

7 Like the seal Paro, intended to help the elderly with Alzheimer disease, see <http://www.parorobots.com/> accessed 4 December 2015.

8 Such as the softbot Watson by IBM, see <http://www.ibm.com/smarterplanet/us/en/ibmwatson/> accessed 4 December 2015.

nature of machines so that they will be more easily accepted in human environments.[9]

Definitions offered by researchers are always more precise and narrowly tailored to accommodate the specific field of interest of the speaker,[10] yet the outcome is fragmented and contradictory if considered together.[11]

Finally, a lowest common denominator approach is unsatisfactory as well. Defining a robot as a machine which autonomously performs a task[12] is at most a synecdoche, since it identifies the peculiar trait of an entire set of applications by reference to one of its possible control mechanisms,[13] and ultimately pointless because it is so general that it fails to provide sufficient guidance when attempting to distinguish a robot from other applications which operate unattended.

The reason why there is not and could never be a satisfactory definition of the term 'robot' is its a-technical nature, both from an engineering and a legal point of view. Being derived from science fiction,[14] the word solely means labour and more precisely enslaved labour. The technologies that have developed and the applications that exist are so diverse that maintaining the use of that term may only serve the purpose of synthesis, allowing one to indicate an extensive set of objects.

The consequence for the purpose of the present analysis is that we may not address the legal issues posed by robots unitarily, since the inherent technical differences between robotic applications cannot be overlooked without losing insight. Hence, attention should rather be devoted to isolating the traits that could be of relevance in changing the paradigm

---

9 See Masahiro Mori, 'The Uncanny Valley' [2012] IEEE Robotics & Automation Magazine 98, translation by Karl F MacDorman and Norri Kageki of the original 1970 seminal article.

10 For a complete survey of technical definitions available, see Pericle Salvini, *Taxonomy of Robotic Technologies* (RoboLaw Deliverable D4.1, 2013) 17.

11 See George A Bekey, 'Current Trends in Robotics: Technology and Ethics' in Patrik Lin, Keith Abney and George A Bekey (eds), *Robot Ethics The Ethical and Social Implications of Robotics* (The MIT Press 2012) 17.

12 This was done by Antonio Santosuosso, Chiara Boscarato and Franco Caroleo, 'Robot e Diritto: una Prima Ricognizione' [2012] La Nuova Giurisprudenza Commentata 494, 498 (in Italian 'una macchina che svolge autonomamente un lavoro').

13 See Salvini 18.

14 Karel Čapek, *R.U.R. (Rossumovi univerzální roboti)* (1922).

within which to frame single robotic applications and the liability issues they raise (*infra* II.2.c and III.1.a).

b) Legal notions applicable to robots and ensuing legal regimes

Not only the notion of robot is *per se* technologically undetermined, but also potentially different and overlapping legal definitions may apply, depending on the nature and function of the specific application. This implies that diverse kinds of products could be framed within several different regimes, each regulating one or more specific aspects, often lacking adequate coordination.

Because most robots are intrinsically mechanical objects[15] they fall under the broad definition of machinery set forth by the Machinery Directive (MD) (Art 2(a)).

At the same time, robots that qualify as products intended for the consumer market are also subject to the General Product Safety Directive (GPSD),[16] unless more specific rules are applicable. The GSPD also regulates those issues non-directly tackled by sector legislation (Art 1(2)) – such as the MD – like the follow up of the product after its distribution on the market, involving a duty to inform public authorities of dangerous products, and taking action to prevent risks (Art 5(3) GSPD). Moreover, it extends its application to other subjects, such as distributors, who instead are not addressed by the MD.[17]

Pursuant to the GPSD a product is deemed safe when it does not 'present any risk or only the minimum risks compatible with the product's use, considered to be acceptable and consistent with a high level of protection for the safety and health of persons' (Art 2(b)), further determined in light of other conditions such as 'the categories of consumers at risk when using the product, in particular children and the elderly' (Art 2(b)(iv)). The relevance of these provisions for some robotic applications is evident.

15 Directive 2006/42/EC of the European Parliament and of the Council of 17 May 2006 on machinery, and amending Directive 95/16/EC [2006] OJ L 157/24.

16 Directive 2001/95/EC of the European Parliament and of the Council of 3 December 2001 on general product safety [2002] OJ L 11/4.

17 See Directorate General Health and Consumer Protection (DG SANCO), 'Guidance document on the relationship between the General Product Safety Directive (GPSD) and certain sector directives with provisions on product safety', second chapter, November 2015.

Care robots, intended for use as assistive devices for people with disabilities and the elderly, or educational robots that could be used in schools or similar environments, are particularly affected by the aforementioned provisions, requiring an appropriate level of safety, both with respect to the contexts in which the product is to be used and the added vulnerability of its users. In turn, compliance with these requirements may help producers demonstrate the product was not defective, hence escaping responsibility.

The field of healthcare robotics presents an interesting case in the perspective of defining robots, and identifying the regime ensuing from this definition. Machinery such as surgical robots,[18] robotic capsules for diagnostic or therapeutic purposes, cochlear or visual implants, advanced robotic prostheses and exoskeletons,[19] and other brain-computer interfaces qualify as medical devices, and thus are covered by the Medical Devices and Active Implantable Medical Devices Directives (MDD and AIMDD).[20] The main problem in this case is not merely the overlap between legal regimes, since this sector-specific legislation prevails over the more general regulation, but the absence of specific rules for multifaceted and multipurpose devices such as robotic products. Both directives are extremely broad in scope and cover a wide range of devices, from sticking plasters to wheelchairs, from stethoscopes to heart valves, and from thermometers to hip implants.

The discipline they provide is therefore very general, and if on the one hand this uniformity might be considered favouring innovation – allowing producers who intend to expand their businesses to other sectors to do so without facing too high transaction costs – on the other hand it may leave some devices if not completely unregulated, most likely under-regulated.[21]

---

18 See Federico Azzarri and Andrea Bertolini, 'Computer integrated surgical systems' in Erica Palmerini (ed), *Guidelines on Regulating Robotics* (2014).

19 See Andrea Bertolini, 'Robotic Prostheses' in Erica Palmerini (ed), *Guidelines on Regulating Robotics* (2014).

20 Council Directive 93/42/EC of 14 June 1993 concerning medical devices [1993] OJ L 169/1; Council Directive 90/385/EC of 20 June 1990 on the approximation of the laws of the Member States relating to active implantable medical devices [1990] OJ L 189/17.

21 Please allow reference to Andrea Bertolini and Erica Palmerini, 'Regulating Robotics. a Challenge for Europe' in *Upcoming Issues of EU Law. Compilation of in-depth analyses.* Workshop for the IURI Committee of the European Parliament, Session II, 94-129 (Office for the Official Publications of the European Communi-

Indeed, this scheme is not tailored for particularly dangerous or ethically sensitive devices such as body or brain implants, and lacks the specificity needed to meet diverse levels of technical complexity and risk.

Moreover, there are several issues that the directives do not cover, or treat only superficially. Firstly, there is the experimentation phase. BCIs, advanced prosthetics, and other neuro-robotic technologies are not common clinical applications. In fact, they are still largely at a research stage, being slowly developed towards introduction into clinical practice. Early experiments in these fields are often carried out in a legal vacuum, because existing regulations simply recall general principles on human experimentation that are not always suitable for innovative products and systems. This regulatory gap is regarded as one of the major hindrances to the flow of new devices along the innovation trajectory,[22] and may also influence the liability problem, for accidents involving the use of a robotic device. The training of neuro-prosthetic devices, for instance, needs to be carried out in controlled environments in order to monitor potential malfunctioning and to avoid putting other people at risk until the wearer has gained sufficient control of the system. Normally the focus of regulation of clinical trials is on the protection of patients and healthy volunteers. However, in the case of complex and advanced devices such as bionic prostheses, lack of attention on training and control may increase the risks not only for the user, leading to accidents that a comprehensive experimentation phase could instead avoid. Ultimately, this would also affect the subjects being held liable, shifting responsibility from the wearer to other subjects – such as the producer, programmer, or the clinician – who had not properly instructed and trained the patient.[23]

Secondly, the medical devices regulation does not seem to address additional risks, in terms of safety and security, which are determined by the use of robotic systems, sometimes even implanted in the body, with data

---

ties 2014), 119 et seq <http://www.europarl.europa.eu/document/activities/cont/201409/20140924ATT89662/20140924ATT89662EN.pdf> accessed 20 November 2015.

22 See Maurits Butter and others, 'Robotics for Healthcare. Final Report' (European Commission, 3 October 2008).

23 Patrick Moore and others, 'Personal Responsibility in the Age of User-Controlled Prosthetics' (WeRobot, 4th Annual Conference on Robotics, Law and Policy, Seattle, April 2015) <www.werobot2015.org/wp-content/uploads/2015/04/Moore-et-al-Personal-Responsibility-in-the-Age-of-User-controlled-Neuroprosthetics.pdf> accessed 20 November 2015.

processing capabilities, real-time communication with external sources and direct connection to the web. Hacking attempts on software-controlled, internet-connected medical devices are a contingency that the current medical device regulation regime does not consider, nor does the undergoing revision process of the MDD and AIMDD, despite the fact that vulnerabilities to external interferences of ICT devices are regarded as one of the most pressing legal issues within this field.[24]

Thirdly, MDD and AIMDD only concern devices that are meant for diagnostic or therapeutic purposes. Due to the phrasing of the directive (Art 2 MDD), this condition fairly exclusively depends on how the manufacturer categorises the device and on the claims he/she makes regarding the product.[25] Such a narrow interpretation adheres to the double-edged rationale underlying this legislation, which is to protect the health of patients through a system of certification, but also to ensure the free movement of goods without posing any unjustified restrictions. Robotic applications purely aimed at human enhancement therefore do not fall within the MDD regime, although they appear to be very similar to devices already in use in clinical environments for the treatment of different types of conditions and diseases, and present the same features and risks.[26] Without the need to comply with the minimal requirements established by the relevant regime, liability may expand and be fuelled by the lack of a

---

24 Bert-Jaap Koops and Mark N Gasson, 'Attacking Human Implants: A New Generation of Cybercrime' (2013) 5 [2] Law, Innovation and Technology 248; Benjamin Wittes and Jane Chong, 'Our Cyborg Future. Law and Policy Implications' (The Brookings Institution, September 2014) <www.brookings.edu/research/reports2/2014/09/cyborg-future-law-policy-implications> accessed 20 November 2015; Stephen S Wu and Marc Goodman, 'Neural Devices Will Change Humankind: What Legal Issues Will Follow?' (2012) 8 The SciTech Lawyer 3.

25 This interpretation has been confirmed by the ECJ, Case C-219/11 *Brain Products GmbH v BioSemi VOF and Others* [2012].

26 Within the revision process, the existence of a regulatory gap with regard to 'implantable or other invasive products without a medical purpose' has been acknowledged. In order to establish some sort of regulatory control over these types of devices, a new option has been proposed, that is to consider implantable or other invasive products included in a special list as medical devices, regardless of whether or not they are intended by the manufacturer to be used for a medical purpose. See Commission, 'Proposal for a Regulation of the European Parliament and of the Council on medical devices, and amending Directive 2001/83/EC, Regulation (EC) No 178/2002 and Regulation (EC) No 1223/2009' COM (2012) 542 final, art 2.1.

framework within which a certain level of safety and efficacy are certified before distribution on the market.

Difficulty in establishing the legal status of robotic products can also be witnessed with respect to autonomous vehicles. According to a detailed analysis of both federal legislation and national US laws, the circulation of self-driving cars is considered to be lawful in the USA, because they would fall within the notion of vehicles adopted by the relevant laws, which at the same time do not explicitly require the driver to be in the constant control of the activity and of traffic conditions.[27] However, several statutes have been enacted in order to experimentally allow the circulation of automated cars in a few states (e.g. Nevada, California, Florida), and to regulate some aspects such as safety requirements, insurance coverage, special plates, notification of crashes to competent authorities, and restrictions to circulation.[28]

In Europe, the legal status of autonomous vehicles is more uncertain.[29] The Vienna Convention on road traffic[30] seems to indicate that autonomous cars should not circulate on public roads, since it states that 'Every moving vehicle […] shall have a driver' (Art 8(1)) and that 'Every driver shall at all times be able to control his vehicle …' (Art 8(5)). The fully automated driving mode would not be consistent with this formulation, which could on the contrary allow highly automated vehicles where a person on board is constantly monitoring the traffic situation and is able to resume control and override the automatic system.[31] At present, standards set by UNECE would also affect the legality of self-driving vehicles, whenever they require a feature that involves a human driver (e.g. that brakes are activated by muscular energy) or that indirectly rules out automatic control.[32]

---

27 Bryant Walker Smith, 'Automated Vehicles Are Probably Legal in the United States' (2014) 1 Texas A&M Law Review 411.

28 Bryant Walker Smith, 'Automated Vehicles?' 500–508.

29 See Maurice Schellekens, 'Self-Driving Cars' in Erica Palmerini (ed), *Guidelines on Regulating Robotics* (2014) 53 et seq.

30 Convention on Road Traffic, Vienna, 8 November 1968.

31 See the amendment to Article 8 introduced by UNECE, which will enter into force on 23 March 2106: Working Party on Road Traffic Safety, 'Report of the Sixty-eighth Session of the Working Party on Road Traffic Safety' (ECE/TRANS/WP. 1/145) (24–26 March 2014, Geneva).

32 For some examples, see Nikolaus Lang and others, 'Revolution Versus Regulation' 20.

2. *The technology's inherent features*

Notwithstanding the difficulties in defining what a robot is, there is some agreement with regard to the minimal features that all robots should exhibit to be recognised as such. The basic features that identify a robot are commonly described referring to the sequence 'sense – think – act', and to the equipment needed to perform these actions.[33] A robot has sensors to enable data collection, which is then processed by embedded software, ultimately leading to an action, normally intended to achieve predetermined goals. Other usual, but not necessary, characteristics include the ability to communicate with an operator, other robots, or an external network, and an ability to learn from experience in a training process that does not involve human inputs. There is, in fact, a certain continuity between an automaton and a real robot, the latter being characterised by a higher complexity than the former.[34] Instead of a clear-cut and qualitative line of discrimination, robots differ from automatic machines in their increasing complexity that enables them to execute high-level tasks without human supervision, and ensures efficient reactions to multiple stimuli from the environment. Advances in diverse fields – perception, space representation, object and facial recognition, movement planning, and the integration of all these functions – will make robots increasingly precise and effective tools to undertake various tasks in unstructured environments.

This very basic description underlines the elements inherent in robotic technologies that could have legal significance.

---

33 Commission de réflexion sur l'Éthique de la Recherche en sciences et technologies du Numerique d'Allistene (CERNA), 'Éthique de la recherche en robotique' (November 2014), 12 <cerna-ethics-allistene.org/digitalAssets/38/ 38704_Avis_ro botique_livret.pdf> accessed 20 November 2015.

34 A good example is that of a fridge, which can autonomously activate its engine when it perceives that the temperature is increasing above the set level. The sequence sense-think-act is reproduced along an extremely simple scheme: only the temperature is sensed, and only one action is performed (turn on and off a switch).

a) Embodiment

A robot is an embodied entity that collects and processes data, thus highlighting the potential and risks of both the physical and digital worlds. By combining these features, robots can perform a wide spectrum of useful tasks, but also expose their users, and bystanders, to the risk of wrongful interactions, leading to financial losses, privacy infringements, and physical harm. 'Robots ... differ from computers and software precisely in that they are organised to act upon the world. The capacity to act physically upon the world translates, in turn, to the potential to physically harm people or property'.[35]

In addition, robots are expected to populate ordinary spaces. When robots are used in industrial settings, clear boundaries separate them from the workers. Protective fences isolate robot workspaces, contact between man and machine is reduced to a minimum, and humans and robots perform distinct tasks without interacting. Robots represent in this case an advanced form of automation, which does not trigger complex legal issues. The robots that may soon inhabit our homes, drive us around, fly over our homes, and assist us in hospitals will on the contrary have many more opportunities for infringing our liberties and fundamental rights.

b) Technical connectivity

Robots are also connected devices. A continuous flow of information and data normally takes place between the robotic system, digital networks and the producer or seller. Data collection and data flows are generated in many ways: by remote software updates, telematic services agreement, and cloud robotics.[36] In fact, outsourcing part of the robot's data processing to remote servers renders the system more efficient, and exploits the Internet to compute and process vast amounts of data. Technical connectivity enables robots to be made lighter, cheaper, and less

---

35 Ryan Calo, 'Robotics and the Lessons of Cyberlaw' (2015) 103 California Law Review 513, 532.

36 On cloud robotics and the legal challenges for consumer law in the US, see Andrew Proia, Drew Simshaw and Kris Hauser, 'Consumer Cloud Robotics and the Fair Information Practice Principles: Recognizing the Challenges and Opportunities Ahead' (2015) 16 Minnesota Journal of Law, Science & Technology 145.

power-consuming, thanks to limited on-board computers, and at the same time improves robots functionality. Robots in fact share knowledge, learn from other robots' experiences, and draw from extensive databases for tasks such as object recognition and navigation planning. For instance, in the future automated vehicles will rely on detailed and up-to-date navigation services; integrate vehicle-to-vehicle (V2V) or vehicle-to-infrastructure (V2I) communication technologies to transmit basic safety information, such as warnings to drivers concerning impending crashes. They will be equipped with in-vehicle 'infotainment' systems, with both information and entertainment services. These systems will increase the collection and use of vehicle data, especially geo-location data, generated and transmitted to and from motor vehicles. Robotic medical devices can also have wireless capabilities that are commonly used to send the data to the patient's physician.

Product connectivity raises different issues. Firstly, it makes the system vulnerable to hacking and external attacks. Security against cyber-attacks is considered to be critical both for automated vehicles[37] and for implanted medical devices.[38]

Secondly, robots will increasingly inhabit private spaces, where they will sense and record their environment, and share that information with third parties (for instance, service providers) or store it in the cloud in order to carry out different functions.[39] Privacy concerns arise, hardened by the fact that robots need to be connected to external networks to operate. Cyber-security and privacy are both a technological and a legal

37 See National Highway Traffic Safety Administration, 'Preliminary Statement of Policy Concerning Automated vehicles', 2013 <www.nhtsa.gov/staticfiles/rulemaking/pdf/Automated_Vehicles_Policy.pdf> accessed 20 November 2015; Gillian Yeomans, 'Autonomous vehicles. Handing over control: opportunities and risks for insurance' (Lloyds 2014) para 6.1.4, 16.

38 FDA, 'Cybersecurity for Networked Medical Devices Containing Off-the-Shelf (OTS) Software' (14 January 2005) <www.fda.gov/downloads/MedicalDevices/DeviceRegulationandGuidance/GuidanceDocuments/ucm077823.pdf> accessed 20 November 2015; FDA, 'Content of Premarket Submissions for Management of Cybersecurity in Medical Devices' (2 October 2014), <www.fda.gov/downloads/MedicalDevices/DeviceRegulationandGuidance/GuidanceDocuments/UCM356190.pdf.> accessed on 20 November 2015.

39 Margot E Kaminsky, 'Robots in the Home: What Will We Have Agreed to?' (2015) 51 Idaho Law Review 661; Ryan Calo, 'Robots and Privacy' in Patrick Lin, George Bekey, and Keith Abney (eds), *Robot Ethics: The Ethical and Social Implications of Robotics* (MIT Press 2012).

challenge, which probably entails embedding privacy (and security) safeguards into the design of products and network architectures, but also entails evaluating the effectiveness of current privacy regulation.

Thirdly, the flow of information between the producer/seller and the robotic device could expand the knowledge of risks to which the users of a product or bystanders are exposed. This phenomenon -- described as proximity to the product, to the product user and to the product use – is considered as a driver of liability.[40] Although many technical challenges still need to be resolved (such as the stability of the connection), thanks to product connectivity, manufacturers/sellers will gradually acquire increasing control over their products, learn more about their post-sale use, and potentially discover risks or unveil misuses which they were not previously aware of. This expanded knowledge could eventually widen the obligations, and subsequent liability, of sellers (see §V).

c) Robots' autonomy

Another distinctive feature of robotic systems is their capacity to operate autonomously, without human supervision. This characteristic is not constantly present – many robots are tele-operated or programmed to execute fully predefined actions – but is generally considered an important attribute, depending on the functions the robot is designed to perform. The importance of autonomy stems from the fact that advanced robots will operate in dynamic and unstructured environments, where they will be exposed to highly varied types of inputs that must be accounted for as they occur. If a robot has to accomplish complex tasks, often unspecified, without human supervision, it needs the capability to efficiently react to external stimuli and to the users' requests.

The increasing complexity of robotic systems potentially raises the possibility of emergent behaviours, i.e., modes of behaviour that were not predicted by the designer but which arise as a result of unexpected interactions among the components of the system or with the operating environment.[41] The fact that designers and engineers cannot always foresee how the robot will act in real-world scenarios, when confronted with new situa-

---

40 Bryant Walker Smith, 'Proximity-Driven Liability' (2014) 102 Georgetown Law Journal 1777.

41 Ronald C Arkin, *Behavior-Based Robotics* (MIT Press 1998).

tions and new inputs, is at times identified as raising an accountability issue. However, it may be disputed that a programming technique – no matter how innovative and enabling – should suffice in excluding the liability of the engineer who designed the device.[42] More sensibly, one may consider that the complex interaction of different actors involved in the creation of the device, may cause the ascertainment of liability – in particular with respect to the causal nexus – to become extremely complex. This aspect, which is definitely not exclusive to robotics, may here become of increasing relevance, reducing – in some cases – human control and oversight,[43] yet does not appear to be *per se* decisive (see III. 1.b).

III. Do robots challenge liability rules?

A common question in the discussion on the regulation of robotics is whether the law is equipped to deal with the robots' particular features or whether the rationale underpinning the current rules is challenged by the intrinsic characteristics of robotic technologies, in particular with respect to liability rules.[44] Answering this question entails analysing the gap between robot capabilities and robot regulation. Notably, liability is allocated on the basis of 'control' that someone exerts over his/her own behaviour, or over the things he/she produces and sells, or owns or uses, or over other persons whose action he/she is deemed responsible for.

The autonomy and emergent behaviour that robots – in some cases – display is deemed to conflict with these very principles, identifying a loss of control on the side of the creator of the device.[45]

42 For a discussion on this point see Andrea Bertolini, 'Robots as Products: The Case for a Realistic Analysis of Robotic Applications and Liability Rules' (2013) 5 Law Innovation and Technology 214, 231 et seq.

43 René von Schomberg, 'From an ethics of technology towards an ethics of knowledge policy: implications for robotics'(2008) 22 *Artificial Intelligence and Society* 331.

44 See Andrea Bertolini, 'Robots and liability - Justifying a change in perspective' in Fiorella Battaglia, Julian Nida-Rümelin and Nikil Mukerji (eds), *Rethinking Responsibility in Science and Technology* (Pisa University Press 2014) 143 et seq.

45 Andreas Matthias, 'The responsibility gap: Ascribing responsibility for the actions of learning automata' (2004) 6 *Ethics and Information Technology* 175; Andreas Matthias, *Automaten als Träger von Rechten* (Logos Verlag 2010); George Bekey,

Alternative solutions are therefore envisioned, which take this problem into account and which attempt to define a plausible framework for the compensation of damages arising from the use of these machines.

One seemingly viable option could be to apply the most severe responsibility scheme associated with the undertaking of dangerous activities to robotic products and activities. However, although robotic behaviour can be unpredictable and software malfunctioning will almost inevitably occur, the deployment of robotic devices may not be enumerated among extra-hazardous activities, neither by referring to their modes of operation nor to the nature of interactions with human beings they presuppose. At a general level, and considering the potentials of those technologies that are more imminent, there are not sufficient grounds to qualify robotic applications as intrinsically dangerous.

In contrast, another proposal is to limit liability, as a way both to boost innovation in the robotic industry, by reducing the fears of liability-related costs, and to exclude producers having to bear responsibility for risks that cannot be avoided, notwithstanding the care in designing the product and informing the users. The 'compromise between the need to foster innovation and the need to incentivise safety' would have a precedent in the immunity of gun manufacturers from what people do with their guns and web providers in terms of how their website may be used.[46] This is based on the assumption that robots can be put to multiple uses not all of which can be predicted and warned against by producers. More precisely, a 'selective immunity' would shield open robotic platform manufacturers from all actions related to improvements made by third parties.[47] Such a proactive approach has drawbacks because it risks shifting the costs of liability onto the victims, if not accompanied by other forms of compensatory remedies.

An alternative approach would be to increase the owner's responsibility. This idea rests on the assumption that the aggrieved party by the robot would encounter many difficulties were he/she to prove the negligence of the owner and/or the causality, due to the complexity and the lack of transparency of highly sophisticated machines to ordinary citizens. The

---

Patrick Lin and Keith Abney, 'Ethical Implications of Intelligent Robots', in Jeffrey L Krichmar and Hiroaki Wagatsuma (eds), *Neuromorphic and Brain-Based Robots* (CUP 2011).

46 Ryan Calo, 'Open Robotics' (2011) 70 Maryland Law Review 571.

47 Ryan Calo, 'Open Robotics'.

reason for applying a strict liability instead of a negligence standard stems from the fact that the owner is a beneficiary of technology and can obtain additional advantages in introducing robots into his/her organisation. Many national liability rules enforce this paradigm for damages brought about by a thing that is owned by the tortfeasor or a person that is included in his/her organisation. Such reinforced owner's accountability would be accompanied, in this proposal, by a liability cap limiting the amount of damages that same person could be required to compensate. In addition there would be some form of insurance, which often supplements the model of strict liability, and which could make the system more feasible and sustainable while innovation progresses.[48]

A third solution is the creation of a legal personhood for robots in order to make them responsible for any damage they may cause.[49] This proposal stems from the observation that robots are being programmed to show increasing adaptive and learning capabilities, and can therefore react unpredictably to the inputs they receive from the environment. In these cases, the attribution of liability to the robot's owner could still apply, based on existing models such as the vicarious liability for injuries caused by animals, or the parental responsibility for damages produced by minors. However another scheme has been explored, because, ultimately, 'it seems that producer, programmer, owner and user are assuming the role of "external controller" of an *entity* that seems to be capable of expressing embryonic but growing levels of autonomy and subjectivity'[50]. Building on the argument regarding the forms of responsibility arising from a robot's action, a more general discourse on the legal subjectivity of robots has been proposed. 'Electronic personhood' is considered to be a plausible approach for embodied robots (or software agents) that display a certain degree of autonomy and interact with people. Robots would have to be registered and equipped with assets in order to compensate for damages or

48 Michael Decker, 'Responsible Innovation for Adaptive Robots', in Fiorella Battaglia, Nikil Mukerji and Julian Nida-Rümelin (eds), *Rethinking Responsibility in Science and Technology* (Pisa University Press 2014).

49 Christophe Leroux and others, 'Suggestions for a green paper on legal issues in robotics. Contribution to Deliverable D3.2.1 on ELS issues in robotics' (31 December 2012) <www.eurobotics.net/cms/upload/PDF/euRobotics_Deliverable_D.3.2.1_Annex_Suggestion_GreenPaper_ELS_IssuesInRobotics.pdf> accessed 20 November 2015.

50 Christophe Leroux and others, 'Suggestions for a green paper on legal issues in robotics' 75.

fulfil obligations. Different options could be included regarding how this financial basis should be established and funded.[51]

1. *A functional approach to liability rules*

To better address plausible alternatives and identify the preferable strategy that jurists ought implement, both in a *de iure condito* and *de iure condendo* perspective, a step back is required. Indeed, the correct framework of analysis and approach needs to be specified, in particular with respect to why a change in extant regulation may be required in order to accommodate robotic technologies. Two are, in fact, the possible alternative perspectives: (i) a difference may be found in the way robots 'are', inducing us to conclude that they could amount to beings – at least within a certain degree; or (ii) their peculiar functioning may suggest the adoption of a technically – in a legal dimension – different scheme. An argument grounded sub (i) may be deemed ontological, sub (ii) functional, the differences – even with respect to the outcomes – are substantial, and deserve some consideration.

In a private law perspective, the ascription of liability fundamentally entails the shifting of a cost – namely of damages[52] – from one party to the other, when the damaging party is either deemed at fault[53] or held strictly liable,[54] pursuant to a general provision or – in some cases – a specific

---

51 Christophe Leroux and others, 'Suggestions for a green paper on legal issues in robotics' 58 et seq.

52 As a quick and necessarily incomplete reference, see Guido Calabresi and Douglas A Melamed, 'Property Rules, Liability Rules, and Inalienability: One View of the Cathedral' (1972) 85 Harvard Law Review 1089 et seq; Richard Posner, *Economic analysis of law* (Aspen 2007).

53 Fault is traditionally the default standard of all tort law systems. See Dan B Dobbs, Robert E Keeton and Daviv G Owen, *Prosser and Keeton on Torts* (West Publishing 1995); David G. Owen, *Products Liability Law. Hornbook series* (second edn, Thompson West 2008); Dan B Dobbs, *The law of torts* (West 2004); Carlo Castronovo, *La nuova responsabilità civile* (Giuffrè 2006); Francesco Donato Busnelli, *voce «Illecito civile»* (Treccani 1989); Gerhard Wagner and Hein Kötz, *Deliktsrecht* (Vahlen 2013).

54 Strict liability differs from a fault based rule since the claimant is not required to demonstrate that the defendant was negligent or violated a specific norm setting a standard of conduct to be held in similar circumstances. It suffices, instead, to establish the existence of a nexus between the harm suffered and the conduct (or

norm.[55] To this end – physical – persons are held liable because (i) they can determine themselves and their actions towards a desired end, and (ii) they – both physical and legal – own assets, with which they can face the claims brought against them for the compensation of damages. In particular because of (i) liability rules may produce that deterrence effect so fundamental to the legal system as a whole, inducing a desirable behaviour on the side of the subjects acting in society; because of (ii) victims may obtain due compensation and achieve the redress of the negative consequences suffered.

Absent the capacity of the subject to determine itself towards a given end the attribution of liability may not serve its harm prevention function; absent autonomous assets – and the ability to earn such assets – another subject needs to be identified in order to provide required compensation to the victim. Things, as well as animals, do not satisfy either the first or the second requirement and cannot therefore be held liable, thus the person 'behind' them is.[56] Robots, until proven otherwise, are objects and thus such liability rules apply to them.

a) The robot as an autonomous agent: a misconception

So in sketching the overall framework, we can easily show that the ontological argument is neither philosophically nor technologically grounded,

---

defect). Such rules are normally deemed more favourable to the claimant, yet it is disputable whether it is not the causal nexus the most relevant burden to be fulfilled. At the same time the idea is challenged that strict liability rules provide additional deterrence incentives, see Posner 182; Mitchell A Polinsky and Steven Shavell, 'The uneasy case for product liability' (2009-2010) 123 Harvard Law Review 1437, 1437 et seq.

55 The most relevant example to the analysis here conducted is the one of the Council Directive 85/374/EEC of 25 July 1985 on the approximation of the laws, regulations and administrative provisions of the Member States concerning liability for defective products [1985] OJ L210/29 (henceforth Product Liability Directive or PLD).

56 Often specific rules provide that the owner of the animal is held liable for the harm caused by its possession, see art. 2052 of the Italian Civil Code, or art 1385 of the French Civil Code, or § 833 BGB.

and even in a purely functional perspective, cannot be agreed upon, much less in a legal one.[57]

In an ethical perspective, a robot does not show that ability of coordinating its actions towards its self-determined end that constitutes the fundamental requisite to be deemed an agent, hence a responsible being.[58] No existing device shows this degree of autonomy and it is disputed – in a purely technological perspective – whether such kind of self-awareness could ever be achieved,[59] or whether it rests in the realm of science fiction, together with Asimov's bicentennial man.

However, were such a technology created, deeming it an agent would still represent a *contradictio in adjecto* – in a Kantian perspective – for it

---

57 See Bryant Walker Smith, 'Proximity-Driven Liability' 102 The Georgetown Law Journal 1779.

58 See Gutman, Rathgeber and Syed.

59 For a discussion see Joachim Hertzberg and Raja Chatila, 'AI Reasoning Methods for Robotics' in Bruno Siciliano and Oussama Khatib (eds), *Handbook of Robotics* (Springer 2008) 208, 'Reasoning requires that the reasoner [...] has an explicit representation of parts or aspects of its environment to reason about'. The engineering problem is that of identifying formalism suitable for representing knowledge to be used by a machine, which will be further distinguished in two sub-problems: 'epistemological adequacy: does the formalism allow the targeted aspects of the environment to be expressed compactly and precisely?' and 'computational adequacy: does formalism allow typical inferences to be drawn effectively or efficiently?'. There is however a trade-off between an epistemologically satisfactory formalism and the possibility of inferring conclusions for the solutions of problems, (see 211).
On the distinction between GOFAI (Good Old Fashioned Artificial Intelligence) LAI (Light Artificial Intelligence) see Floridi, pos. 2862 et eq. Essentially the former entails the construction of a machine 'whose behaviour would eventually be at least comparable, if not superior, to the behaviour characterizing intelligent human beings in similar circumstances'; the latter instead simply aims at achieving a specific functionality or capability, to perform a task efficiently, such as driving in the traffic avoiding collisions and other accidents.
Discussing artificial intelligence Curtis E.A. Karnow, 'The Application of Traditional Tort Theory to Embodied Machine Intelligence' (WeRobot), 3 states that 'The notion of intelligence as applied to machines is often just shorthand for "I don't know how they do that so quickly" an amazement borne of ignorance. We might in that way ascribe intelligence to Apple's Siri, which can respond to basic voice commands with vaguely contextually correct responses, missile defense systems which distinguish hostile intruders, and stock market programs which in fractions of a second calculate the best price and execute trades. The apparent, magic of these advanced technologies is generally a function of speed outside human scale, and of the observer's ignorance of the programs being used'.

would not represent and end-in-itself,[60] but simply another artefact, created with and for a purpose – whatever that may be, even simply to exist and be free.[61] A utilitarian stance would instead lead us to conclude that no sound argument could be formulated to legitimise the creation of such an artificial-being. Since the very purpose of robotics is to improve the human condition, designing applications that would freely determine themselves according to their own desires and preferences, eventually disobeying the orders issued to them, would be – to say the least – contradictory.[62]

Short of that kind of full-fledged autonomy, all robots are plainly completing the tasks they were designed to fulfil, in the ways that were made possible to them by their creators – designers, researchers, producers, programmers. Thence, no matter what sort of emergent behaviour they might display, such machines would still not defy their classification as mere objects, heteronomously determined in their actions by the real agent, a human being, who alone might be held responsible.[63]

---

60 This is a mere application of the Kantian categorical imperative, pursuant to which '*vernünftige Wesen stehen aller unter dem Gesetz, dass jedes derselben sich selbst und alle andere niemals bloß als Mittel, sondern jederzeit zugleich als Zweck an sich selbst behandeln solle*'.

61 See Gutman, Rathgeber and Syed 223 et seq.

62 This very question is asked by Dieter Sturma, 'Autonomie. Über Personen Künstliche Intelligenz und Robotik' in T Christaller and J Wehner (eds), *Autonome Machinen* (Westdeutscher Verlag 2003) 52, 'Auf die Frage einer künstlichen Person, warum wir sie in maschineller Form überhaupt zur Existenz gebracht hätten, wären wir kaum besser vorbereitet als der unglückliche Dr. Frankestein. Wenn aber ernsthaft Projekte der künstliche Erzeugung von Bewusstsein erwogen werden sollen, dann wäre es ratsam zu fragen, ob es überhaupt rechtfertigungsfähige Gründe dafür geben kann, auf technologischem Wege neue Bewusstseinsformen mit existenziellen und ethischen Eigenschaften zu entwickeln'. At the same time, if such a being was created we could even expect it to take control and decide for itself what degree of freedom and rights to grant us, Bert-Jaap Koops, Hildebrandt-Mireille and David-Oliver Jaquet-Chiffelle, 'Bridging the Accountability Gap: Rights for New Entities in the Information Society?' (2010) 11(2) Minnesota Journal of Law, Science & Technology 497, 561. For a more detailed discussion, please allow reference to Bertolini, 'Robots as Products' 225.

63 Gutman, Rathgeber and Syed 246–247.

b) The ability to learn and the alleged loss of control. A criticism

Even the robot's ability to 'learn', defined – by some authors – as the machine's ability to acquire and elaborate data in order to complete its tasks,[64] does not constitute a sound argument to identify a loss of control on the side of the 'creator'[65] and determine a responsibility of the machine itself.

The different techniques that are normally considered – neural networks[66] and evolutionary robotics[67] – represent in fact alternative programming techniques, intended to influence the way the device is conceived and elaborated, rather than its daily operation. It is thence the producer's decision as to what kind of technique to use in order to achieve the best result possible, both in terms of sophistication and functionality of the robot as well as safety.[68]

Moreover, even if we assumed that an ability to modify itself was granted to the robot after the moment it was introduced into the market that would still represent a heteronomously determined choice of the 'creator', which should only be allowed when sufficiently safe.[69]

---

64 See Andreas Matthias, 'The Responsibility Gap: Ascribing Responsibility for the Actions of Learning Automata' 6 Ethics and Information Technology 177.

65 See Andreas Matthias, 'From Coder to Creator. Responsibility Issues in Intelligent Artifact Design' in Rocci Luppicini and Rebecca Adell (eds), *Handbook of Research in Technoethics*, vol Handbook of Research in Technoethics (Hersher 2008) 175 et seq.

66 See Hertzberg and Chatila 220.

67 See Dario Floreano, Phil Husbands and Stefano Nolfi, 'Evolutionary Robotics' in Bruno Siciliano and Oussama Khatib (eds), *Handbook of Robotics* (Springer 2008) 1424 'Here, instead of programming a robot with detailed instructions on how to complete a specific task, [a]n initial population of different artificial chromosomes, each encoding the control system . . . of a robot is randomly created. Each of these chromosomes is then decoded into a corresponding controller . . . and downloaded into the processor of the robot. The robot is then let free to act . . . according to a genetically specified controller while its performance of a given task is automatically evaluated . . . The fittest individuals are allowed to reproduce by generating copies of their chromosomes . . . the newly obtained population is tested again on the same robot. This process is repeated for a number of generations until an individual is born which satisfies the fitness function set by the user'.

68 For a more detailed discussion, see Andrea Bertolini, 'Robots and liability - Justifying a change in perspective' (Pisa University Press 2014) 155 et seq.

69 See the discussion of the learning elevator example at Andrea ibid (Pisa University Press 2014) 157 et seq.

Therefore, in a legal perspective no real loss of control may be appreciated, invalidating existing liability principles. Indeed, *but-for* the human who designed and produced the robot in a given fashion, the robot would not have had those capacities, which in hypothesis later led to the tortious outcome. To the contrary, new technologies will enable producers to exert a higher degree of control, extending their *Einwirkungsmöglickeit* in the postcontractual phase (see V).[70]

c) Picking the gifts of the evil deity: a policy-approach to liability issues in robotics

Rejecting the ontological argument does not necessarily entail stating that extant rules need not be revised, rather that the grounds so to do shall be purely functional, the consequence of a well formulated policy argument aimed at designing adequate incentives.[71]

To explain this concept we could recall the powerful example originally conceived by *Guido Calabresi* for his tort law classes, in order to address traffic accidents and the use of automobiles in modern society.[72] If an evil deity offered mankind a gift intended to substantially improve people's lives and make the more enjoyable, yet demanding a certain number of – innocent – victims every year, choosing whether to accept the gift and what sacrifice tolerate in exchange would simply be a matter of public policy.

---

70 See also Bryant Walker Smith, 'Proximity-Driven Liability' 102 The Georgetown Law Journal 1777, 1777 et seq.

71 Please allow reference to Andrea Bertolini, 'Robotic prostheses as products enhancing the rights of people with disabilities. Reconsidering the structure of liability rules' 29 International Review of Law, Computers & Technology 116 et seq. Here Art 4(g) of the UN Convention on the Rights of People with Disabilities is expressly considered in order to support a reshaping of applicable product liability rules to favour both the producers of such devices and the victims involved in accident where use of those very devices is made.

72 Guido Calabresi, *Il dono dello spirito maligno. Gli ideali, le convinzioni, i modi di pensare, nei loro rapporti col diritto* (Giuffrè 1996). The example here subsequently recalled starts at page 10.

The gift corresponds to any form of technological progress,[73] bringing new and unconceived opportunities to society and yet demanding a cost,[74] even to those who may decide not to make a direct or even indirect use of it. Robotics being one of the most relevant form of technological progress, perfectly fits the sketched narrative, and thus forces us to ponder what kind of applications we are willing to favour, what potential we desire to unleash and exploit, as well as what burden we are willing to bear. To this end, liability rules, placing a direct incentive on all subjects involved, clearly represent – as they did in *Calabresi's* example – a privileged tool to engineer society.

The analysis conducted up to here has shown that no ontological grounds can be identified to exclude the application of existing norms to new technologies. However, different sets of rules may overlap, triggering higher levels of litigation among different actors and producing inefficiencies and market failures. A detailed assessment of extant norms in light of their possible application to specific classes of devices needs thence be undergone, starting with product liability rules.[75]

2. The theoretical and empirical limits of products liability rules

The historical rationales for the development of product liability rules are to be identified in the problem of privity of contract.[76] Considering that in modern society consumers purchase their products from a reseller, who normally does not have any way to influence the quality of the good sold,

---

73 Guido Calabresi, *Il dono dello spirito maligno. Gli ideali, le convinzioni, i modi di pensare, nei loro rapporti col diritto* (Giuffrè 1996) 23.

74 See also Mark Coeckelbergh, *Human Being @ Risk* (Springer 2013) 103 et seq.

75 Conclusions achieved could most certainly be of strategic relevance for the development of a European industry of robotic products, but may even induce a more profound rethinking of some of the theoretical grounds upon which the current civil liability system is built. This is a frequently observable phenomenon in the legal discourse, whereby solutions elaborated for specific sub-fields and subtopics, appearing to be at the frontier of the traditional debate, may then in turn prove more efficient in addressing a fundamental problem, and then become generalised solutions. This phenomenon is described by Carlo Castronovo, 'Diritto privato generale e diritti secondi la ripresa di un tema' Europa e diritto privato 397et seq.

76 See Owen 27; Filippo Busoni, 'Responsabilità per danno da prodotti difettosi' in Giuseppe Vettori (ed), *Codice del consumo commentario* (Cedam 2007) 824.

it is devoid of purpose to hold that intermediary liable for the damages suffered even by the occasional user.[77] With product liability rules, the legislator successfully circumvented such a problem, while balancing on the one hand the right to produce and on the other hand that of receiving compensation when harm was suffered.[78]

Ideally, by forcing the internalisation of the costs associated with the marketing of the good, the legislator intends to provide appropriate incentives to invest in high safety standards for the items commercialised, at the same time ensuring that the inevitable victim is not left to bear the entire consequences.

However, several studies, both theoretical[79] and empirical[80] – have challenged the adequacy of existing rules in attaining this otherwise desirable effect. In particular, it was argued that no observable incentive is provided by product liability regulation towards the commercialisation of safer products.[81] Apparently, market mechanisms – among which is reputation – play the most relevant role in ensuring the reliability of devices. At the same time, it was observed that the introduction of an exemption, preventing a specific class of manufactures[82] to be sued under product

---

77 Art 1 PLD, which holds the producer liable for the damage caused by a defect in his product, is intended as not limited to the person owning the good, but rather includes even those who make unauthorised use of it, see Busoni 834.

78 See Owen 7 '[b]y choosing to expose product users and others to certain types and degrees of risk, manufacturers appropriate to themselves certain interests in safety and bodily integrity that may belong to those other persons. Similarly by choosing to make claims against manufacturers for harm resulting from such risks or uses victims of product accidents seek to appropriate to themselves economic interests that may belong to manufacturers and other consumers'.

79 See Posner, 182; Polinsky and Shavell, 1437 et seq.

80 See Eric A Helland and Alexander Tabarrok, 'Product Liability and Moral Hazard: Evidence from General Aviation' (2012) 55 The Journal of Law and Economics 593, 593 et seq.

81 Polinsky and Shavell, 1437 ff.

82 Liability exemptions were introduced in the US legal system for commercial aircrafts in 1994 with the General Aviation Revitalization Act (Act Aug. 17, 1994, P.L. 103–298, § 1–4, 108 Stat. 1552; Nov. 20, 1997, P.L. 105-102, § 3(e), 111 Stat. 2215, henceforth GARA). The particularly high number of product liability actions brought against civil aviation aircrafts manufacturers was causing the entire industry to collapse when the US government decided to intervene; shielding producers from all actions eighteen years after the airplane was first sold. A recent econometric study (see below fn. 83) aimed at showing the impact of moral hazard concluded that, despite the exemption, the number of accidents

liability rules did not lead to an increase in the number of accidents, preventing moral hazard on the side of the – sophisticated – user of the device.[83]

Moreover, the limited number of cases in Europe, as opposed to the United States,[84] that resort to product liability in order to claim compensation[85] could only be explained by arguing that: (i) products traded in the European market are substantially safer than those sold on the North-American one, or that (ii) the overall system is less favourable to the victim. As the first argument appears *ictu oculi* implausible, the latter seems a more reasonable justification.

Undergoing a detailed analysis of the Product Liability Directive (PLD) falls beyond the purposes of the current study. The mentioned considerations however, certainly suffice in raising the doubt about the adequacy of existing norms, and overall effect they produce when overlapping with alternative liability rules.

---

declined in subsequent years, due to an allegedly greater investment in safety on the side of the user. Three relevant aspects are though observed: (i) commercial aviation is a highly regulated industry, with high technical requirements imposed on producers; (ii) users – namely pilots – are sophisticated parties, with considerable knowledge on the technical aspects of the products and able to understand and process complex information about the correct usage of the machine; (iii) the safety investment decision made by the producer was undertaken – in the vast majority of cases – before the exemption was enacted, and thus when the producer was expected to be held liable pursuant to an objective rule. For a more detailed discussion, see Bertolini, 'Robotic Prostheses' 142–143.

83 Helland and Tabarrok, 593 et seq.

84 Indeed the PLD is based on comparable principles to those of the Restatement Third (and Second) of Torts, Product Liability.

85 See Sara Biglieri, Andrea Pupeschi and Christian Di Mauro, 'The Italian Product Liability Experience' in Dennis Campbell (ed), *Liability for Products in a Global Economy* (Kluwer 2005); Miguel Torres Mingot, 'Civil Liability for Defective Products in Spain' in Dennis Campbell and S. Woodley (eds), *Liability for products in a Global Economy* (Kluwer 2005); John Meltzer and Rod Freeman, *Product Liability for the European Union. A report for the European Commission* (available at http://eceuropaeu/enterprise/policies/single-market-goods/files/goods/docs/liability/studies/lovells-study_enpdf, 2003).

a) Uncertainty: the problem of the assessment of the causal nexus and the overlapping of different sets of rules

To better show how complicated the application of the PLD may be when technologically advanced products are considered, two examples may be taken into account, namely robotic prostheses, and cars with increasing degrees of automation.

Let us assume the case of a robotic hand implanted onto the human body of a person with disability, used by the wearer to perform various daily activities, including driving.[86] If an accident occurred, in order to establish the liability of the producer, the victim – be it the wearer or third party – would need to show that the functioning of the device is the cause of the accident, and that the malfunctioning would not have verified, had the implant been designed otherwise. To operate, a robotic prosthesis[87]

86 This example is derived from the real-life case of Christian Kandlbauer, the Austrian bilateral amputee, whose arms were replaced by two different prostheses by Otto Bock, one of which made use of the biological signal derived from the nervous system, see <http://www.ottobock.com/cps/rde/xchg/ob_com_en/hs.xsl/11443.html.> accessed 4 December 2015. Mr. Kandlbauer died in a car crash while driving a vehicle especially designed for his needs, and approved by traffic authorities. See also the information available on the press of the time of the accident <http://www.theguardian.com/world/2010/oct/22/christian-kandlbauer-arm-dies-crash> accessed 4 December 2015. In the case, it was impossible to ascertain whether the accident was due to a malfunctioning of the prosthesis, and in no way in the present document we are assuming that it indeed may have been. The example is just used to exemplify the reasoning by making purely fictional assumptions.

87 A prosthesis is defined as 'a device that physically replaces a missing body part, which may be lost due to physical injury, disease, or congenital conditions' (Oxford English Dictionary 2014). The term prosthesis – originally used in linguistics in 1550, meaning in late Latin, 'addition of a letter or syllable to a word' – was first referred to an 'artificial body part' in 1900 (Oxford English Dictionary, 2014). While the prosthetic field also includes internally implanted artificial body parts (such as hip bones, auditory prostheses, teeth), this analysis will focus on limb prostheses – which may include both upper and lower body extremities – since they are more related to biomechanics and kinesthetics. Within such still broad spectrum of devices, the adjective 'robotic' helps to distinguish simply passive adjustable applications from – usually electrically – powered mechatronic systems, but also specifically addresses the presence into this device of actuators, sensors and microcontrollers, together with an intelligent control system implementing a desired behaviour (i.e., actuators return given responses on the basis of sensors' data), see Pericle Salvini and Marco Cempini, 'Robotic Pros-

interprets the biological signal sent by the human nervous system and transforms it into commands to the motors and actuators of which it consists, finally leading to the movement.[88] To show a causal nexus thence, one would need to (i) isolate the one of the many movements performed – or failed to perform – that determined the accident, and (ii) identify a malfunctioning or error in the interpretation of the signal by the machine, and finally (iii) demonstrate that it is due to a defective design of the system. The proof is evidently burdensome, and might lead the victim not to sue the producer in the first place, or – in case it was a third party – sue the implantee.

Autonomous vehicles[89] provide an even clearer example, inasmuch as they might trigger strategic behaviour on the side of both the producer and the owner/driver. Considering a scenario of increasing automation, where human interaction is at times required – for technical reasons, namely the incapacity of the system to handle specific weather or traffic conditions – or allowed – according to the user's preferences, to the extent he is left free to decide whether to take over control – the liability of the driver, of the owner, and of the producer intertwine.

Let us assume that a vehicle is proceeding in driverless mode on an urban road when it encounters unexpected traffic, which it estimates it cannot safely handle, hence signals the driver to take control. The driver, having chosen the mode – even if he could have driven himself all along, for that was just a function his vehicle enabled him to select – was

---

theses' in Erica Palmerini (ed), *Guidelines on Regulating Robotics* (2014) 108 et seq. Prostheses, together with orthoses and exoskeletons, can be grouped together under the class of hybrid bionic systems (henceforth HBS), see Silvestro Micera, *Hybrid Bionic Systems for the Replacement of Hand Function* (2006)1752 et seq. An HBS is a system consisting of three elements: (i) biological (i.e., human or animal), linked to (ii) an artificial part (i.e., prosthesis), by means of (iii) a control interface. Depending on the configuration, HBSs can be 'artificial systems with biological elements or subsystems, where the biological system is a complementary or supplementary element to the technical system or a biological systems with artificial elements or subsystems, in which the artificial subsystem, e.g., a robotic artefact, is a complementary or supplementary element to the biological system' (ibid 1753).

88 For a more detailed description see Salvini and Cempini117 et seq.

89 For a comprehensive discussion of the technical aspects of driverless vehicles, see Alberto Broggi and others, 'Intelligent Vehicles' in Bruno Siciliano and Oussama Khatib (eds), *Handbook of Robotics* (Springer 2008).

distracted, causing his reaction not to be prompt and, consequently, an accident occurs.

The accident may be seen as due to human error, consisting in the delayed reaction, or as a design defect, for the warning may be considered not sufficiently timely either. However, the choice to let the vehicle drive in urban settings may be deemed negligent on the side of the user, taking excessive risk, but also the design – intended eminently as programming – could again be blamed for enabling such a choice, instead of forcing the person to attentively sit behind the wheel. In all these cases then, at least in legal systems such as the Italian,[90] also the owner, even when not sitting in the cabin, could still be called to repay damages, to some extent easing the position of the victim. Yet, this would only apparently solve the issue, for he could still sue in recourse either the driver or the producer, or both, leading to *ex ante* uncertainty with respect to whom may then be called to – ultimately – bear the costs of the accident.

The substantial difference with current traffic accidents rests on the tighter human-machine interaction[91] that causes the otherwise clear cut line between human error and technical malfunctioning to become increasingly more blurred with growing automation.

b) The shift towards product liability and the technology-chilling effect

The closer interaction of man and machine that robotic products bring about causes a shift towards the application of product liability rules in fields that as of today are preeminently, if not exclusively, regulated through alternative sets of rules, such as the tort of negligence or specific norms, e.g. the liability of the owner of the vehicle. Over time, absent legal reform, the overlapping of alternative schemes will become more evident, leading to a twofold consequence. The inefficiencies that appear to characterise extant norms – and the PLD in particular – will assume greater relevance. The number of cases that may require their application will increase, and the difficulties that claimants today face in showing the

---

90 Art 2054, 2° co. of the Italian Civil Code holds the owner of the vehicle jointly and severally liable with the driver.

91 Currently over 90% of the cases can be traced back to human error, see Broggi and others 1177.

defectiveness of design and the existence of a clear causal nexus will most likely be exacerbated by the technological complexity of such devices.

At the same time, the uncertainty of the legal outcome, associated with the multiplicity of uses and scenarios in which the same robotic application may be employed, causes the risk resting on the producer to be hard to assess and hence manage, in particular by acquiring adequate insurance coverage.[92]

Technological complexity, lack of clarity in the applicable legal paradigm, and informational asymmetry[93] will cause decisions by courts to be highly random, increasing the cost of litigation and causing the outcome to be hard to foresee *ex ante.*[94]

Overall, this might lead to a technology-chilling effect,[95] delaying the emergence of innovative products and the development of a – European – industry for advanced robotic products.

IV. From the attribution of liability to a risk management strategy

The picture briefly sketched may lead us to conclude that even with respect to robotics there is no paradigmatic change in the legal issues that

---

92 Following up with the prosthesis example, we may consider that the same malfunctioning may cause very different consequences, ranging from the breaking of eggs in the basket, to the injury of the wearer when training in a gym, to a car accident. The difficulty in restraining the scenarios and uses of the device depends on the very reason why it is developed. For a more detailed discussion, see Bertolini, 'Robotic prostheses as products' 116 et seq.

93 Informational asymmetry in economic terms, is due to the impossibility for one party (the independent one – judge) to observe a phenomenon known at least to one of the litigants, leading to the frustration of the otherwise legitimate and legally relevant interest brought before him. See, Benjamin E Hermalin, Avery W Katz and Richard Craswell, 'Contract Law' in Mitchell A Polinsky and Steven Shavell (eds), *Handbook of Law and Economics*, vol I (North-Holland 2007); Ian Ayres and Robert Gertner, 'Filling Gaps in Incomplete Contracts' The Yale Law Journal 87 et seq.

94 See Alan Schwartz and Robert E Scott, 'Contract Interpretation Redux' 119 Yale Law Journal 926 et seq.

95 Despite resorting to different arguments, see Aneta Podsiadla, 'What robotics can learn from the contemporary problems of Information Technology sector. Privacy by Design as a product safety standard - compliance and enforcement' (We Robot: Getting Down to Business); Schellekens 57 et seq; Ryan Calo, 'Open Robotics' 70 Maryland Law Rev 571.

need to be addressed and solved. After all causality has always been one of the most complex aspects of civil liability in all its applications,[96] and the overlapping of alternative schemes may occur in other, more established, fields of law.

However, given that there seem to be grounds to doubt the efficiency of existing rules in serving their own rationales – in particular in providing incentives to investments in product safety and in easing the position of the victim in obtaining compensation – the functional question may legitimately be posed. Possibly, the two rationales that product liability rules aim at achieving could be disentangled and addressed with different and autonomous strategies.

The example of civil aviation in the United States shows that reputation and merely economic incentives, together with narrow tailored technical standards best ensure product safety. Technical standardisation instead, in particular at the European level, seems to be insufficient so long as robotic products are taken into account. Either completely missing – for instance with respect to robots provided with learning capacities – or too broad and all-encompassing, hence inadequate.[97]

Compensation instead, may be ensured through criteria that burden the party better placed to (i) identifying risks, (ii) managing them, and (iii) minimising administrative costs associated therewith.

Such an approach is not foreign to European legal systems, where similar solutions are adopted in well-established fields such as the liability of the owner of the vehicle for traffic accidents. Bringing this argument forward may entail adopting – at least with respect to some classes of

---

96 See for instance Luca Nocco, *Il «sincretismo causale» e la politica del diritto: spunti dalla responsabilità sanitaria* (Giappichelli 2010).

97 This is the case with the AIMDD and MDD, for instance when their application to robotic prostheses and exoskeletons is considered, see Bertolini, 'Robotic prostheses as products' 123 et seq. The European Commission in its Communication to the European Parliament, the Council and the European Economic and Social Committee of 1 June 2011 – A strategic vision for European standards: Moving forward to enhance and accelerate the sustainable growth of the European economy by 202059, COM (2011) 311 final, deems standardisation of strategic relevance, stating that: '[...] in the future, European standardization will play a crucial role in a wide variety of areas, wider than today, ranging from supporting European competitiveness, protecting the consumer, improving the accessibility of disabled and elderly people to tackling climate change and the resource efficiency challenge'.

applications – no-fault plans, compulsory insurance schemes, and absolute liability rules, eventually coupled with damage caps.

Exploring the full range of possibilities falls beyond the purposes of the current analysis, and rests on the peculiarities of the single classes of applications and their potential market – and market failures. In some cases, compulsory insurance schemes may suffice, requiring minimal adaptation of existing norms. This could happen with driverless vehicles, where a large market can reasonably be anticipated and pooling and spreading of costs easily attained. However, the problems briefly sketched above (above § III.2) together with the material difficulties in acquiring data with respect to the new risks such devices pose,[98] demand the development of new risk management strategies, and may support a call for legal reform, identifying with certainty whom – between the owner or the producer – ought to be called to compensate.[99]

Simply providing for new legal obligations to insure is *per se* insufficient. This was the case with the Italian regulation of civilian drones, set forth by the competent authority (*Ente Nazionale Aviazione Civile*)[100] that left insurance companies with a duty to contract, absent any data for the quantification of potential damages and of the frequency of their occurrence. Premiums, as of today, are thence being determined according to criteria that are totally unrelated to the risk managed, such as the size and cash-flow of the professional service provider.

When robotic prostheses are concerned instead, lacking as large a market, considering the high cost of said devices and the limited economic capacities of potential users, no-fault schemes may prove a more viable option.[101]

---

98 The statistical data upon which insurance companies calculate their premiums risks becoming soon obsolete, being fundamentally centered on the human driver, his age, sex, and area of residence. When automation will reduce the influence of the man in the loop, this information will be less relevant, while new vulnerabilities will emerge, in particular cybersecurity, whose consequences can only partially be anticipated and assessed.

99 Price mechanisms and the elasticity of the demand curve for driverless vehicles will ultimately determine whom, among the different actors, has to bear the burden associated with the purchasing of insurance.

100 Regolamento ENAC 'Mezzi Aerei a Pilotaggio Remoto', Deliberazione n. 42/2013 of December 16th 2013, and subsequent modifications

101 For a more detailed discussion please allow reference to Bertolini, 'Robotic prostheses as products' 127 et seq.

V. Connectivity and the balancing of opposing interests. Privacy-by-design, access-to-data and postcontractual duties

The ever increasing volume of data robotic devices will generate over time through their sensors represents at once a potential threat to users' privacy and a precious element for risk management and the filling of the informational gaps that prevent adequate insurance products from being developed.

If some authors claim liability rules could be 'proximity driven'[102] – however still allowing a high degree of *ex ante* uncertainty that should instead be reduced – the exchange between fully anonymised data and postcontractual services may prove a viable solution.

The European Union had discussed the possibility to introduce a uniform regulation of post-sale services in the occasion of the adoption of the Directive 1999/44/EC of the European Parliament and the Council of 25 May 1999 on certain aspects of the sale of consumer goods and associated guarantees, given that many states already had similar provisions.[103]

Some European national systems set forth detailed obligations, for instance for the supply of replacement parts for durable products,[104] but the debate on the matter is fragmented and underdeveloped.

---

102 See Walker Smith, 1779 et seq.

103 See the Green book on guarantees for consumer goods and after-sale services, COM (93) 509 final.

104 See Sale of Goods and Supply of Services Act (SGSSA) of 1980, § 12 on which Mary Donnelly and Fidelma White, *Consumer Law: Rights and Regulation* (Round Hall 2014) 132; Sales Law Review Group, *Report on the legislation governing the sale of goods and supply of services*, of October 18th 2011, available at <www.djei.ie/publications/commerce/2011/saleslawreviewgroupreport2011.pdf.> accessed 4 December 2015.Under Spanish law, see *Real Decreto Legislativo, 1/2007, de 16 de noviembre, por el que se aprueba el texto refundido de la Ley General para la Defensa de los Consumidores y Usuarios y otras leyes complementarias*, (LGDCU), art 127, 1° co. stating «*En los productos de naturaleza duradera, el consumidor y usuario tendrá derecho a un adecuado servicio técnico y a la existencia de repuestos durante el plazo mínimo de cinco años a partir de la fecha en que el producto deje de fabricarse*», on which Juan José Marin Lopez, *sub art. 127* (Aranzadi 2009) 1595 et seq.
Under German law cases and doctrinal articles elaborated an *Ersatzteilbereithaltungspflicht* of substantially equivalent content, see AG München, 6.5.1970, in [1971] BB 62; AG Rüsselsheim, 30.1.2004 – 3C 769/03, in *Deutsches Autorecht*,

Post-sale services may become of increasing relevance embracing all fields of robotics.[105] Their refinement may lead us to reconsider the overall access-to-data issue in a different perspective. Requiring users to share information generated by their own devices – once safely handled through a privacy-compliant design of the application itself, ensuring highest standards of anonymity and protection[106] – may become justified once they receive a wide and articulated array of maintenance, updating and safety-oversight services[107] in exchange.

As of today, postcontractual obligations and duties have not been a central topic of discussion in the legal debate. However, an attempt at categorising and analysing them as regulated with respect to single

---

2004, 280 et seq with a comment by Schattenkirchner; see also Greulich, 'Nachwirkungen bei Liefverträgen' [1955] Betriebs-Berater 208, 208 et seq; Peter Finger, 'Die Verpflichtung des Herstellers zur Lieferung von Ersatzteilen' [1970] Neue Juristische Wochenschrift 2049; Hans-Georg Rodig, 'Verpflichtung des Herstellers zuer Bereithaltung von Ersatzteilen für langlebige Wirtschaftsgüter und ausgelaufene Serien' [1971] Betriebs-Berater 854; Ludwig-Philipp Kühne, 'Die nachvertragliche Ersatzteilbelieferung' [1986] Betriebs-Berater 15271527; Claus Ullrich and Thomas Ulbrich, 'Das Bevorraten von Ersatzteilen' [1995] Betriebs-Berater 371; Wolfgang Kühnel and Peter Spamer, 'Vertraglich vereinbarte Vorratslager für Ersatzteile von Maschinen und Anlagen' [1976] Betriebs-Berater 339, 340; Roland Michael Beckmann, *sub § 433* (Sellier - de Gruyter 2004) 120, Rn 121.

Under Austrian law, see Alexander Schopper, *Nachvertragliche Pflichten. Das Pflichtenprogramm nach Erlöschen der vertraglichen Hauptleistungspflicht* (Manzsche 2009) 518.

105 Take for instance the case of service robotics, see Andrea Bertolini and Giuseppe Aiello, 'Robot Companions: a Legal and Ethical Analysis' forthcoming [2016] The Information Society

106 See the Proposal for a Regulation of the European Parliament and of the Council on the protection of individuals with regard to the processing of personal data and on the free movement of such data (General Data Protection Regulation), of January 25th 2012, COM (2012) 11 final; the Federal Trade Commission Report on Protecting Consumer Privacy in an Era of Rapid Change, Recommendation for Businesses and Policy Makers, of March 2012, available at <https://www.ftc.gov/sites/default/files/documents/reports/federal-trade-commission-report-protecting-consumer-privacy-era-rapid-change-recommendations/120326privacyreport.pdf.> accessed 4 December 2015.

107 Such as the *Beobachtungs-* and *Rückrufspflichten*, see Theo Bodewig, *Der Rückruf fehlerhafter Produkte* (Mohr Siebeck 1999); with respect to financial services also Jens-Hinrich Binder, 'Nachsorgende Vertragspflichten? Begründung und Reichweite fortdauerender Schutzpflichten nach Leistungsaustausch in Schuldverhältnissen' Archiv für die civilistische Praxis 587 et seq.

contractual kinds has been undergone in different European legal systems, also aiming at identifying grounds to support their imposition absent a specific legal or contractual provision.[108]

A more comprehensive discussion at the European level and in particular the reshaping of after-sale services in light of technological advancement may prove a plausible approach to handle a multiplicity of deeply interconnected problems, ranging from privacy to access to data and consumer protection for users of robotic devices.

108 See M. E. André, P. Grignon and P. Dumont, *Après contrat* (2005); critical towards the category Christian von Bar, '"Nachwirkende" Vertragspflichten' 179 Archiv für die civilistische Praxis 452 et seq; instead Theo Bodewig, 'Vertragliche Pflichten «post contractum finitum»' Juristische Ausbildung505 et seq; Binder 587 et seq.; Schopper; please also allow reference to Andrea Bertolini, *Il postcontatto e la responsabilità postcontrattuale* (2016), forthcoming.

Panel Discussion on the Internet of Things

Statement*

Prof. Dr. Rolf H. Weber

The Internet of Things (IoT) technologies are based on data gathered by various sensors built into devices. A new technological environment always raises questions in relation to the contract conditions and the liability regime. To a far extent, however, in the context of the IoT the traditional contract rules can deal with the newly emerging issues; the most critical topic concerns the distinction between the notion of 'goods' (sale) and 'services' being a topic that should be reconsidered in the forthcoming legislative activities.

The liability regime is confronted with the difficulty that a clear relation (i.e. a causality) between a wrongful act and the occurred damage cannot always easily be established. The discussions around big data have shown that the traditional notion of causality governing legal relations since the time of Roman law is more and more replaced by the notion of correlation. The confidence of users (consumers, business entities) in the IoT must reflect this new appearance of correlation.

Nevertheless, the legal situation is not completely new; as in case of the protection of personality the discussions should be centred around the definition of spheres of responsibility that can lead to liability. Following such kind of approach delineating responsibility spheres of the involved stakeholders, major gaps in the liability regime do not seem to exist.

Improvements of the legal framework are always possible, however, too hectic legislative activities are not in the interest of civil society and business due to legal uncertainty and legal instability. All over all, the existing framework appears to be fit for the new technological opportunities. But legislative activities could be done in respect of the mentioned traditional categorization of goods and services and of the clearer delineation of responsibility spheres.

---

* The following contributions are statements during the Panel Discussion on the Internet of Things at the conference on which this volume is based on.

A specific issue that merits closer attention concerns the different treatment of Internet intermediaries and search engines under the E-Commerce Directive 2000 and the Data Protection Directive 1995: The scope of liability is much broader if an intermediary transfers data and is subject to the Data Protection Directive than if an intermediary is involved in electronic contracting due to the liability limitation contained in Arts 12–14 of the E-Commerce Directive; this difference does not appear to be justified.

The Digital Single Market Strategy mainly concentrates on contract/liability issues and regulatory topics (telecommunications, competition, intellectual property). However, the most critical issues of the IoT in the future do not seem to occur in these fields but in other areas: (i) Privacy/data protection is a major challenge in connection with the IoT; even the new General Data Protection Regulation that might be adopted within the next few months does not fully address the technological risks caused by the IoT. Therefore, more emphasis must be placed on the realization of an appropriate data protection framework. (ii) The Digital Single Market Strategy remains almost silent about payment mechanisms; the revised E-Money Directive and the revised Payment Services Directive do not sufficiently tackle the challenges caused by cryptocurrencies that will certainly gain importance during the next few years. In respect of payments, the blockchain technology will become a driving factor in the development of 'monetary' systems. Not only data protection and data security but also trust and confidence in the new payment schemes are becoming important regulatory issues. These challenges need to be addressed before too many misuses are undermining the trust and confidence of consumers and business entities.

Statement*

Robert MacDougall

In advance of the panel, we have been asked to consider problems stemming from either an *unclear* liability regime or the *non-existence* of a clear cut liability regime in this area. We have also been asked to consider whether this affects in any way the offer of IoT services/goods of suppliers or the confidence of users (consumers, business users) in IoT and/or data driven services and connected tangible goods.

With this in mind, I would first like to provide some introductory context to set out Vodafone's observations on the IoT market. Each year we publish our M2M Barometer to track market development and establish how businesses are adopting this technology. We do this through interviews with over 650 executives, in conjunction with Circle Research and Analysys Mason, publishing the final report on our website. As part of this research, we ask companies what they perceive to be the main barriers to IoT adoption, and liability has not, to date, been identified. Security and privacy are seen as the most common concerns – not a barrier to adoption per se – but a barrier to increasing use. In our 2015 M2M Barometer, 33% of businesses interviewed said that security is a barrier to them increasing their use of M2M. But there were important distinctions between sectors. Retail and health ranked highest for security and privacy concerns: 41% of healthcare organisations agreed 'strongly' that security breaches are a major concern, compared to 36% across all sectors. Conversely, sectors like transportation ranked lower — just 23% of transportation and logistics companies agree strongly that security breaches are a major concern. This is probably because businesses in these sectors hold less personal data.

But that is not to say we do not take issues around liability seriously – we do. But our view is that we should be able to manage it contractually and via innovative, industry led initiatives. This is something I will elabo-

---

* Robert MacDougall is Head of Enterprise Regulation, Vodafone Group Services Limited. The author thanks Rod Freeman and Valerie Kenyon at Hogan Lovells for their invaluable contribution to these speaking points.

rate on in relation to the other questions that have been posed by Professor Staudenmayer.

1. Do suppliers and users find the legal framework balanced and clear?

The obvious frame of reference for product liability considerations in Europe is the Product Liability Directive.[1] At a high-level, the Directive establishes the principle that the 'producer' of a 'product' is liable for damages caused by a 'defect' in his product. The Directive was notified to the Member States of the EU (who then needed to bring into force national laws and provisions to implement the Directive) in 1985. The result of a long period of negotiation and consideration, the Directive's drafting involved a careful balancing of the various interests in order to produce a workable and appropriate liability regime for products in Europe.

At a broader policy level, the question does arise as to whether it is appropriate to extend this 'no fault' liability regime to technologies that are more in the nature of a service than a product. An obvious consideration is whether certain IoT technologies are 'products' within the meaning of the Product Liability Directive. Some clarification may be needed over time in that regard. There are also a number of other questions that could arise in relation to certain IoT applications. In particular:

- who is responsible for safety compliance of an IoT product on an on-going basis?
- Who will be liable in the event that an IoT product causes damage?
- What will that person be liable for?
- How should their liability be assessed?
- How should the risks be insured?

So, in answer to the question raised, there are potentially areas of ambiguity in relation to the existing regime and its application to IoT products. However, many of these risks are not unique to IoT; for example, these risks exist in established technology industries. As an example, the development of after-market third party components for a product – where that component may have a fundamental impact on the use and safety of the original product – raises considerations similar to those raised about the

1 Directive 85/374/EEC

application of the existing product liability regime to IoT products and systems. For many reasons, careful consideration and dialogue should take place before making amendments to the existing regulatory regime specifically with IoT in mind.

2. *In any legal or voluntary framework or guidelines that cover liability issues of IoT, are there problems or gaps touching the aspects of liability in relation to such services and tangible products (e.g connected cars etc.)?*

This question focuses on the role of legal or voluntary frameworks or guidelines in the context of IoT.

As a starting point, it's crucial to keep in mind the important role that certain existing standards have to play, for example the activity that the European Commission is sponsoring to develop a common methodology for applying Privacy by Design (Mandate 530) which will be of equal relevance to IoT, as well as existing ISO standards such as ISO/IEC 27018 and ISO/IEC 27034. These technical standardisation initiatives and methodologies have an important role to play in relation to potential liability issues associated with IoT.

The question is right to highlight the important role of guidelines in this area. Within the mobile industry, the GSMA has a key part to play in developing guidelines to embed best practice. Although we don't yet have GSMA IoT liability guidelines, which perhaps reflects the fact that liability is still something of an emerging issue, there are plenty of other guidelines which are relevant and which highlight why there is no reason why industry cannot develop liability guidelines as required.

I would highlight the work the GSMA is doing in relation to IoT security to demonstrate this, as in practice I think that issues of IoT liability and IoT security will be related. The GSMA's IoT security guidelines are industry agnostic. They highlight the role of the IoT Service Provider – and make recommendations about how the IoT service provider can mitigate risks by selecting partners competent in security and by supporting standards-based approaches. They also introduce a set of 'best practice' security and privacy principles, guidance for IoT devices (e.g. secure local interfaces), network operators (e.g. subscription management), and platforms (e.g. cloud security configuration). All of this will help drive best practice and reduce risk associated with IoT applications.

3. *When it comes to liability issues of these services and connected tangible products (e.g. connected car etc.) is the existing framework fit for purpose, in particular is the legal framework future proof?*

With respect to whether the existing regime is fit for purpose, there are some important features of IoT to keep in mind – and I'll discuss these in a moment. But it's also important to recognise the inherent challenges of seeking to 'future-ready' any legal framework. To a large extent, the existing legal framework may be able to cover many of the issues relevant to IoT – but where it can't, careful consideration in advance of any regulatory development is crucial to avoid a 'knee-jerk' reaction that could unnecessarily slow-down the pace of beneficial change and innovation. At this stage, we haven't fully explored all the potential advantages and applications of IoT products and systems.

The rapid development of IoT technology raises a number of product compliance, product liability and insurance-related issues. Whilst aspects of the IoT give rise to special considerations in these areas, the compliance and liability issues do not give rise to a clear need for new legislation or new types of regulation. As a result of this, and as I have already set out, we should first look to manage those issues within the structure of existing legislation and regulatory regimes.

Interdependency is also a key consideration. Increasingly, the development of IoT technologies creates complex interdependencies between product and service producers. Products are designed so that they are dependent on third party technologies in order for the product to perform its basic functions, and in order to maximise the benefit of the product for the user. Those dependencies can increase and become more complex over the life of the product.

This gives rise to questions of who is responsible for certifying safety of the product, who is responsible for ensuring safety on an ongoing basis, and how liabilities should be allocated in the event that the technology behaves in an unsafe way causing damage. These issues can also give rise to challenges in identifying the root cause of product failures, and in determining where fault lies in the event of a problem. Issues relating to liability when products involve third party components are not new but are highlighted when products are increasingly connected and complex.

But I do not consider that new, detailed IoT/M2M legislation is the answer. The question highlights 'connected cars' in particular and I think we can take note of developments in the USA on this point. On July 21,

2015, new legislation was proposed directing the National Highway Traffic Safety Administration (NHTSA) and the Federal Trade Commission (FTC) to promulgate federal regulations setting minimum cybersecurity and privacy standards for all motor vehicles manufactured for sale in the United States, the so-called Security and Privacy in Your Car Act, abbreviated as the 'SPY Car Act'.

The SPY Car Act imposes new regulatory requirements and potential liability. It has also been suggested that the SPY Car Act might overlook existing automotive safety requirements enforced by regulation and common law and gives regulators nearly unlimited power. The SPY Car Act also uses terms that leave the NHTSA and FTC with very significant power to define what constitutes 'reasonable measures' and 'best practices' to protect against hacking and to define what will be considered a 'violation' of the statute. It has also been suggested that it does not consider existing industry initiatives to address both privacy and security concerns. Existing provisions of the FTC Act have already been relied on in relation to enforcement activity in the area of IoT and are effective at providing privacy protections to consumers. Indeed, the automotive industry in the United States has already adopted privacy principles for connected cars – binding as public commitments enforceable under the FTC Act.

We should also not lose sight of the fact that liability provisions exist in the existing EU regulatory framework which govern the provision of electronic communications services and the operation of electronic communications networks in the EU. The Framework Directive requires Members States to ensure that the integrity and security of public communications are maintained. Article 4 of Directive on Privacy and Electronic Communications (the 'ePrivacy Directive') also contains specific provisions that could be relevant to liability, for example that subscribers and users of such services be fully informed by their service provider of any existing security risks which lie outside the scope of possible remedies by the service provider. Therefore, we should seek to apply existing regulation to these new and emerging areas before we seek to introduce new law and regulation designed to address specific IoT liability concerns.

4. *If not, what, in the view of the participants, should be the liability regime for these services and connected tangible goods?*

Interaction with the Insurance industry will be vital to the liability regime for IoT, as the insurance industry will need to be ready to offer insurance products which respond to the relevant risks run in a cost effective way. Where the scale and complexity of potential liabilities is too great to be managed at corporate level through conventional liability insurance it may be necessary to develop arrangements for certain IoT products whereby there is a 'pooling' of risk. At its simplest, this could be an arrangement whereby all the participants in the development of a particular technology pay in to an insurance scheme designed to meet the cost of claims arising from the operation of that technology. This is a system which already operates successfully in the context of certain risk events in certain jurisdictions. Such schemes are often statutory in nature.

But let's not forget about the benefits of IoT, it's not all about risk. For some IoT products, technology can enable and empower consumers so that insurers are able to calculate risk more effectively. Adoption of new technology will lead to risk pools becoming smaller, according to research published earlier this year by Morgan Stanley together with the Boston Consulting Group. This research predicted that damage to insured homes may fall by 40-60% if smart-home devices are adopted. The risk pools for home and car insurance might shrink by up to $102 billion, the report considers.

Legislators may also need to consider existing requirements in relation to insurance to ensure they are meaningful in the light of developments in IoT technology. An example is that of compulsory motor insurance covering individual users of vehicles. It will be necessary to determine whether this model will be appropriate in an age where a fully autonomous vehicle is not operated by an individual user but by a remote operating system.

5. *Do participants think the European Union should have a role when it comes to liability issues of these services and connected tangible goods?*

The role of the European Commission is especially important given the relevance of IoT to the creation a Digital Single Market. A harmonised approach is also vital to maximise the success of the global product market (including in terms of market access for the industry, and supporting innovation in the context of the ease of product compliance and launch), and to maintain high and consistent standards of safety for consumers regardless of their home address.

With regards to product regulation and the importance of a harmonised approach, one factor that becomes increasingly relevant is that consumers are becoming more sophisticated in their approach to sourcing products. Purchasing products from a market other than the one closest to home is now the norm, and consumers can circumvent hurdles that sellers put in place to prevent the use of products/software in non-intended countries with relative ease. For this reason, a harmonised approach to product regulation and product liability is key. That said, this issue is not restricted to the IoT. It is important that the the Commission pushes for a harmonised soft-law approach.

In this respect I would highlight the role of the Alliance for Internet of Things Innovation (AIOTI), an initiative that has recently been set up by the European Commission. The Policy Working Group of the AIOTI, which I Chair, consists of over 200 companies, active across many sectors of the economy. We are making a number of policy recommendations to address barriers that could prevent the take-up of the IoT in the context of the Digital Single Market, with a particular focus on privacy, security and liability. This highlights the role that the European Commission is already playing here to help develop an approach that is relevant to both the demand and supply sides of the economy, which is, after all, one of the key considerations associated with IoT.

FSC
www.fsc.org
MIX
Papier | Fördert
gute Waldnutzung
FSC® C083411

Kolibri 360 GmbH
Ferdinand-Jühlke-Straße 7
99095 Erfurt, Deutschland
produktsicherheit@kolibri360.de